the AMAZING SPIDER-MAN

LIZARD

NO TURNING BACK

Writer: **DAN SLOTT**
Penciler: **GIUSEPPE CAMUNCOLI** WITH **MARIO DEL PENNINO**
Inkers: **VICTOR OLAZABA** WITH **DANIEL GREEN** & **GIUSEPPE CAMUNCOLI**
Colorist: **FRANK D'ARMATA**
Letterers: **VC'S JOE CARAMAGNA** & **CHRIS ELIOPOULOS**
Assistant Editor: **ELLIE PYLE**
Senior Editor: **STEPHEN WACKER**

UNTOLD TALES OF SPIDER-MAN #9
Writer: **KURT BUSIEK**
Penciler: **RON FRENZ**
Inker: **BRETT BREEDING**
Colorist: **STEPHEN MATTSSON**
Letterer: **RICHARD STARKINGS** & **COMICRAFT**
Editor: **TOM BREVOORT**

Collection Editor: **JENNIFER GRÜNWALD**
Assistant Editors: **ALEX STARBUCK** & **NELSON RIBEIRO**
Editor, Special Projects: **MARK D. BEAZLEY**
Senior Editor, Special Projects: **JEFF YOUNGQUIST**
Senior Vice President of Sales: **DAVID GABRIEL**
SVP of Brand Planning & Communications: **MICHAEL PASCIULLO**

Editor in Chief: **AXEL ALONSO**
Chief Creative Officer: **JOE QUESADA**
Publisher: **DAN BUCKLEY**
Executive Producer: **ALAN FINE**

SPIDER-MAN: LIZARD — NO TURNING BACK. Contains material originally published in magazine form as AMAZING SPIDER-MAN #688-691 and UNTOLD TALES OF SPIDER-MAN #9. First printing 2012. Hardcover ISBN# 978-0-7851-6007-6. Softcover ISBN# 978-0-7851-6008-3. Published by MARVEL WORLDWIDE, INC., a subsidiary of MARVEL ENTERTAINMENT, LLC. OFFICE OF PUBLICATION: 135 West 50th Street, New York, NY 10020. Copyright © 1996 and 2012 Marvel Characters, Inc. All rights reserved. Hardcover: $19.99 per copy in the U.S. and $21.99 in Canada (GST #R127032852). Softcover: $16.99 per copy in the U.S. and $18.99 in Canada (GST #R127032852). Canadian Agreement #40668537. All characters featured in this issue and the distinctive names and likenesses thereof, and all related indicia are trademarks of Marvel Characters, Inc. No similarity between any of the names, characters, persons, and/or institutions in this magazine with those of any living or dead person or institution is intended, and any such similarity which may exist is purely coincidental. **Printed in the U.S.A.** ALAN FINE, EVP - Office of the President, Marvel Worldwide, Inc. and EVP & CMO Marvel Characters B.V.; DAN BUCKLEY, Publisher & President - Print, Animation & Digital Divisions; JOE QUESADA, Chief Creative Officer; TOM BREVOORT, SVP of Publishing; DAVID BOGART, SVP of Operations & Procurement, Publishing; RUWAN JAYATILLEKE, SVP & Associate Publisher, Publishing; C.B. CEBULSKI, SVP of Creator & Content Development; DAVID GABRIEL, SVP of Publishing Sales & Circulation; MICHAEL PASCIULLO, SVP of Brand Planning & Communications; JIM O'KEEFE, VP of Operations & Logistics; DAN CARR, Executive Director of Publishing Technology; SUSAN CRESPI, Editorial Operations Manager; ALEX MORALES, Publishing Operations Manager; STAN LEE, Chairman Emeritus. For information regarding advertising in Marvel Comics or on Marvel.com, please contact Niza Disla, Director of Marvel Partnerships, at ndisla@marvel.com. For Marvel subscription inquiries, please call 800-217-9158. **Manufactured between 7/30/2012 and 9/10/2012 (hardcover), and 7/30/2012**

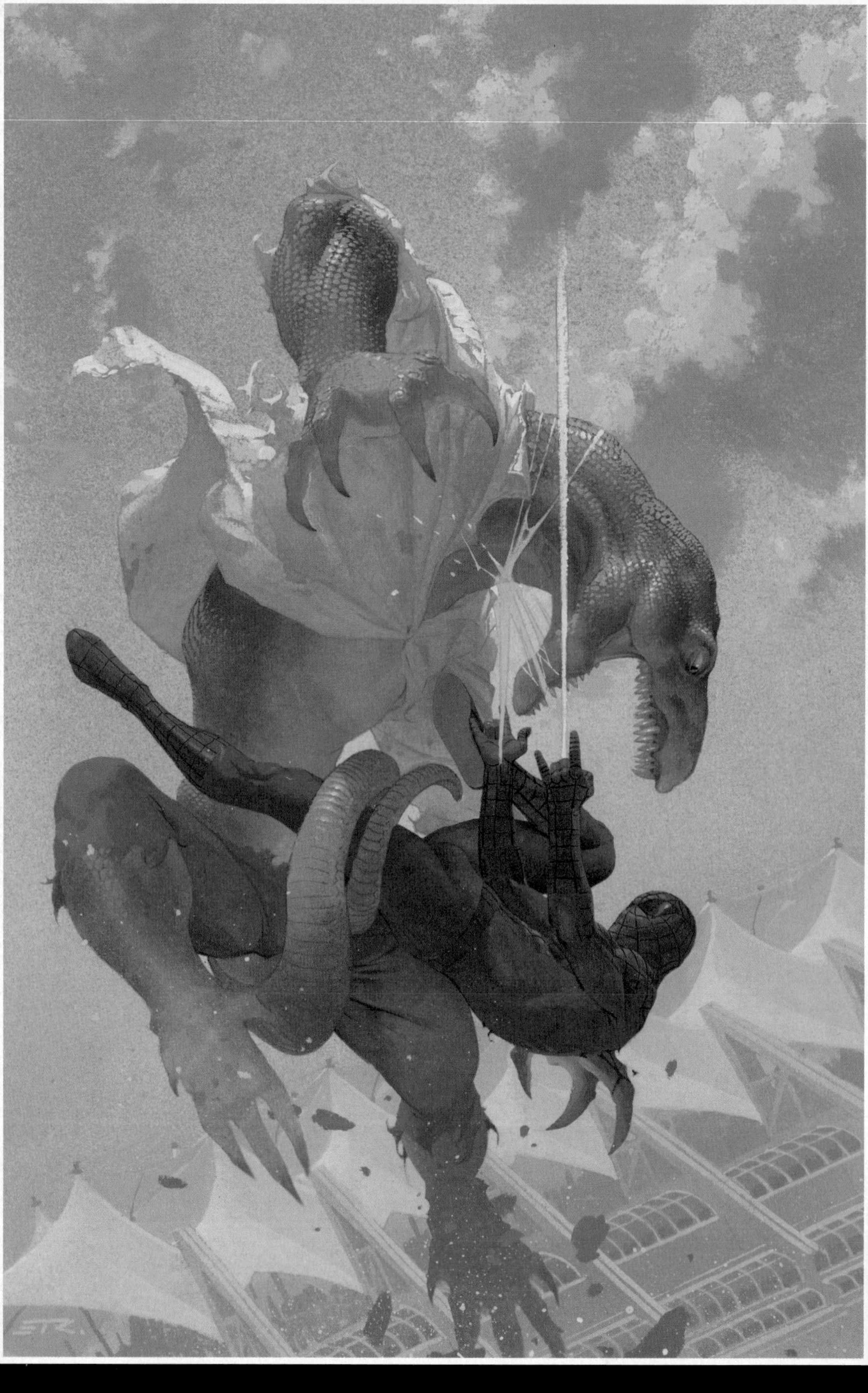

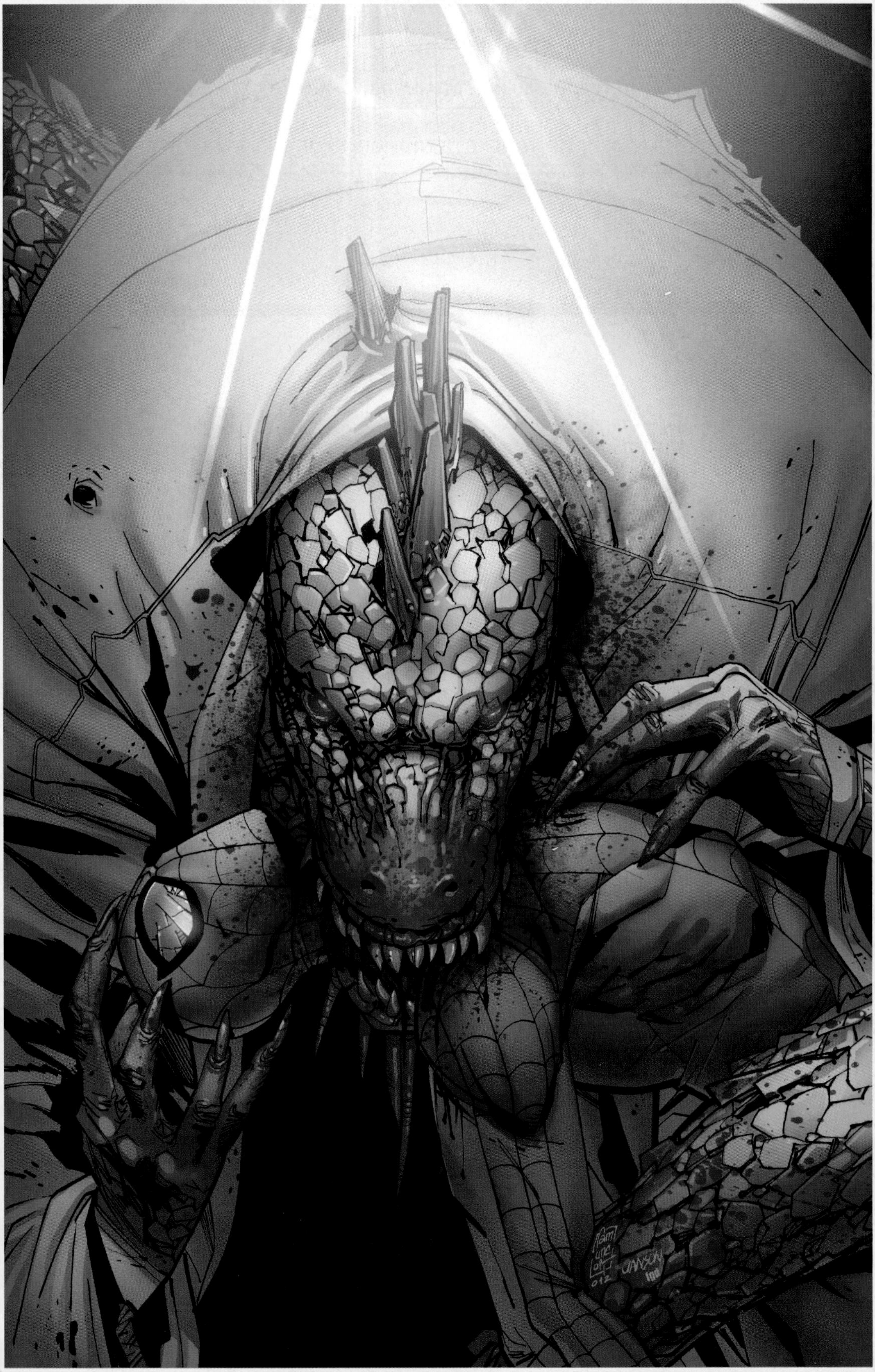

AMAZING SPIDER-MAN #688

COVER BY GIUSEPPE CAMUNCOLI, KLAUS JANSON & FRANK D'ARMATA

FINAL ☆☆☆☆

DAILY BUGLE®

NEW YORK'S FINEST DAILY NEWSPAPER

SINCE 1897 ☆☆☆☆
$1.00 (in NYC)
$1.50 (outside city)

INSIDE: MARY JANE WATSON COURTS CLUBBERS!; MATT MURDOCK STILL MISSING!; RACHEL COLE-ALVES: VICTIM OR VIGILANTE? RUMOR: RAGE-FILLED REPTILES RUN RAMPANT!

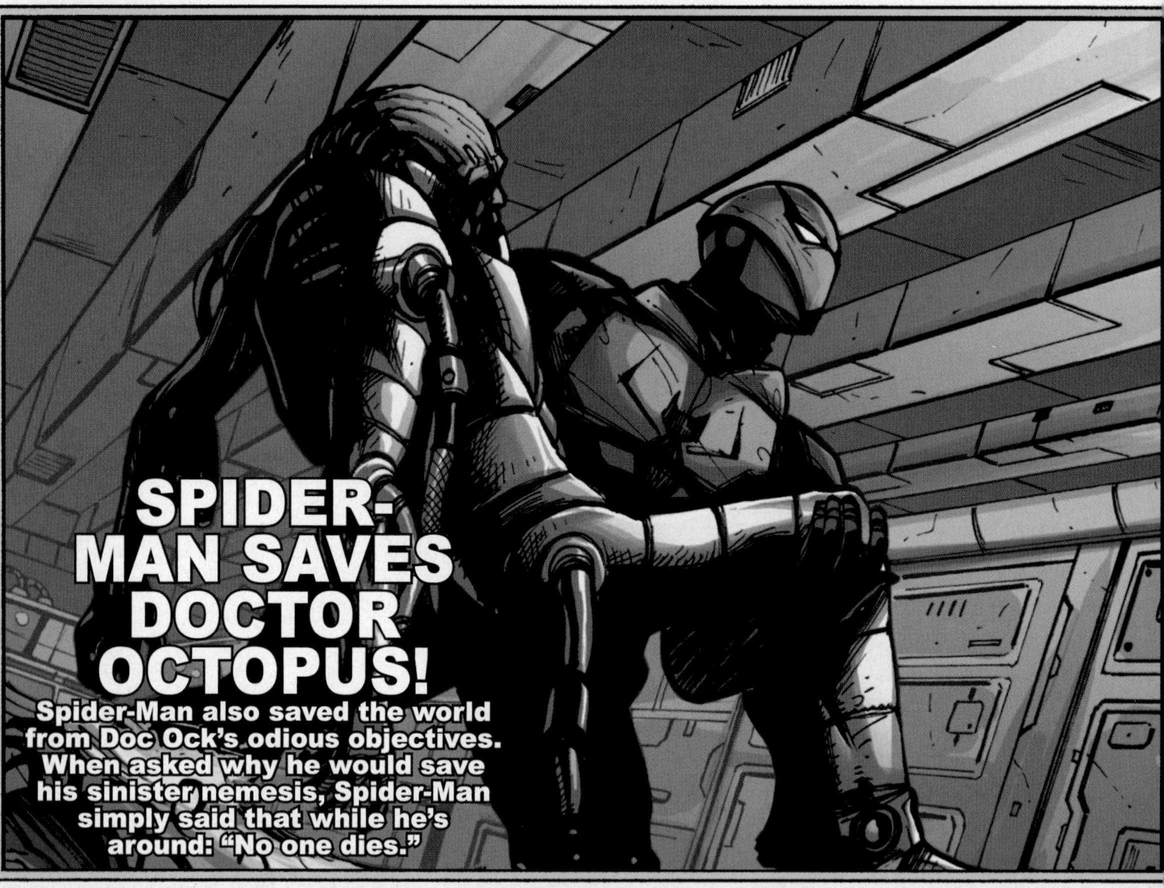
SPIDER-MAN SAVES DOCTOR OCTOPUS!
Spider-Man also saved the world from Doc Ock's odious objectives. When asked why he would save his sinister nemesis, Spider-Man simply said that while he's around: "No one dies."

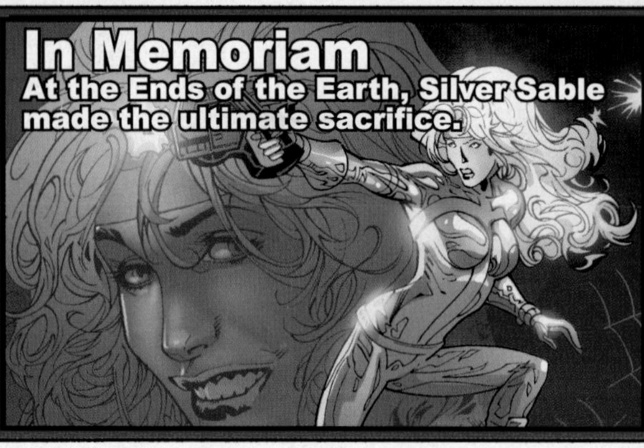
In Memoriam
At the Ends of the Earth, Silver Sable made the ultimate sacrifice.

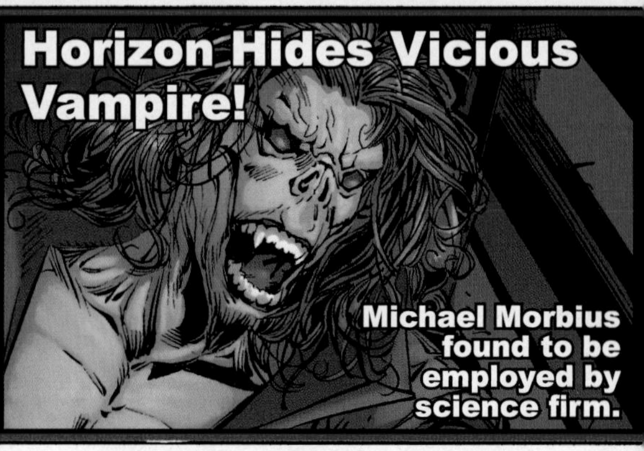
Horizon Hides Vicious Vampire!
Michael Morbius found to be employed by science firm.

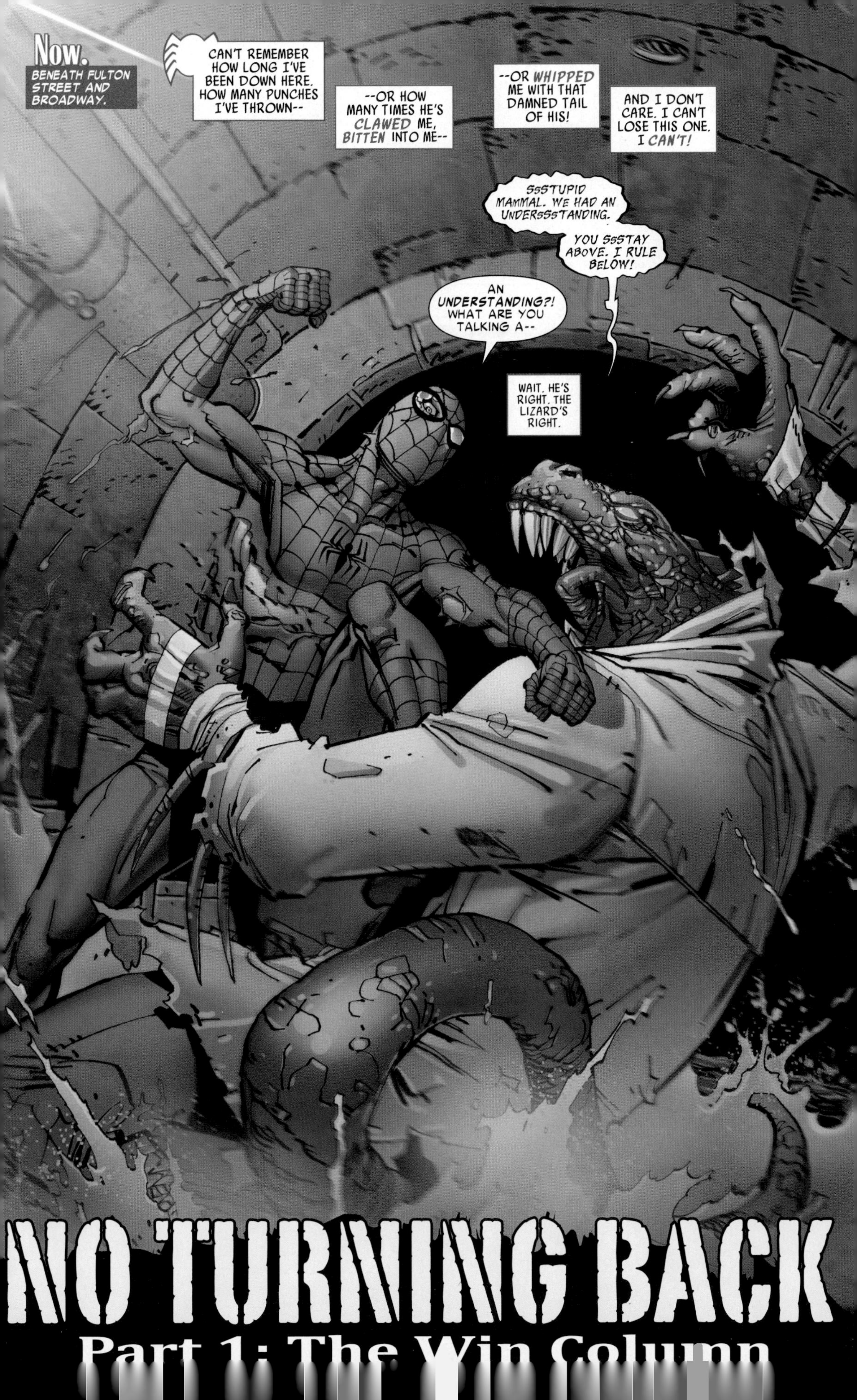
Now.
BENEATH FULTON STREET AND BROADWAY.
CAN'T REMEMBER HOW LONG I'VE BEEN DOWN HERE. HOW MANY PUNCHES I'VE THROWN--
--OR HOW MANY TIMES HE'S CLAWED ME, BITTEN INTO ME--
--OR WHIPPED ME WITH THAT DAMNED TAIL OF HIS!
AND I DON'T CARE. I CAN'T LOSE THIS ONE. I CAN'T!
SsSTUPID MAMMAL. WE HAD AN UNDERSsSTANDING.
YOU SsSTAY ABOVE. I RULE BELOW!
AN UNDERSTANDING?! WHAT ARE YOU TALKING A--
WAIT. HE'S RIGHT. THE LIZARD'S RIGHT.
NO TURNING BACK
Part 1: The Win Column

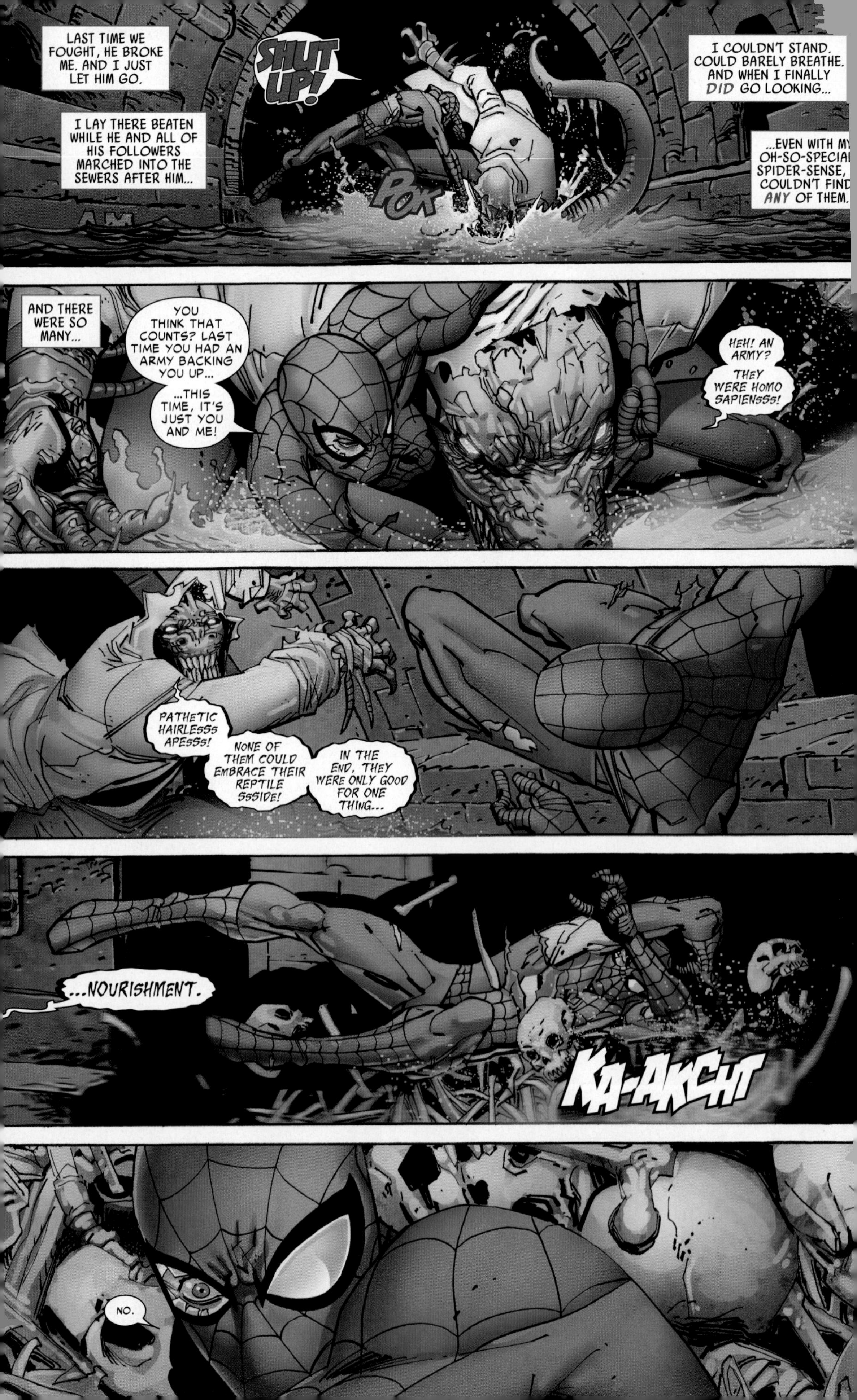
LAST TIME WE FOUGHT, HE BROKE ME. AND I JUST LET HIM GO.
I LAY THERE BEATEN WHILE HE AND ALL OF HIS FOLLOWERS MARCHED INTO THE SEWERS AFTER HIM...
SHUT UP!
POK
I COULDN'T STAND. COULD BARELY BREATHE. AND WHEN I FINALLY DID GO LOOKING...
...EVEN WITH MY OH-SO-SPECIAL SPIDER-SENSE, COULDN'T FIND ANY OF THEM.
AND THERE WERE SO MANY...
YOU THINK THAT COUNTS? LAST TIME YOU HAD AN ARMY BACKING YOU UP...
...THIS TIME, IT'S JUST YOU AND ME!
HEH! AN ARMY?
THEY WERE HOMO SAPIENSSS!
PATHETIC HAIRLESSS APESSS!
NONE OF THEM COULD EMBRACE THEIR REPTILE SSSIDE!
IN THE END, THEY WERE ONLY GOOD FOR ONE THING...
...NOURISHMENT.
KA-AKCHT
NO.

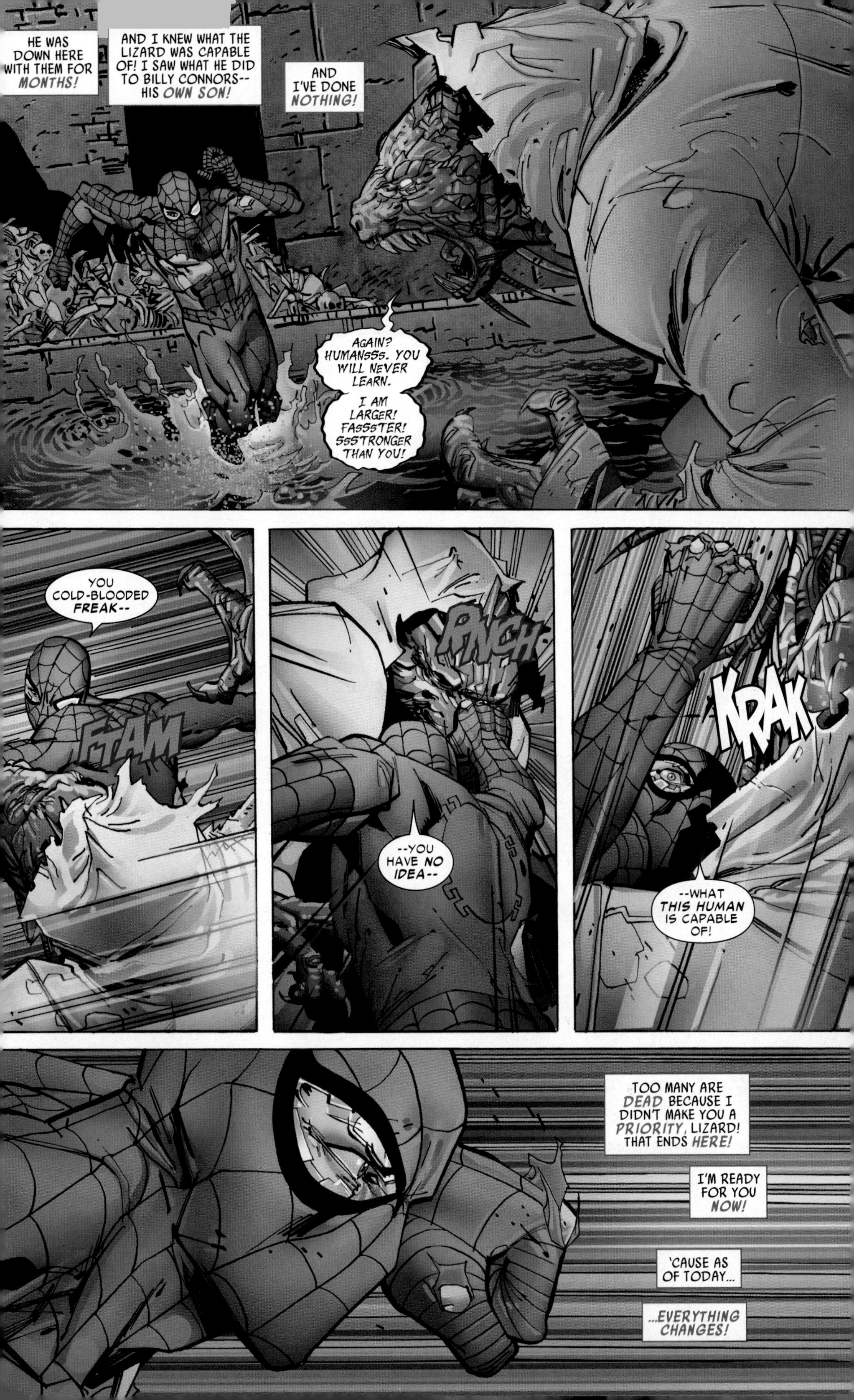

HE WAS DOWN HERE WITH THEM FOR MONTHS!
AND I KNEW WHAT THE LIZARD WAS CAPABLE OF! I SAW WHAT HE DID TO BILLY CONNORS-- HIS OWN SON!
AND I'VE DONE NOTHING!
AGAIN? HUMANSSS. YOU WILL NEVER LEARN.
I AM LARGER! FASSSTER! SSSTRONGER THAN YOU!
YOU COLD-BLOODED FREAK--
FTAM
PTNCH
--YOU HAVE NO IDEA--
KRAK
--WHAT THIS HUMAN IS CAPABLE OF!
TOO MANY ARE DEAD BECAUSE I DIDN'T MAKE YOU A PRIORITY, LIZARD! THAT ENDS HERE!
I'M READY FOR YOU NOW!
'CAUSE AS OF TODAY...
...EVERYTHING CHANGES!

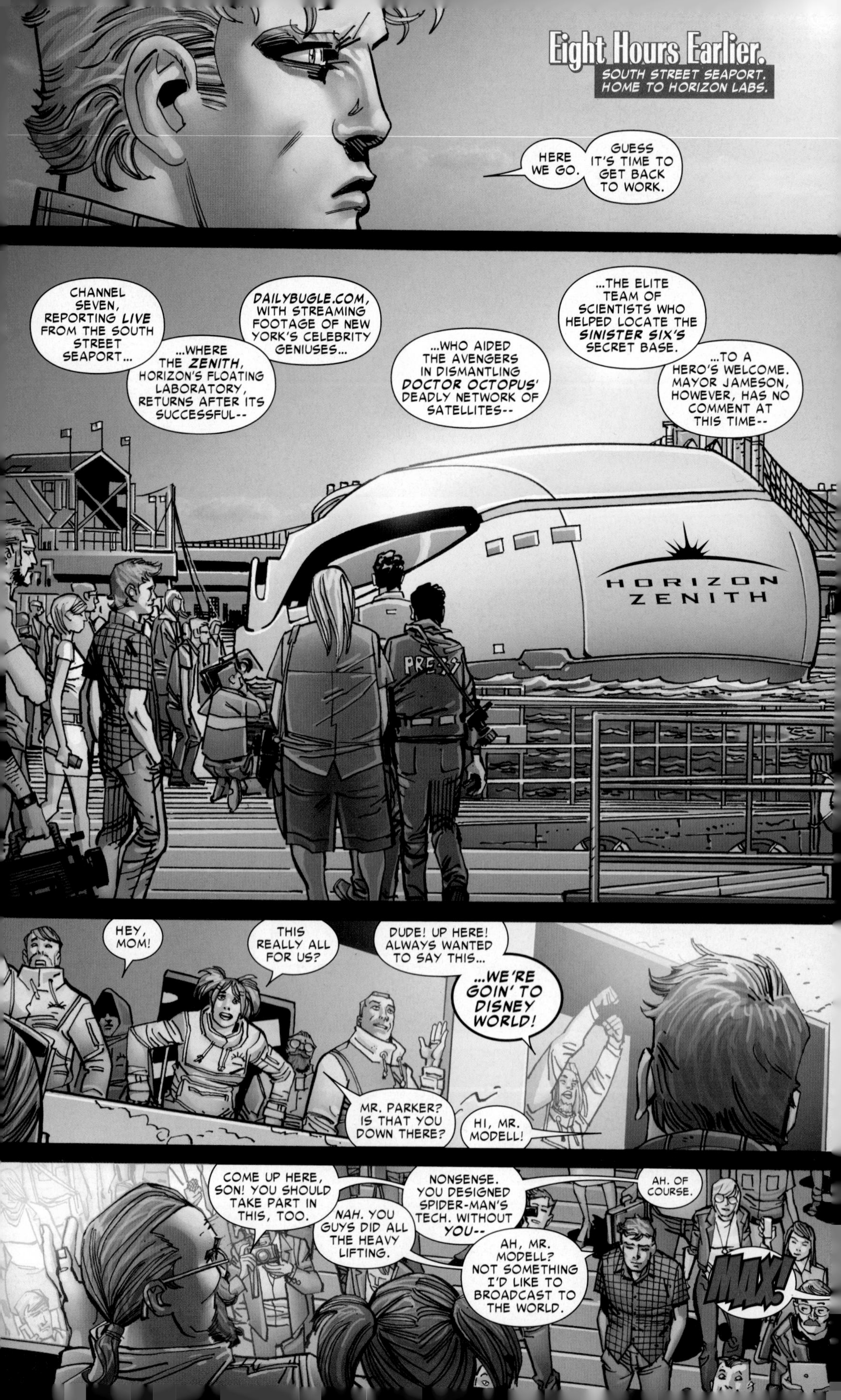
Eight Hours Earlier.
SOUTH STREET SEAPORT. HOME TO HORIZON LABS.
HERE WE GO.
GUESS IT'S TIME TO GET BACK TO WORK.
CHANNEL SEVEN, REPORTING LIVE FROM THE SOUTH STREET SEAPORT...
...WHERE THE ZENITH, HORIZON'S FLOATING LABORATORY, RETURNS AFTER ITS SUCCESSFUL--
DAILYBUGLE.COM, WITH STREAMING FOOTAGE OF NEW YORK'S CELEBRITY GENIUSES...
...WHO AIDED THE AVENGERS IN DISMANTLING DOCTOR OCTOPUS' DEADLY NETWORK OF SATELLITES--
...THE ELITE TEAM OF SCIENTISTS WHO HELPED LOCATE THE SINISTER SIX'S SECRET BASE.
...TO A HERO'S WELCOME. MAYOR JAMESON, HOWEVER, HAS NO COMMENT AT THIS TIME--
HORIZON ZENITH
PRESS
HEY, MOM!
THIS REALLY ALL FOR US?
DUDE! UP HERE! ALWAYS WANTED TO SAY THIS...
...WE'RE GOIN' TO DISNEY WORLD!
MR. PARKER? IS THAT YOU DOWN THERE?
HI, MR. MODELL!
COME UP HERE, SON! YOU SHOULD TAKE PART IN THIS, TOO.
NAH. YOU GUYS DID ALL THE HEAVY LIFTING.
NONSENSE. YOU DESIGNED SPIDER-MAN'S TECH. WITHOUT YOU--
AH, MR. MODELL? NOT SOMETHING I'D LIKE TO BROADCAST TO THE WORLD.
AH. OF COURSE.
MAX!

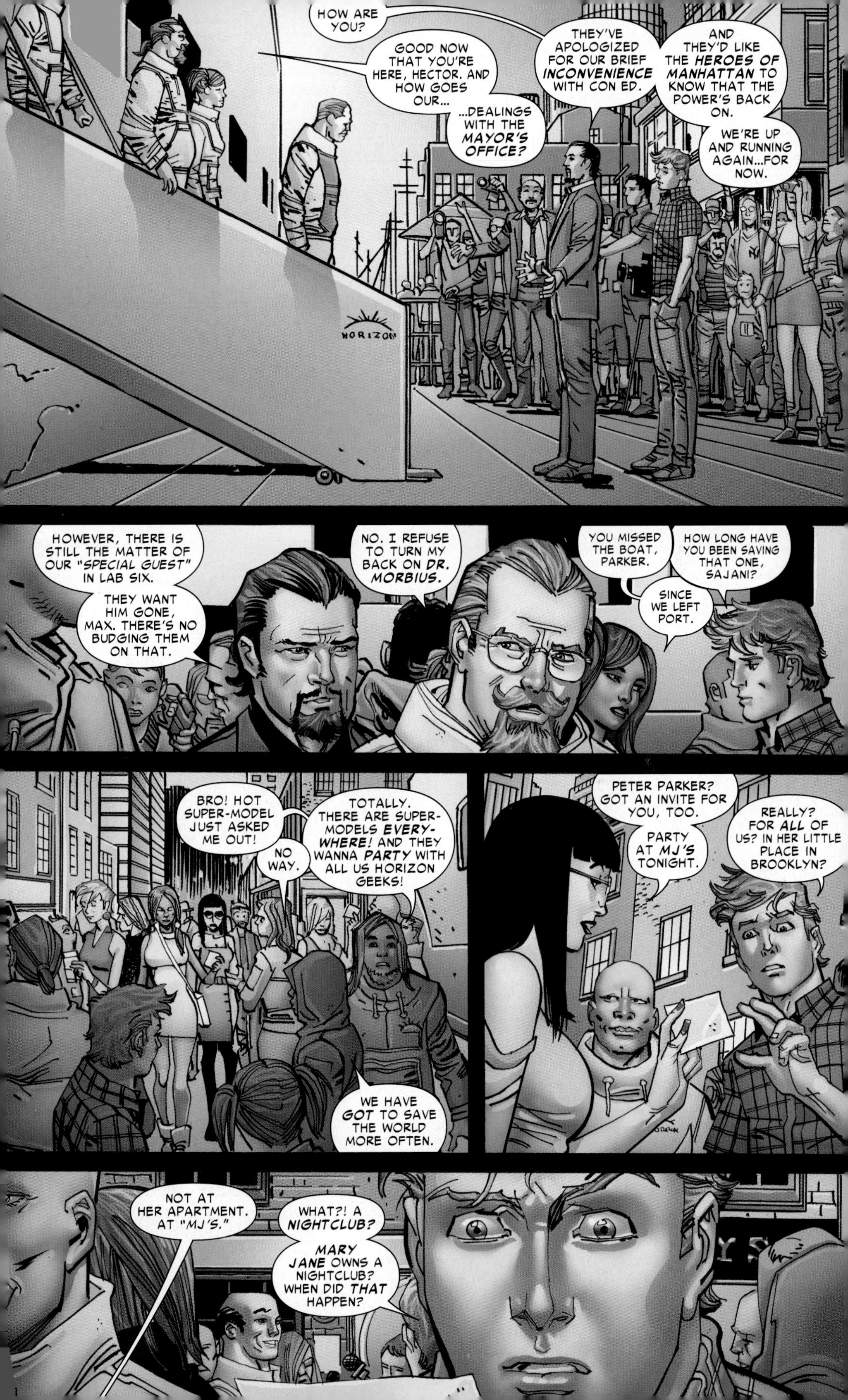

HOW ARE YOU?
GOOD NOW THAT YOU'RE HERE, HECTOR. AND HOW GOES OUR...
...DEALINGS WITH THE MAYOR'S OFFICE?
THEY'VE APOLOGIZED FOR OUR BRIEF INCONVENIENCE WITH CON ED.
AND THEY'D LIKE THE HEROES OF MANHATTAN TO KNOW THAT THE POWER'S BACK ON.
WE'RE UP AND RUNNING AGAIN...FOR NOW.
HORIZON
HOWEVER, THERE IS STILL THE MATTER OF OUR "SPECIAL GUEST" IN LAB SIX.
THEY WANT HIM GONE, MAX. THERE'S NO BUDGING THEM ON THAT.
NO. I REFUSE TO TURN MY BACK ON DR. MORBIUS.
YOU MISSED THE BOAT, PARKER.
HOW LONG HAVE YOU BEEN SAVING THAT ONE, SAJANI?
SINCE WE LEFT PORT.
BRO! HOT SUPER-MODEL JUST ASKED ME OUT!
NO WAY.
TOTALLY. THERE ARE SUPER-MODELS EVERY-WHERE! AND THEY WANNA PARTY WITH ALL US HORIZON GEEKS!
WE HAVE GOT TO SAVE THE WORLD MORE OFTEN.
PETER PARKER? GOT AN INVITE FOR YOU, TOO.
PARTY AT MJ'S TONIGHT.
REALLY? FOR ALL OF US? IN HER LITTLE PLACE IN BROOKLYN?
NOT AT HER APARTMENT. AT "MJ'S."
WHAT?! A NIGHTCLUB?
MARY JANE OWNS A NIGHTCLUB? WHEN DID THAT HAPPEN?

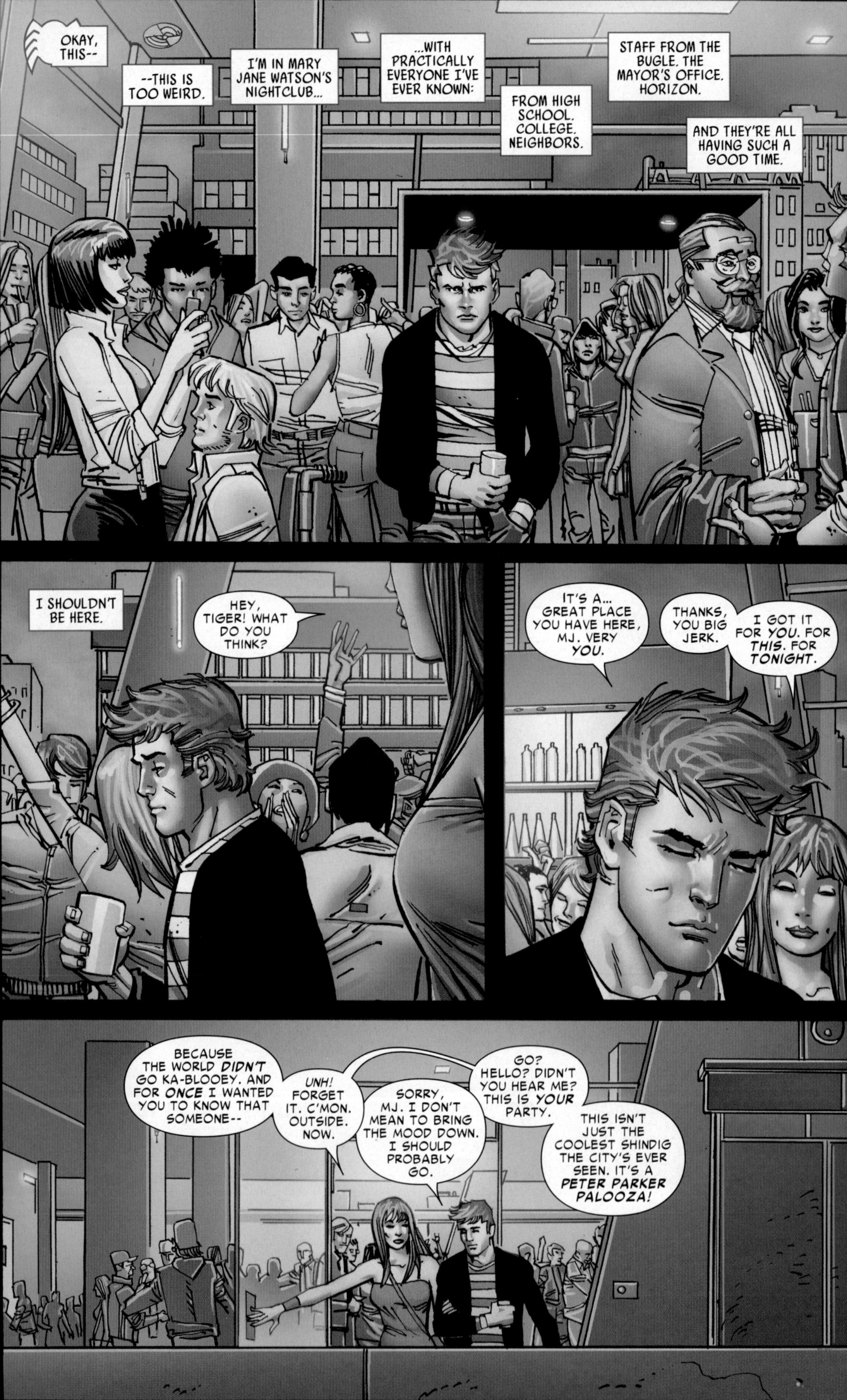
OKAY, THIS--
--THIS IS TOO WEIRD.
I'M IN MARY JANE WATSON'S NIGHTCLUB...
...WITH PRACTICALLY EVERYONE I'VE EVER KNOWN:
FROM HIGH SCHOOL. COLLEGE. NEIGHBORS.
STAFF FROM THE BUGLE. THE MAYOR'S OFFICE. HORIZON.
AND THEY'RE ALL HAVING SUCH A GOOD TIME.
I SHOULDN'T BE HERE.
HEY, TIGER! WHAT DO YOU THINK?
IT'S A... GREAT PLACE YOU HAVE HERE, MJ. VERY YOU.
THANKS, YOU BIG JERK.
I GOT IT FOR YOU. FOR THIS. FOR TONIGHT.
GO? HELLO? DIDN'T YOU HEAR ME? THIS IS YOUR PARTY.
THIS ISN'T JUST THE COOLEST SHINDIG THE CITY'S EVER SEEN. IT'S A PETER PARKER PALOOZA!
SORRY, MJ. I DON'T MEAN TO BRING THE MOOD DOWN. I SHOULD PROBABLY GO.
UNH! FORGET IT. C'MON. OUTSIDE. NOW.
BECAUSE THE WORLD DIDN'T GO KA-BLOOEY. AND FOR ONCE I WANTED YOU TO KNOW THAT SOMEONE--

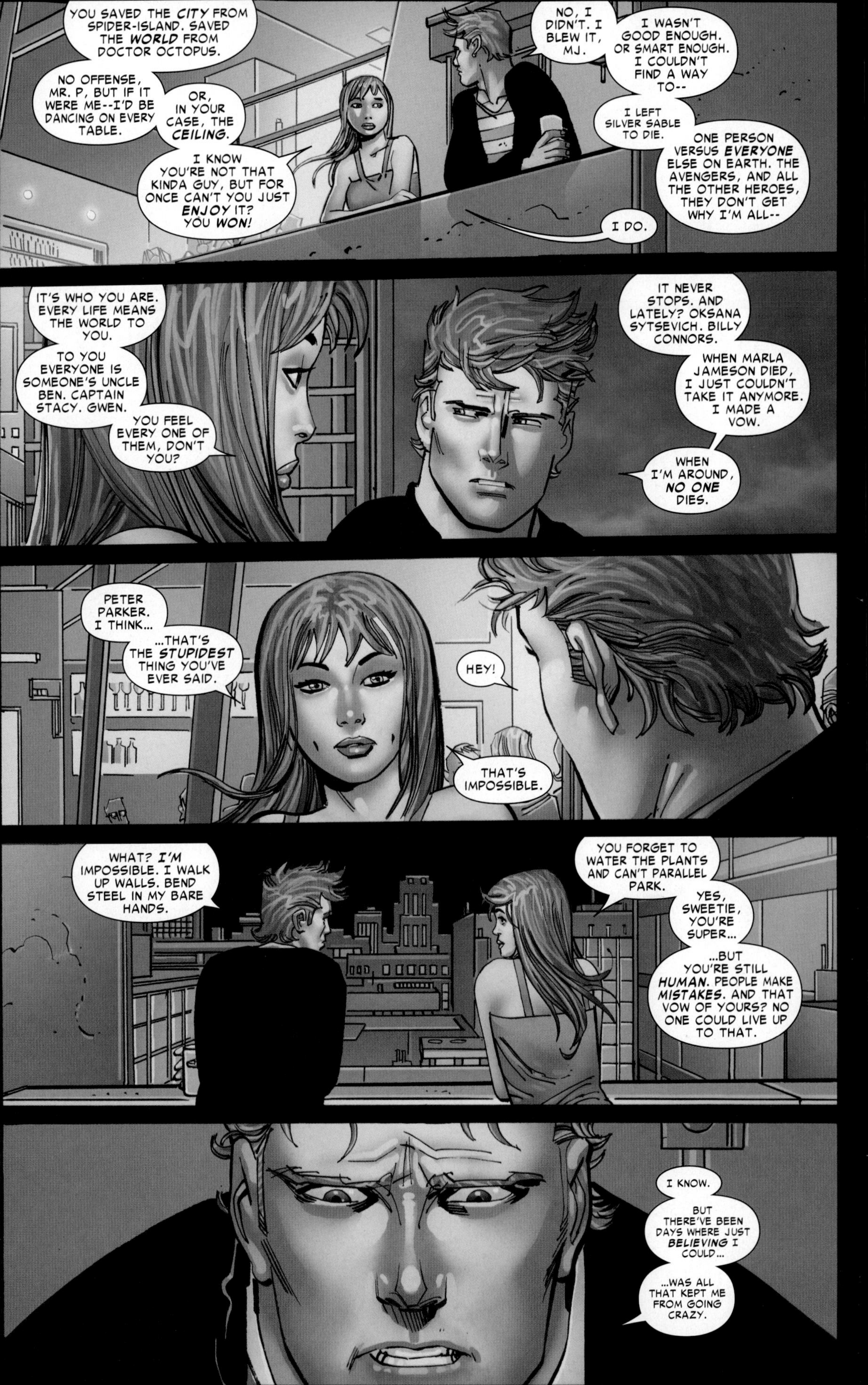
YOU SAVED THE CITY FROM SPIDER-ISLAND. SAVED THE WORLD FROM DOCTOR OCTOPUS.
NO OFFENSE, MR. P, BUT IF IT WERE ME--I'D BE DANCING ON EVERY TABLE.
OR, IN YOUR CASE, THE CEILING.
I KNOW YOU'RE NOT THAT KINDA GUY, BUT FOR ONCE CAN'T YOU JUST ENJOY IT? YOU WON!
NO, I DIDN'T. I BLEW IT, MJ.
I WASN'T GOOD ENOUGH. OR SMART ENOUGH. I COULDN'T FIND A WAY TO--
I LEFT SILVER SABLE TO DIE.
ONE PERSON VERSUS EVERYONE ELSE ON EARTH. THE AVENGERS, AND ALL THE OTHER HEROES, THEY DON'T GET WHY I'M ALL--
I DO.
IT'S WHO YOU ARE. EVERY LIFE MEANS THE WORLD TO YOU.
TO YOU EVERYONE IS SOMEONE'S UNCLE BEN. CAPTAIN STACY. GWEN.
YOU FEEL EVERY ONE OF THEM, DON'T YOU?
IT NEVER STOPS. AND LATELY? OKSANA SYTSEVICH. BILLY CONNORS.
WHEN MARLA JAMESON DIED, I JUST COULDN'T TAKE IT ANYMORE. I MADE A VOW.
WHEN I'M AROUND, NO ONE DIES.
PETER PARKER. I THINK...
...THAT'S THE STUPIDEST THING YOU'VE EVER SAID.
HEY!
THAT'S IMPOSSIBLE.
WHAT? I'M IMPOSSIBLE. I WALK UP WALLS. BEND STEEL IN MY BARE HANDS.
YOU FORGET TO WATER THE PLANTS AND CAN'T PARALLEL PARK.
YES, SWEETIE, YOU'RE SUPER...
...BUT YOU'RE STILL HUMAN. PEOPLE MAKE MISTAKES. AND THAT VOW OF YOURS? NO ONE COULD LIVE UP TO THAT.
I KNOW.
BUT THERE'VE BEEN DAYS WHERE JUST BELIEVING I COULD...
...WAS ALL THAT KEPT ME FROM GOING CRAZY.

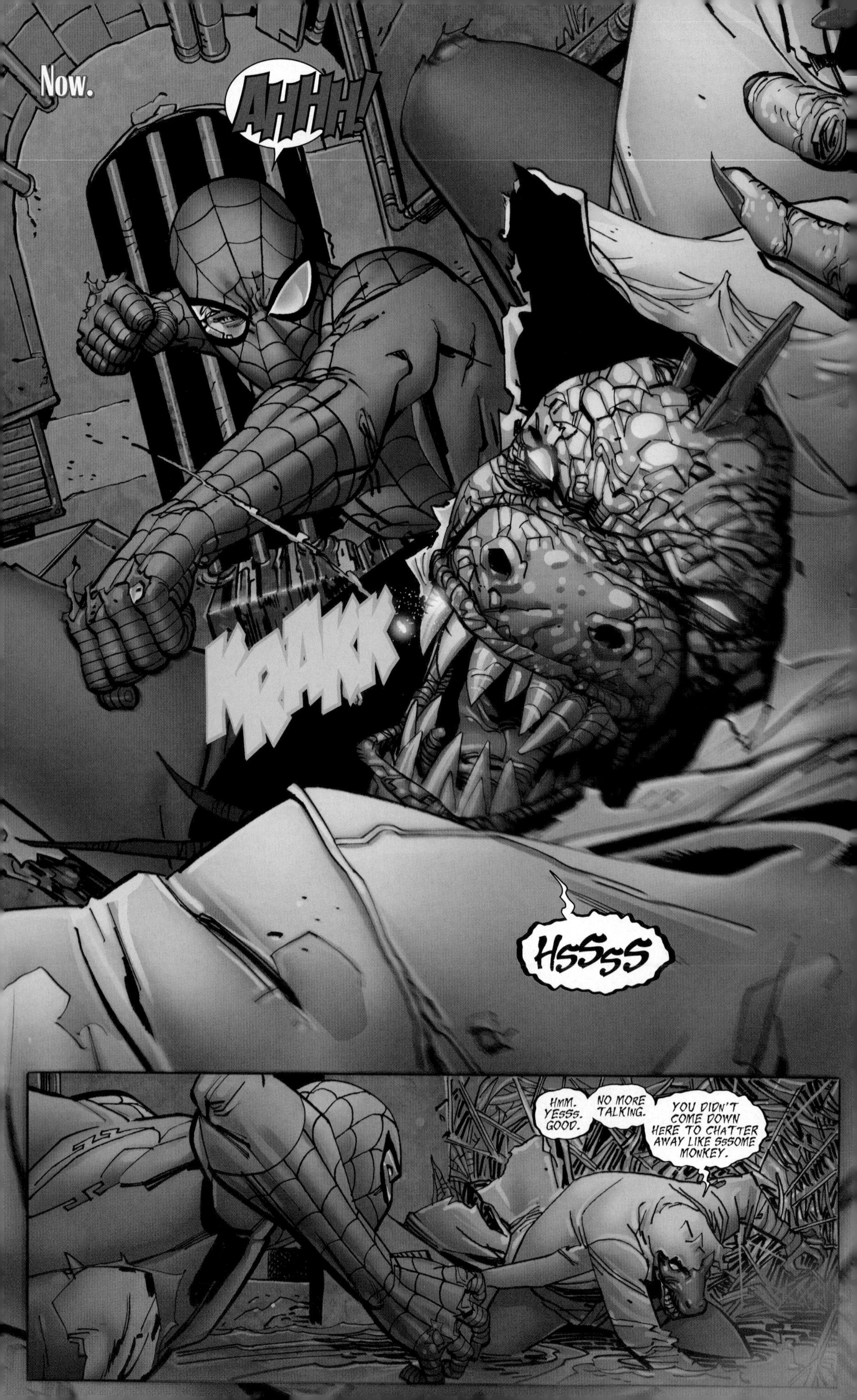
Now.
AHHH!
KRAKK
HSSSS
HMM. YESSS. GOOD.
NO MORE TALKING.
YOU DIDN'T COME DOWN HERE TO CHATTER AWAY LIKE SSSOME MONKEY.

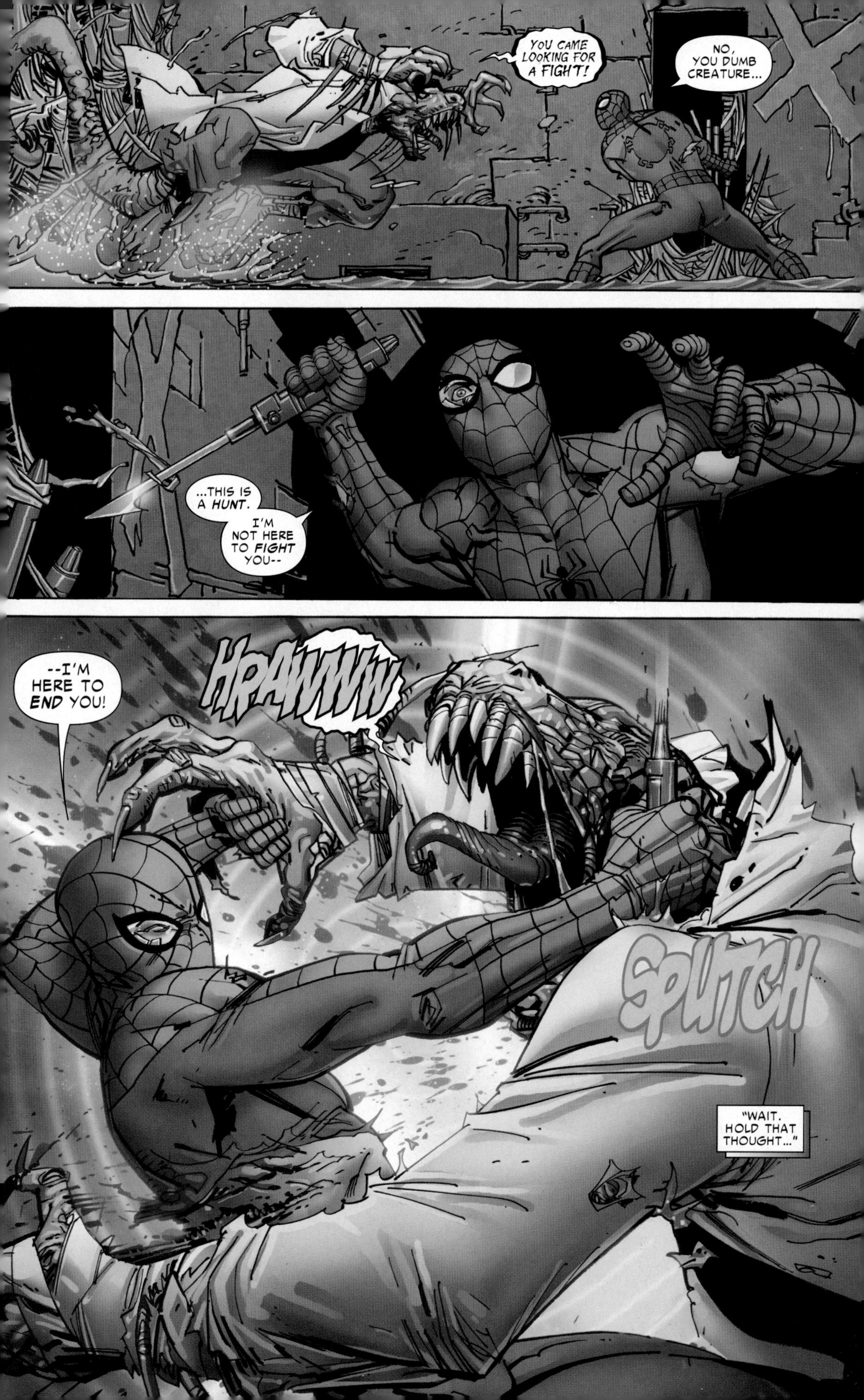
YOU CAME LOOKING FOR A FIGHT!
NO, YOU DUMB CREATURE...
...THIS IS A HUNT.
I'M NOT HERE TO FIGHT YOU--
--I'M HERE TO END YOU!
HRAWWWW
SPLITCH
"WAIT. HOLD THAT THOUGHT..."

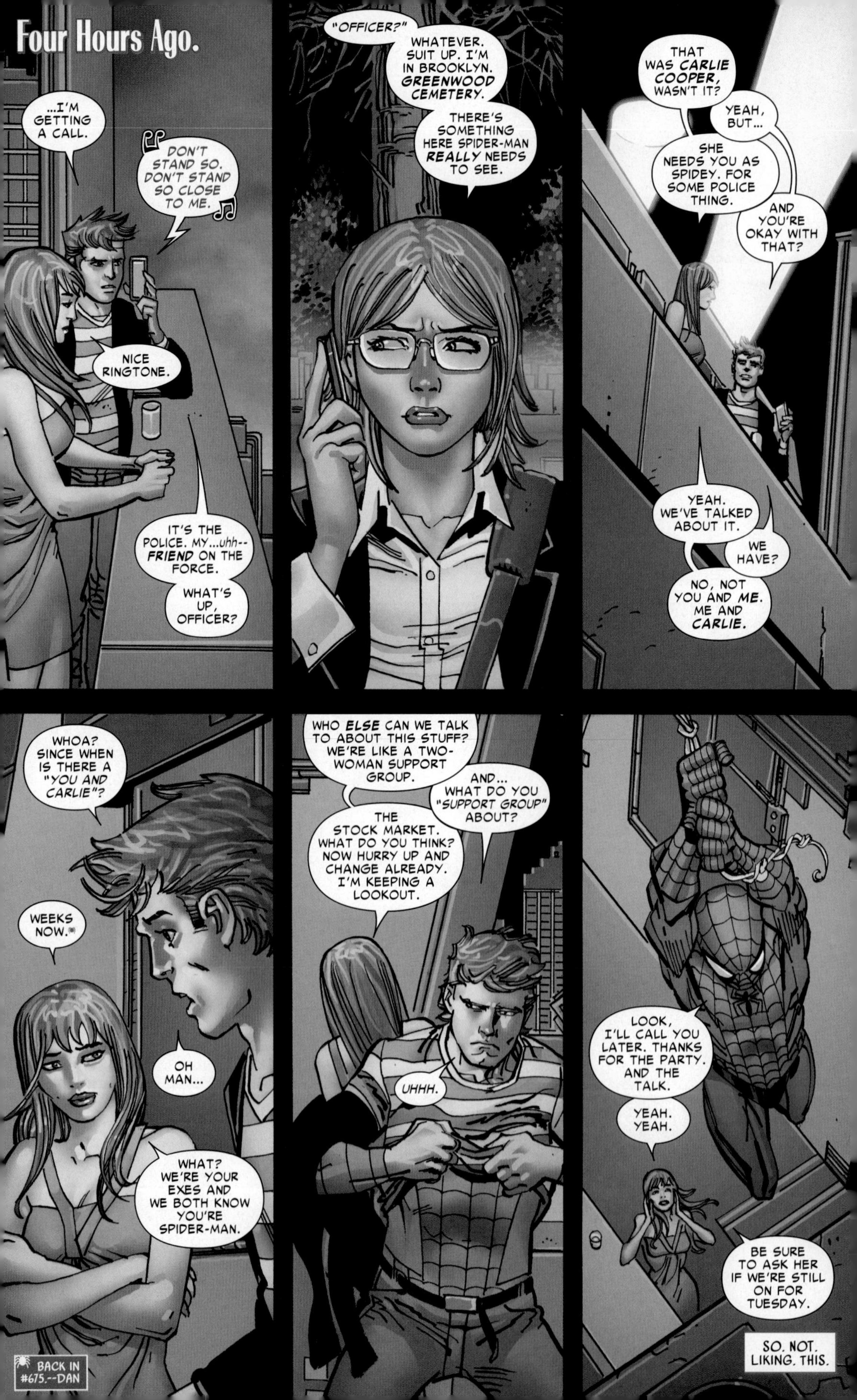
Four Hours Ago.
...I'M GETTING A CALL.
DON'T STAND SO. DON'T STAND SO CLOSE TO ME.
NICE RINGTONE.
IT'S THE POLICE. MY...uhh-- FRIEND ON THE FORCE.
WHAT'S UP, OFFICER?
"OFFICER?"
WHATEVER. SUIT UP. I'M IN BROOKLYN. GREENWOOD CEMETERY.
THERE'S SOMETHING HERE SPIDER-MAN REALLY NEEDS TO SEE.
THAT WAS CARLIE COOPER, WASN'T IT?
YEAH, BUT...
SHE NEEDS YOU AS SPIDEY. FOR SOME POLICE THING.
AND YOU'RE OKAY WITH THAT?
YEAH. WE'VE TALKED ABOUT IT.
WE HAVE?
NO, NOT YOU AND ME. ME AND CARLIE.
WHOA? SINCE WHEN IS THERE A "YOU AND CARLIE"?
WEEKS NOW.*
OH MAN...
WHAT? WE'RE YOUR EXES AND WE BOTH KNOW YOU'RE SPIDER-MAN.
*BACK IN #675.--DAN
WHO ELSE CAN WE TALK TO ABOUT THIS STUFF? WE'RE LIKE A TWO-WOMAN SUPPORT GROUP.
AND... WHAT DO YOU "SUPPORT GROUP" ABOUT?
THE STOCK MARKET. WHAT DO YOU THINK? NOW HURRY UP AND CHANGE ALREADY. I'M KEEPING A LOOKOUT.
UHHH.
LOOK, I'LL CALL YOU LATER. THANKS FOR THE PARTY. AND THE TALK.
YEAH. YEAH.
BE SURE TO ASK HER IF WE'RE STILL ON FOR TUESDAY.
SO. NOT. LIKING. THIS.

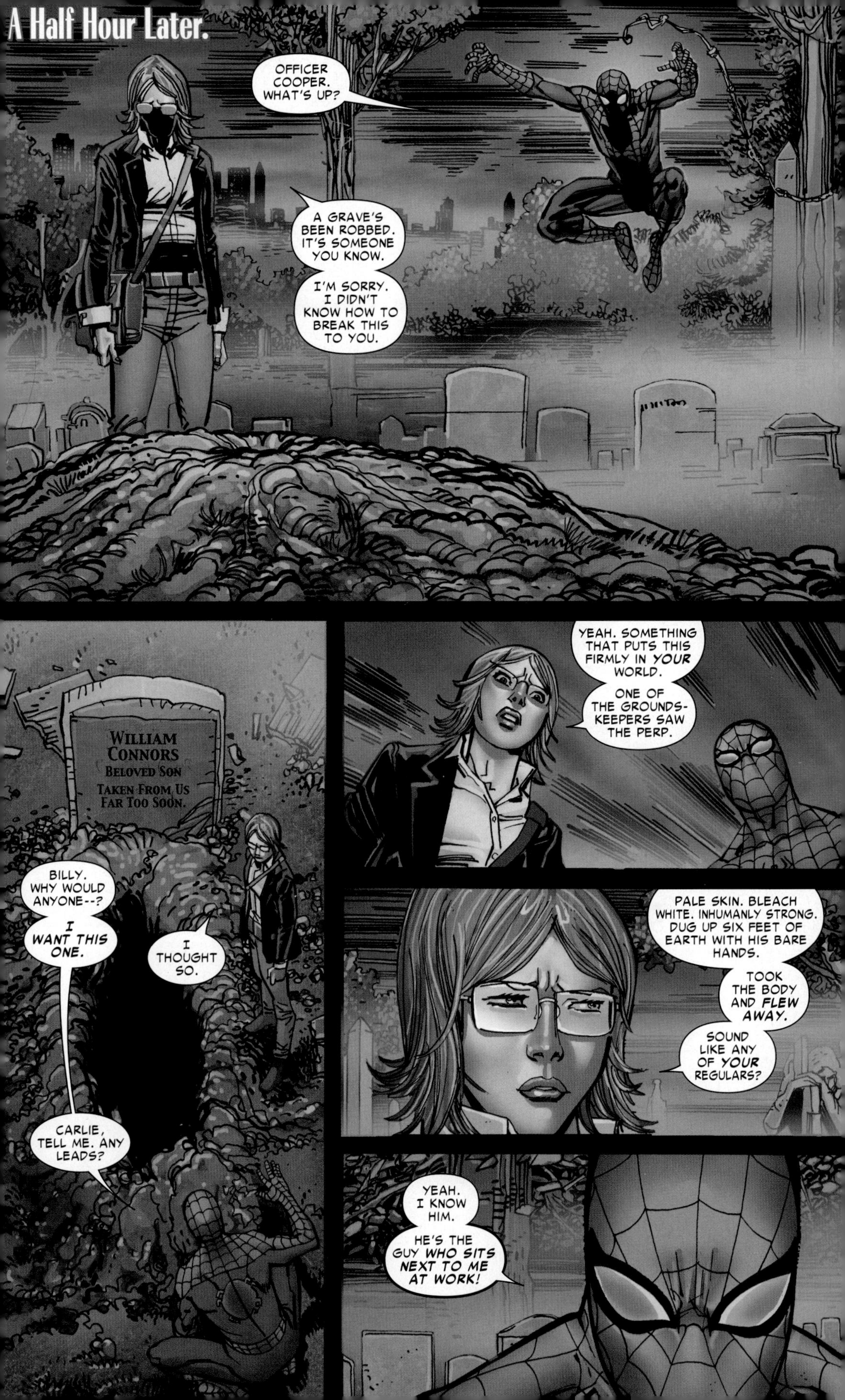
A Half Hour Later.
OFFICER COOPER. WHAT'S UP?
A GRAVE'S BEEN ROBBED. IT'S SOMEONE YOU KNOW.
I'M SORRY. I DIDN'T KNOW HOW TO BREAK THIS TO YOU.
WILLIAM CONNORS
BELOVED SON
TAKEN FROM US FAR TOO SOON.
BILLY. WHY WOULD ANYONE--?
I WANT THIS ONE.
I THOUGHT SO.
CARLIE, TELL ME. ANY LEADS?
YEAH. SOMETHING THAT PUTS THIS FIRMLY IN YOUR WORLD.
ONE OF THE GROUNDS-KEEPERS SAW THE PERP.
PALE SKIN. BLEACH WHITE. INHUMANLY STRONG. DUG UP SIX FEET OF EARTH WITH HIS BARE HANDS.
TOOK THE BODY AND FLEW AWAY.
SOUND LIKE ANY OF YOUR REGULARS?
YEAH. I KNOW HIM.
HE'S THE GUY WHO SITS NEXT TO ME AT WORK!

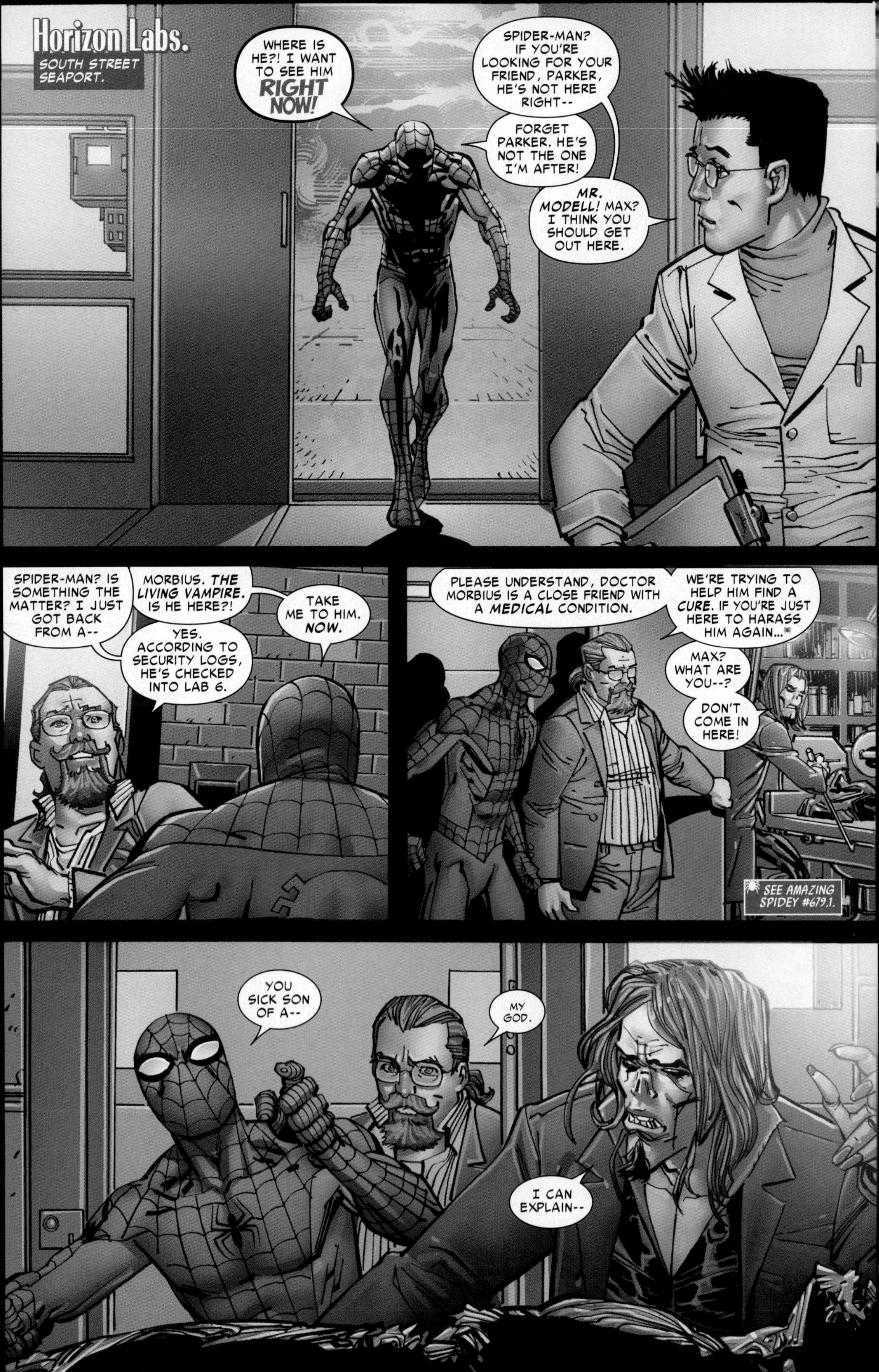
Horizon Labs.
SOUTH STREET SEAPORT.
WHERE IS HE?! I WANT TO SEE HIM RIGHT NOW!
SPIDER-MAN? IF YOU'RE LOOKING FOR YOUR FRIEND, PARKER, HE'S NOT HERE RIGHT--
FORGET PARKER. HE'S NOT THE ONE I'M AFTER!
MR. MODELL! MAX? I THINK YOU SHOULD GET OUT HERE.
SPIDER-MAN? IS SOMETHING THE MATTER? I JUST GOT BACK FROM A--
MORBIUS. THE LIVING VAMPIRE. IS HE HERE?!
YES. ACCORDING TO SECURITY LOGS, HE'S CHECKED INTO LAB 6.
TAKE ME TO HIM. NOW.
PLEASE UNDERSTAND, DOCTOR MORBIUS IS A CLOSE FRIEND WITH A MEDICAL CONDITION.
WE'RE TRYING TO HELP HIM FIND A CURE. IF YOU'RE JUST HERE TO HARASS HIM AGAIN...*
MAX? WHAT ARE YOU--?
DON'T COME IN HERE!
* SEE AMAZING SPIDEY #679.1.
YOU SICK SON OF A--
MY GOD.
I CAN EXPLAIN--

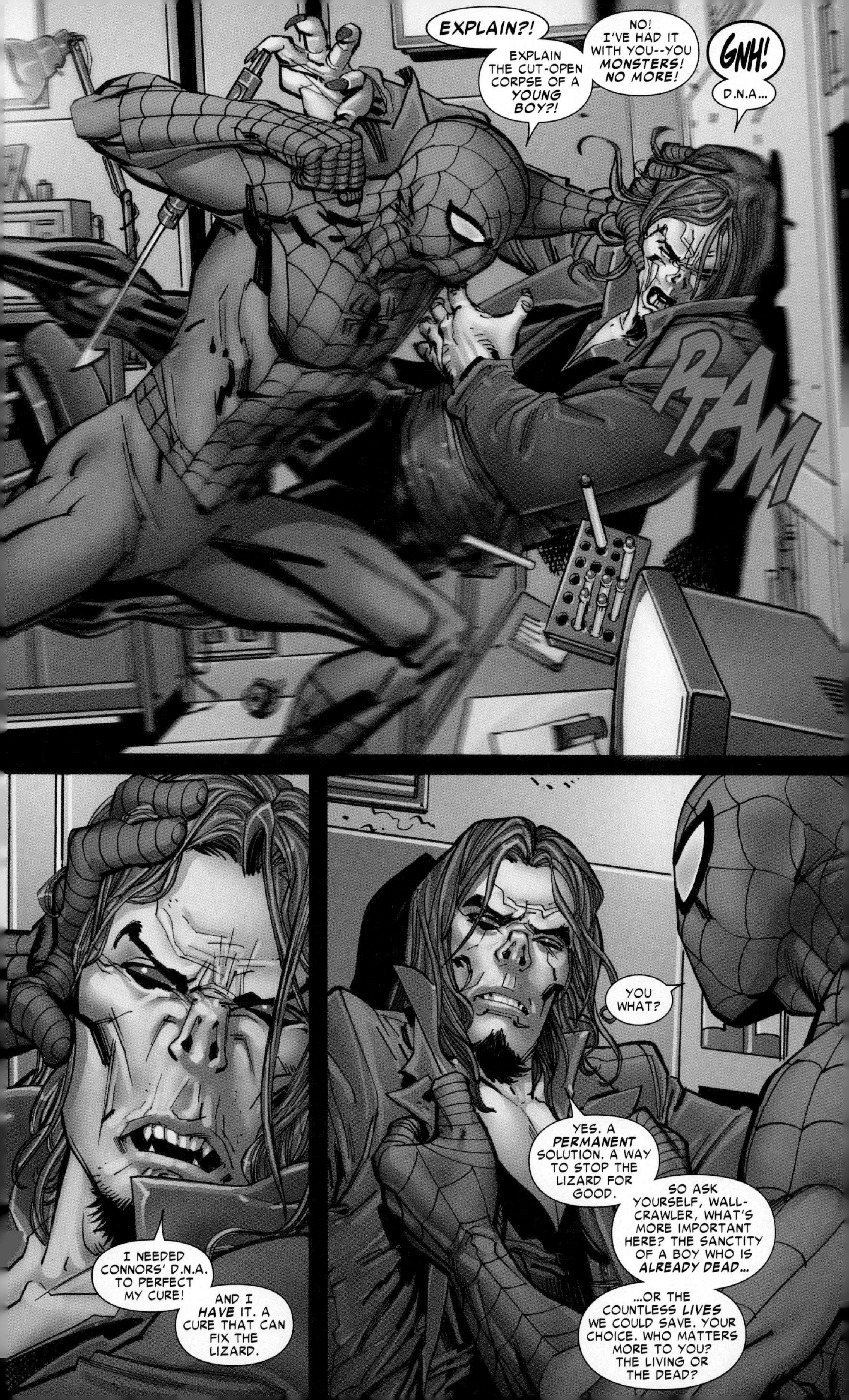
EXPLAIN?!
EXPLAIN THE CUT-OPEN CORPSE OF A YOUNG BOY?!
NO! I'VE HAD IT WITH YOU--YOU MONSTERS! NO MORE!
GNH!
D.N.A...
RAM
I NEEDED CONNORS' D.N.A. TO PERFECT MY CURE!
AND I HAVE IT. A CURE THAT CAN FIX THE LIZARD.
YOU WHAT?
YES. A PERMANENT SOLUTION. A WAY TO STOP THE LIZARD FOR GOOD.
SO ASK YOURSELF, WALL-CRAWLER, WHAT'S MORE IMPORTANT HERE? THE SANCTITY OF A BOY WHO IS ALREADY DEAD...
...OR THE COUNTLESS LIVES WE COULD SAVE. YOUR CHOICE. WHO MATTERS MORE TO YOU? THE LIVING OR THE DEAD?

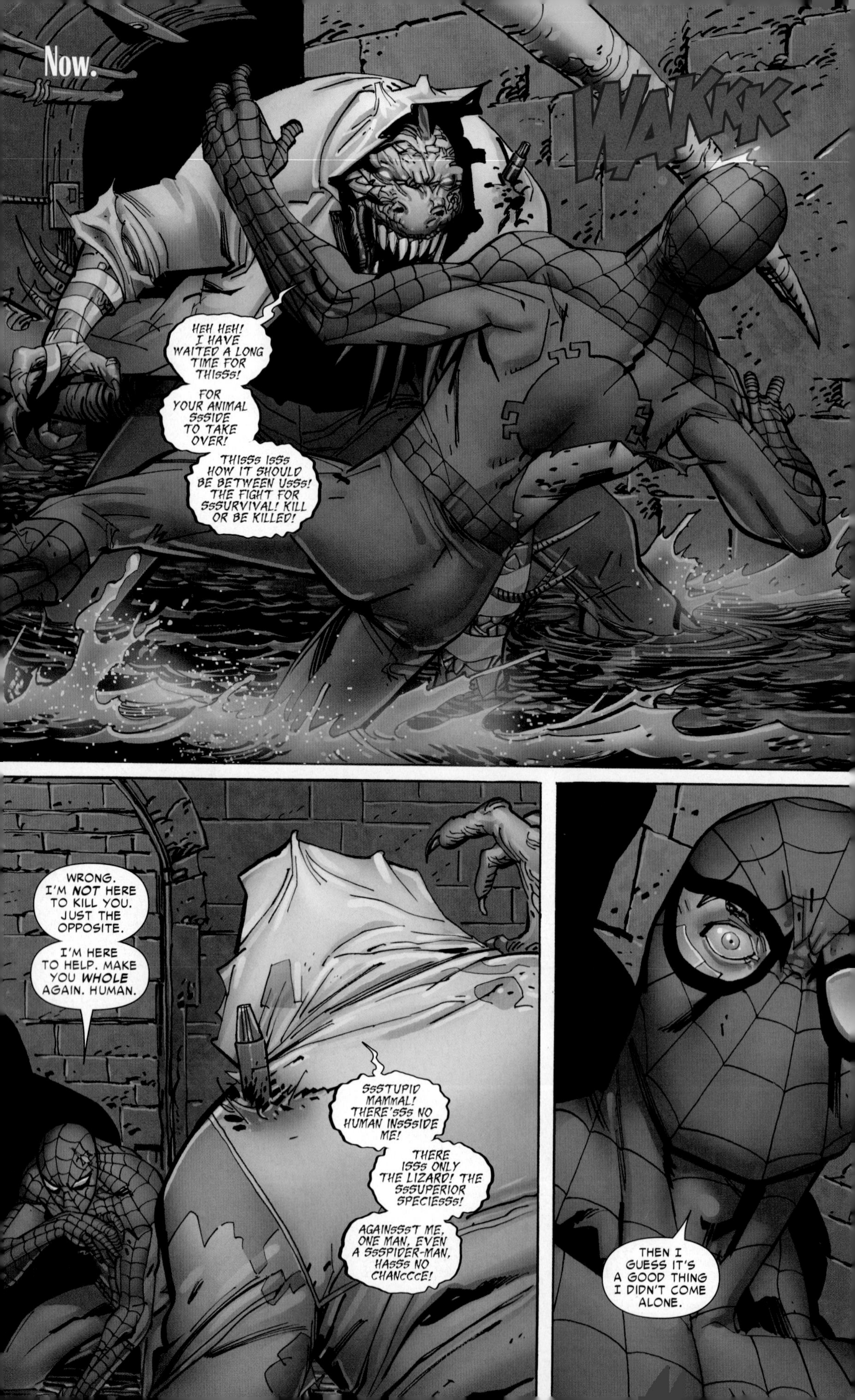
Now.
WAKKK
HEH HEH! I HAVE WAITED A LONG TIME FOR THISSS!
FOR YOUR ANIMAL SSSIDE TO TAKE OVER!
THISSS ISSS HOW IT SHOULD BE BETWEEN USSS! THE FIGHT FOR SSSURVIVAL! KILL OR BE KILLED!
WRONG. I'M **NOT** HERE TO KILL YOU. JUST THE OPPOSITE.
I'M HERE TO HELP. MAKE YOU **WHOLE** AGAIN. HUMAN.
SSSTUPID MAMMAL! THERE'SSS NO HUMAN INSSSIDE ME!
THERE ISSS ONLY THE LIZARD! THE SSSUPERIOR SPECIESSS!
AGAINSSST ME, ONE MAN, EVEN A SSSPIDER-MAN, HASSS NO CHANCCCE!
THEN I GUESS IT'S A GOOD THING I DIDN'T COME ALONE.

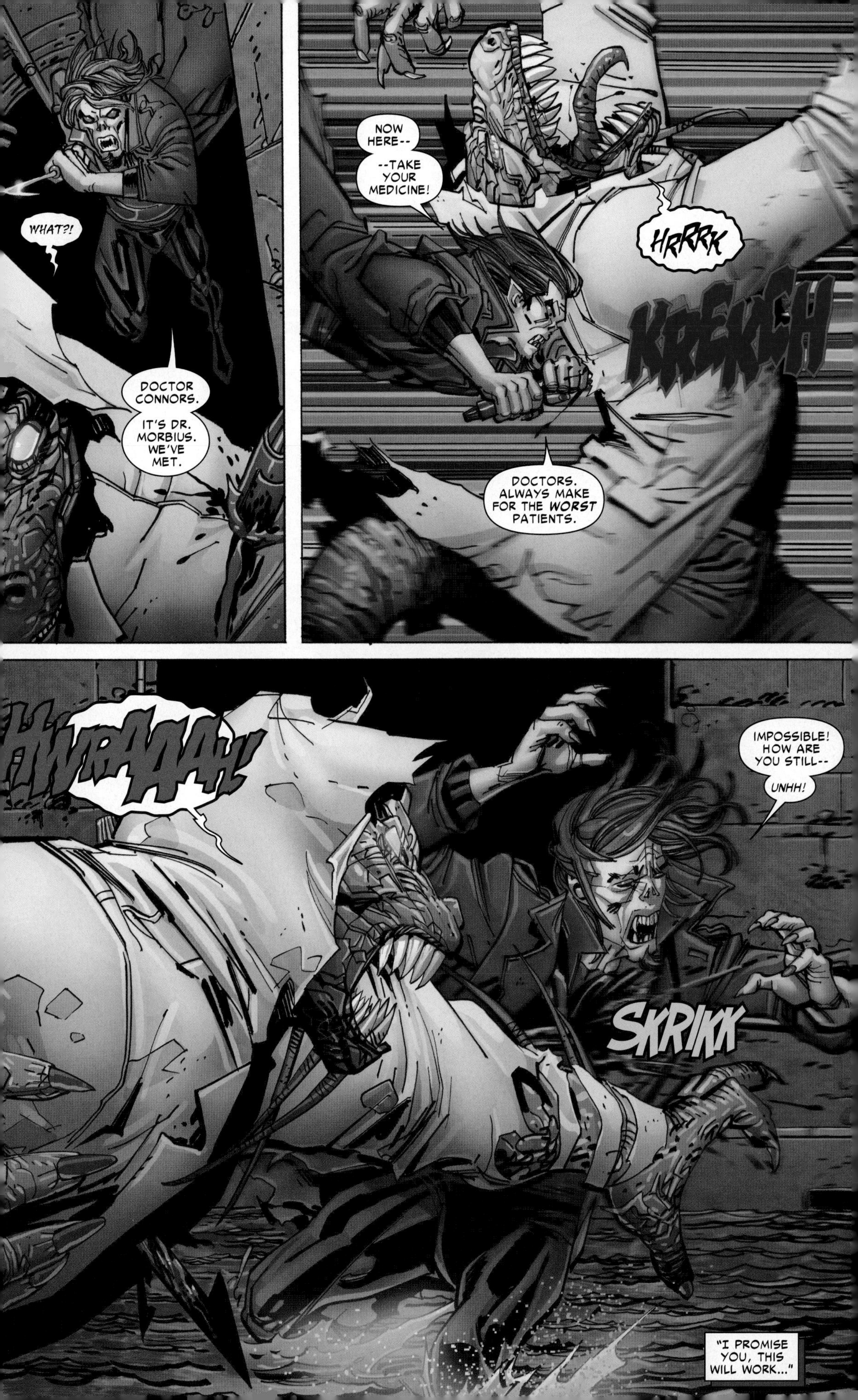
WHAT?!
DOCTOR CONNORS.
IT'S DR. MORBIUS. WE'VE MET.
NOW HERE--
--TAKE YOUR MEDICINE!
HRRRK
KRESCH
DOCTORS. ALWAYS MAKE FOR THE WORST PATIENTS.
HWRAAAH!
IMPOSSIBLE! HOW ARE YOU STILL--
UNHH!
SKRIKK
"I PROMISE YOU, THIS WILL WORK..."

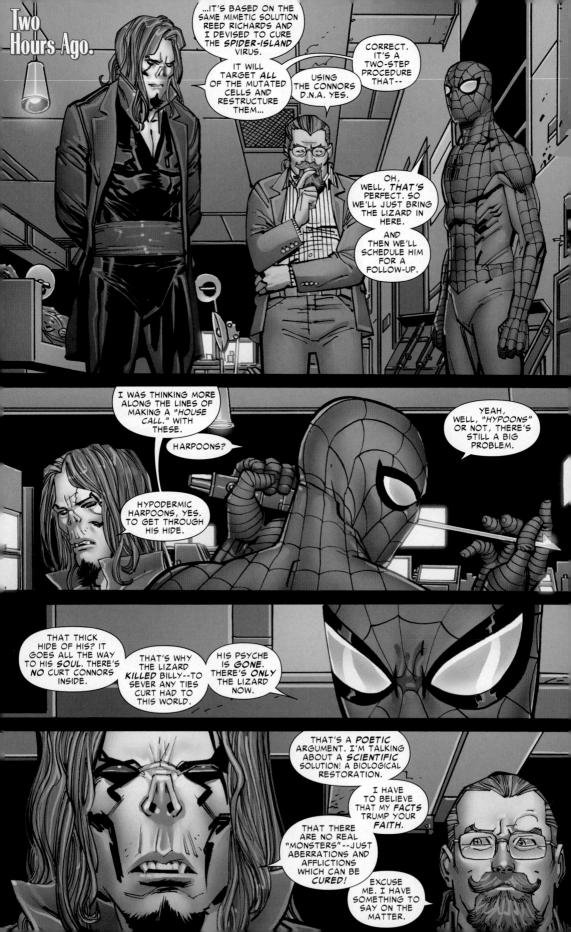

Two Hours Ago.

...IT'S BASED ON THE SAME MIMETIC SOLUTION REED RICHARDS AND I DEVISED TO CURE THE *SPIDER-ISLAND* VIRUS.

IT WILL TARGET *ALL* OF THE MUTATED CELLS AND RESTRUCTURE THEM...

USING THE CONNORS D.N.A. YES.

CORRECT. IT'S A TWO-STEP PROCEDURE THAT--

OH, WELL, *THAT'S* PERFECT. SO WE'LL JUST BRING THE LIZARD IN HERE.

AND THEN WE'LL SCHEDULE HIM FOR A FOLLOW-UP.

I WAS THINKING MORE ALONG THE LINES OF MAKING A "HOUSE CALL." WITH THESE.

HARPOONS?

HYPODERMIC HARPOONS, YES. TO GET THROUGH HIS HIDE.

YEAH, WELL, "HYPOONS" OR NOT, THERE'S STILL A BIG PROBLEM.

THAT THICK HIDE OF HIS? IT GOES ALL THE WAY TO HIS *SOUL*. THERE'S *NO* CURT CONNORS INSIDE.

THAT'S WHY THE LIZARD *KILLED* BILLY--TO SEVER ANY TIES CURT HAD TO THIS WORLD.

HIS PSYCHE IS *GONE*. THERE'S *ONLY* THE LIZARD NOW.

THAT'S A *POETIC* ARGUMENT. I'M TALKING ABOUT A *SCIENTIFIC* SOLUTION! A BIOLOGICAL RESTORATION.

I HAVE TO BELIEVE THAT MY *FACTS* TRUMP YOUR *FAITH*.

THAT THERE ARE NO REAL "MONSTERS"--JUST ABERRATIONS AND AFFLICTIONS WHICH CAN BE *CURED!*

EXCUSE ME. I HAVE SOMETHING TO SAY ON THE MATTER.

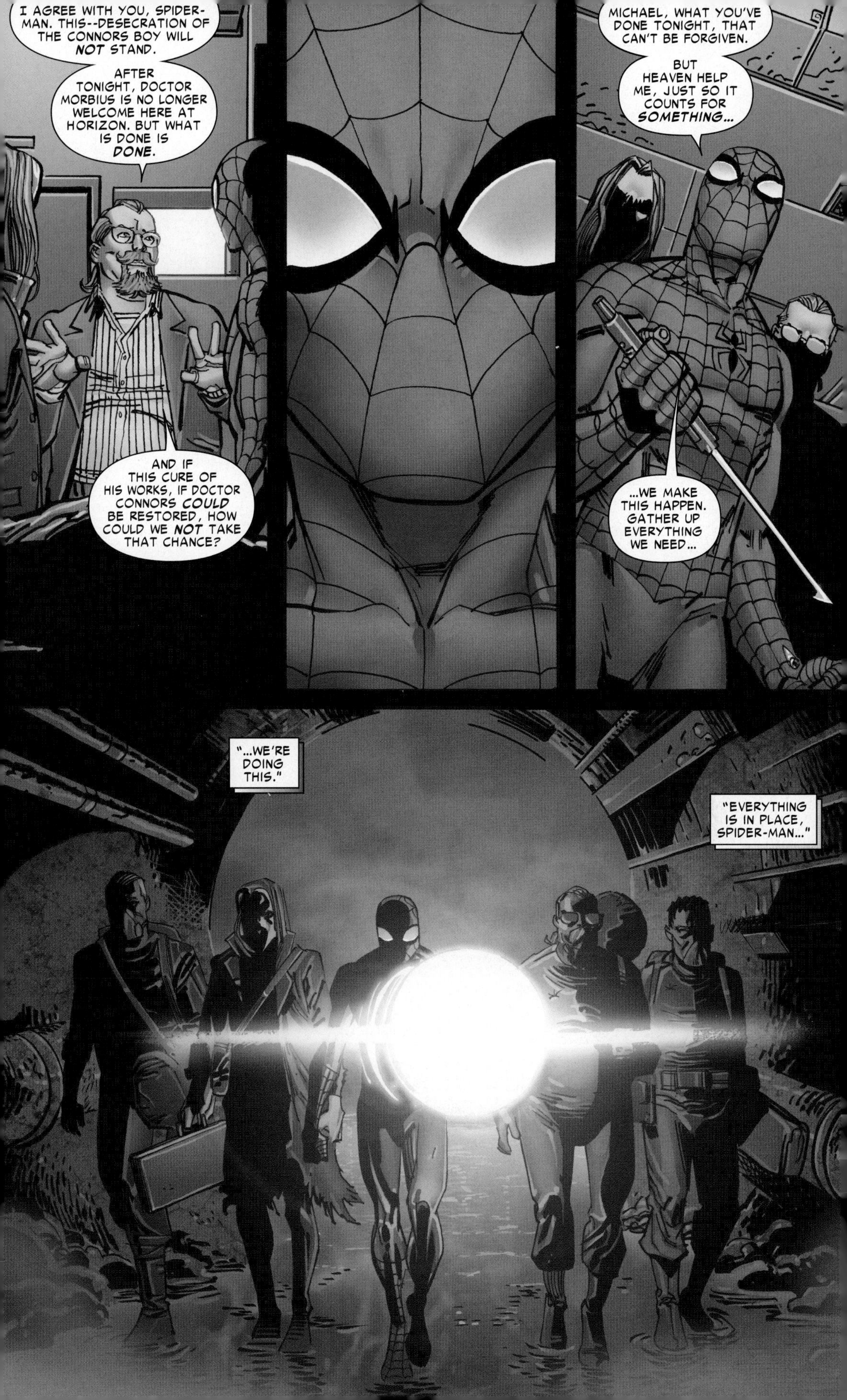
I AGREE WITH YOU, SPIDER-MAN. THIS--DESECRATION OF THE CONNORS BOY WILL *NOT* STAND.
AFTER TONIGHT, DOCTOR MORBIUS IS NO LONGER WELCOME HERE AT HORIZON. BUT WHAT IS DONE IS *DONE*.
AND IF THIS CURE OF HIS WORKS, IF DOCTOR CONNORS *COULD* BE RESTORED, HOW COULD WE *NOT* TAKE THAT CHANCE?
MICHAEL, WHAT YOU'VE DONE TONIGHT, THAT CAN'T BE FORGIVEN.
BUT HEAVEN HELP ME, JUST SO IT COUNTS FOR *SOMETHING*...
...WE MAKE THIS HAPPEN. GATHER UP EVERYTHING WE NEED...
"...WE'RE DOING THIS."
"EVERYTHING IS IN PLACE, SPIDER-MAN..."

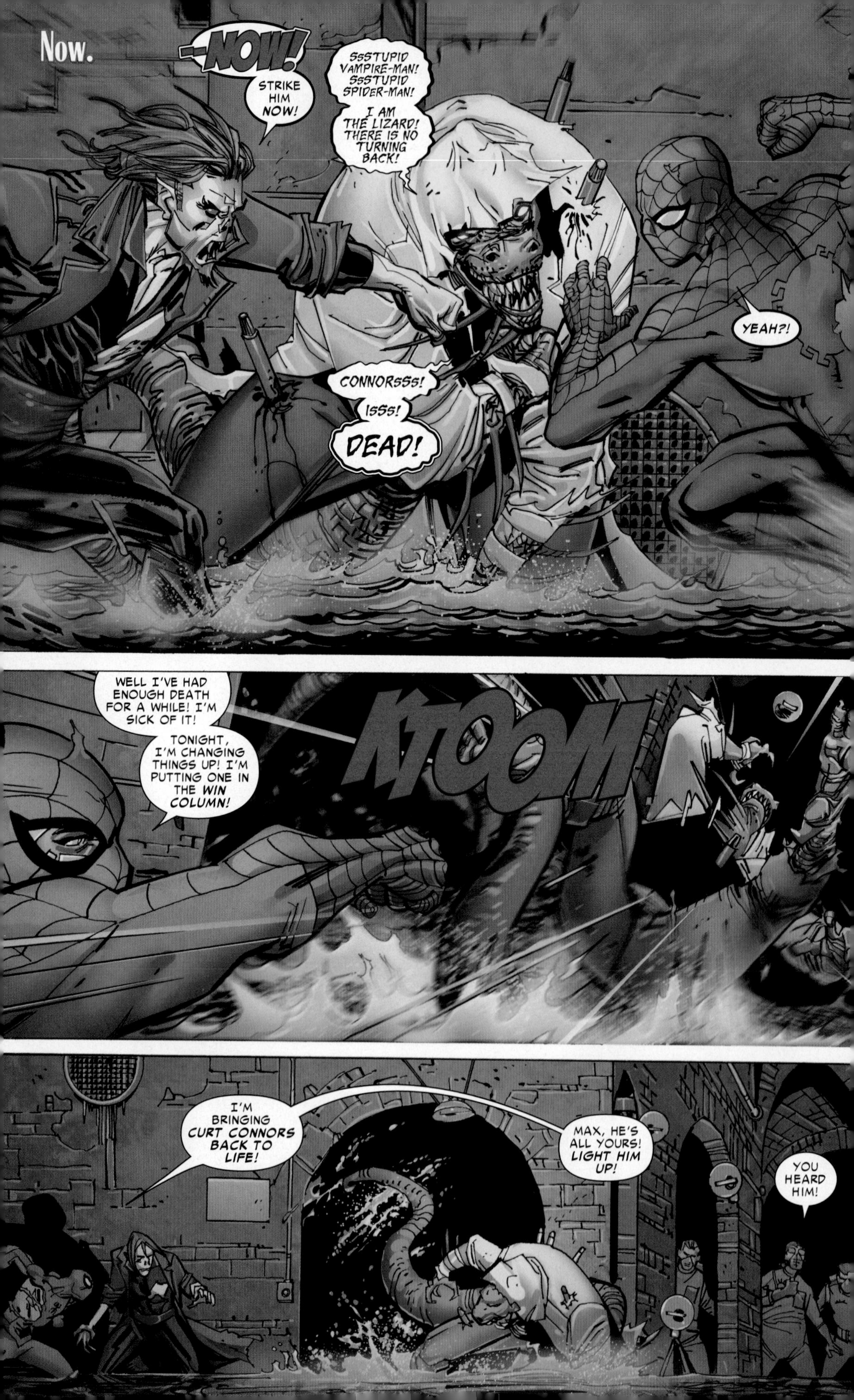
Now.
--NOW!
STRIKE HIM NOW!
SSSTUPID VAMPIRE-MAN! SSSTUPID SPIDER-MAN!
I AM THE LIZARD! THERE IS NO TURNING BACK!
YEAH?!
CONNORSSS!
ISSS!
DEAD!
WELL I'VE HAD ENOUGH DEATH FOR A WHILE! I'M SICK OF IT!
TONIGHT, I'M CHANGING THINGS UP! I'M PUTTING ONE IN THE WIN COLUMN!
KTOOM
I'M BRINGING CURT CONNORS BACK TO LIFE!
MAX, HE'S ALL YOURS! LIGHT HIM UP!
YOU HEARD HIM!

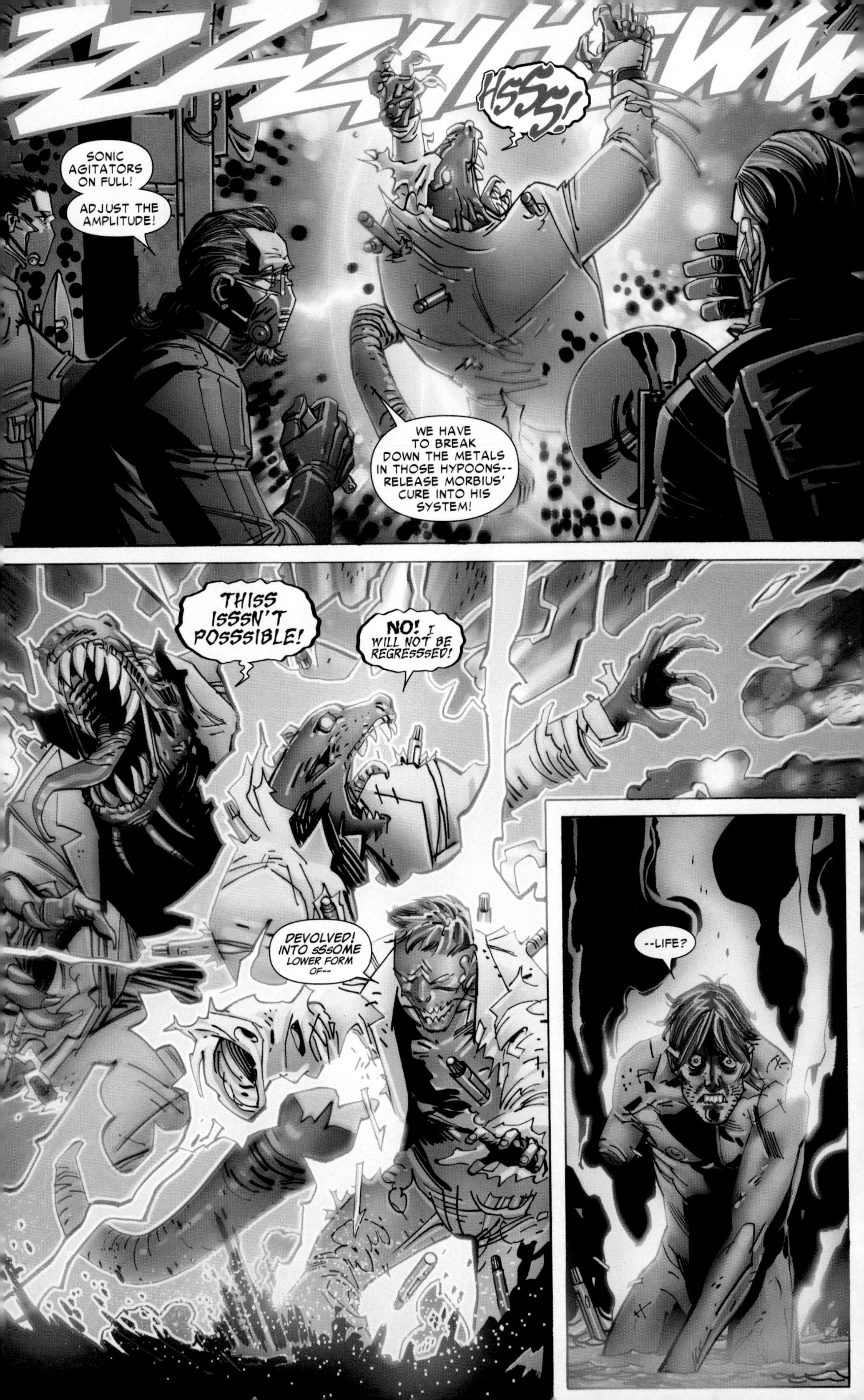
ZZZZHHEWW
HSSS!
SONIC AGITATORS ON FULL!
ADJUST THE AMPLITUDE!
WE HAVE TO BREAK DOWN THE METALS IN THOSE HYPOONS-- RELEASE MORBIUS' CURE INTO HIS SYSTEM!
THISS ISSSN'T POSSSIBLE!
NO! I WILL NOT BE REGRESSSED!
DEVOLVED! INTO SSSOME LOWER FORM OF--
--LIFE?

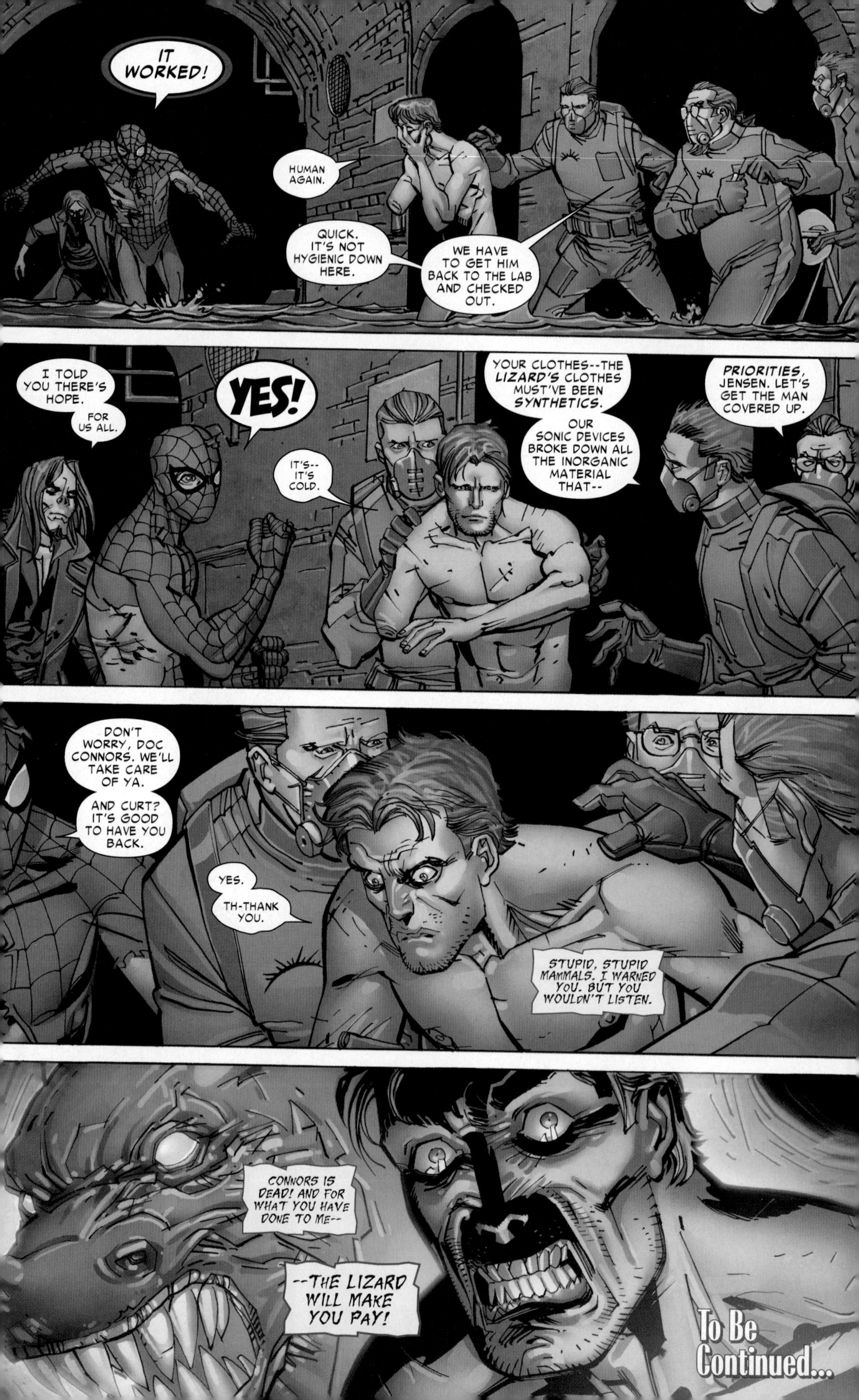
IT WORKED!
HUMAN AGAIN.
QUICK. IT'S NOT HYGIENIC DOWN HERE.
WE HAVE TO GET HIM BACK TO THE LAB AND CHECKED OUT.
I TOLD YOU THERE'S HOPE.
FOR US ALL.
YES!
IT'S-- IT'S COLD.
YOUR CLOTHES--THE LIZARD'S CLOTHES MUST'VE BEEN SYNTHETICS.
OUR SONIC DEVICES BROKE DOWN ALL THE INORGANIC MATERIAL THAT--
PRIORITIES, JENSEN. LET'S GET THE MAN COVERED UP.
DON'T WORRY, DOC CONNORS. WE'LL TAKE CARE OF YA.
AND CURT? IT'S GOOD TO HAVE YOU BACK.
YES.
TH-THANK YOU.
STUPID, STUPID MAMMALS. I WARNED YOU. BUT YOU WOULDN'T LISTEN.
CONNORS IS DEAD! AND FOR WHAT YOU HAVE DONE TO ME--
--THE LIZARD WILL MAKE YOU PAY!
To Be Continued...

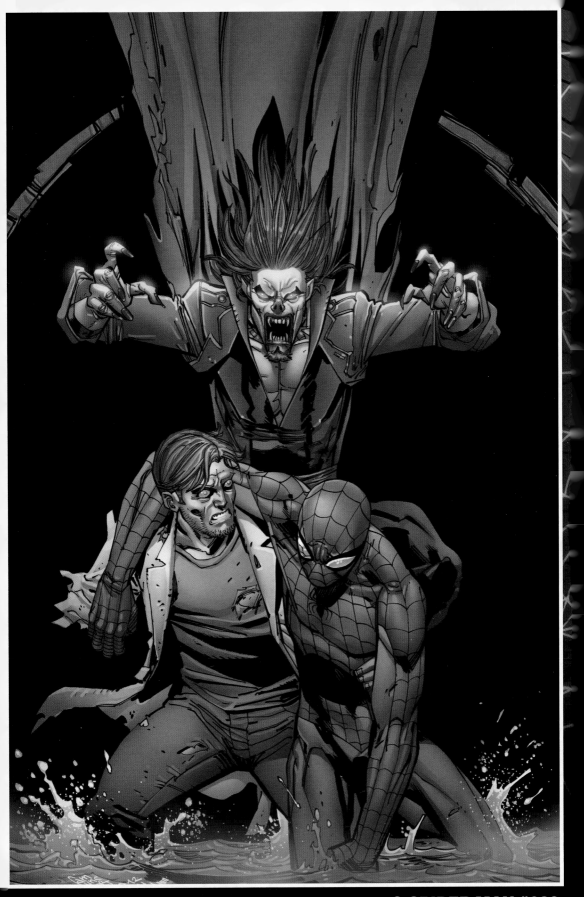

AMAZING SPIDER-MAN #689
COVER BY GIUSEPPE CAMUNCOLI, KLAUS JANSON & FRANK D'ARMATA

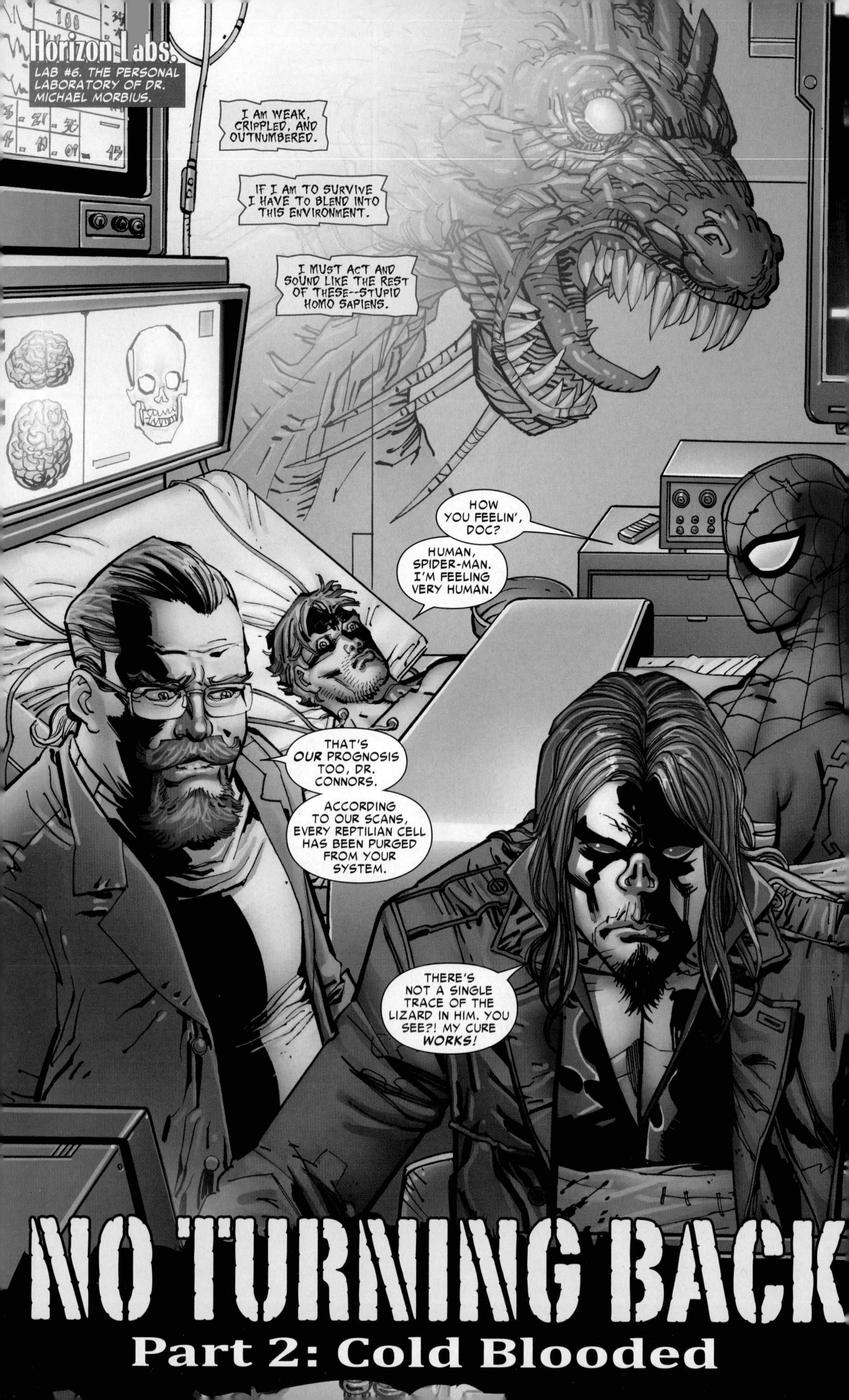
Horizon Labs.
LAB #6. THE PERSONAL LABORATORY OF DR. MICHAEL MORBIUS.
I AM WEAK, CRIPPLED, AND OUTNUMBERED.
IF I AM TO SURVIVE I HAVE TO BLEND INTO THIS ENVIRONMENT.
I MUST ACT AND SOUND LIKE THE REST OF THESE--STUPID HOMO SAPIENS.
HOW YOU FEELIN', DOC?
HUMAN, SPIDER-MAN. I'M FEELING VERY HUMAN.
THAT'S OUR PROGNOSIS TOO, DR. CONNORS.
ACCORDING TO OUR SCANS, EVERY REPTILIAN CELL HAS BEEN PURGED FROM YOUR SYSTEM.
THERE'S NOT A SINGLE TRACE OF THE LIZARD IN HIM. YOU SEE?! MY CURE WORKS!
NO TURNING BACK
Part 2: Cold Blooded

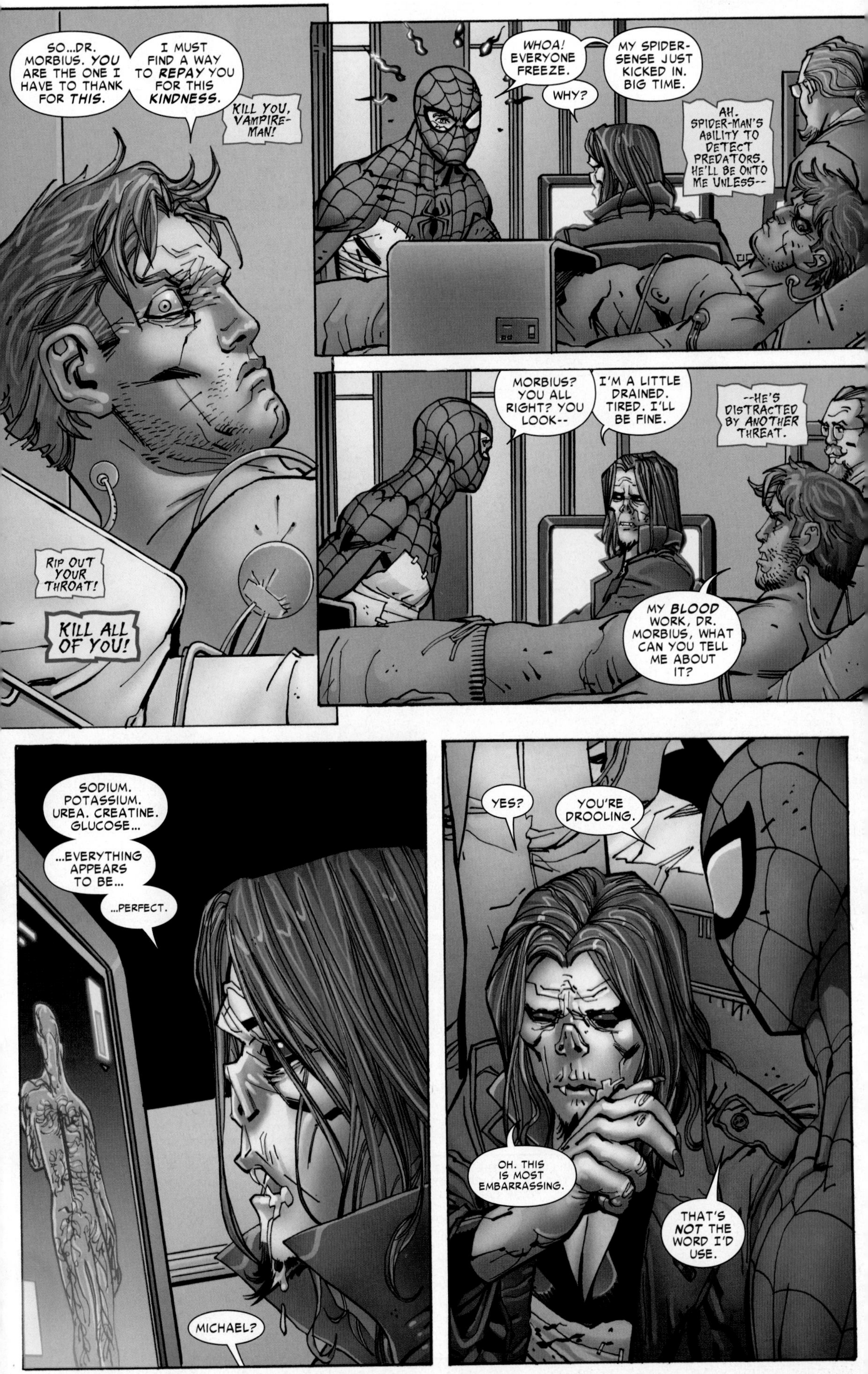
SO...DR. MORBIUS. YOU ARE THE ONE I HAVE TO THANK FOR THIS.
I MUST FIND A WAY TO REPAY YOU FOR THIS KINDNESS.
KILL YOU, VAMPIRE-MAN!
RIP OUT YOUR THROAT!
KILL ALL OF YOU!
WHOA! EVERYONE FREEZE.
WHY?
MY SPIDER-SENSE JUST KICKED IN. BIG TIME.
AH. SPIDER-MAN'S ABILITY TO DETECT PREDATORS. HE'LL BE ONTO ME UNLESS--
MORBIUS? YOU ALL RIGHT? YOU LOOK--
I'M A LITTLE DRAINED. TIRED. I'LL BE FINE.
--HE'S DISTRACTED BY ANOTHER THREAT.
MY BLOOD WORK, DR. MORBIUS, WHAT CAN YOU TELL ME ABOUT IT?
SODIUM. POTASSIUM. UREA. CREATINE. GLUCOSE...
...EVERYTHING APPEARS TO BE...
...PERFECT.
MICHAEL?
YES?
YOU'RE DROOLING.
OH. THIS IS MOST EMBARRASSING.
THAT'S NOT THE WORD I'D USE.

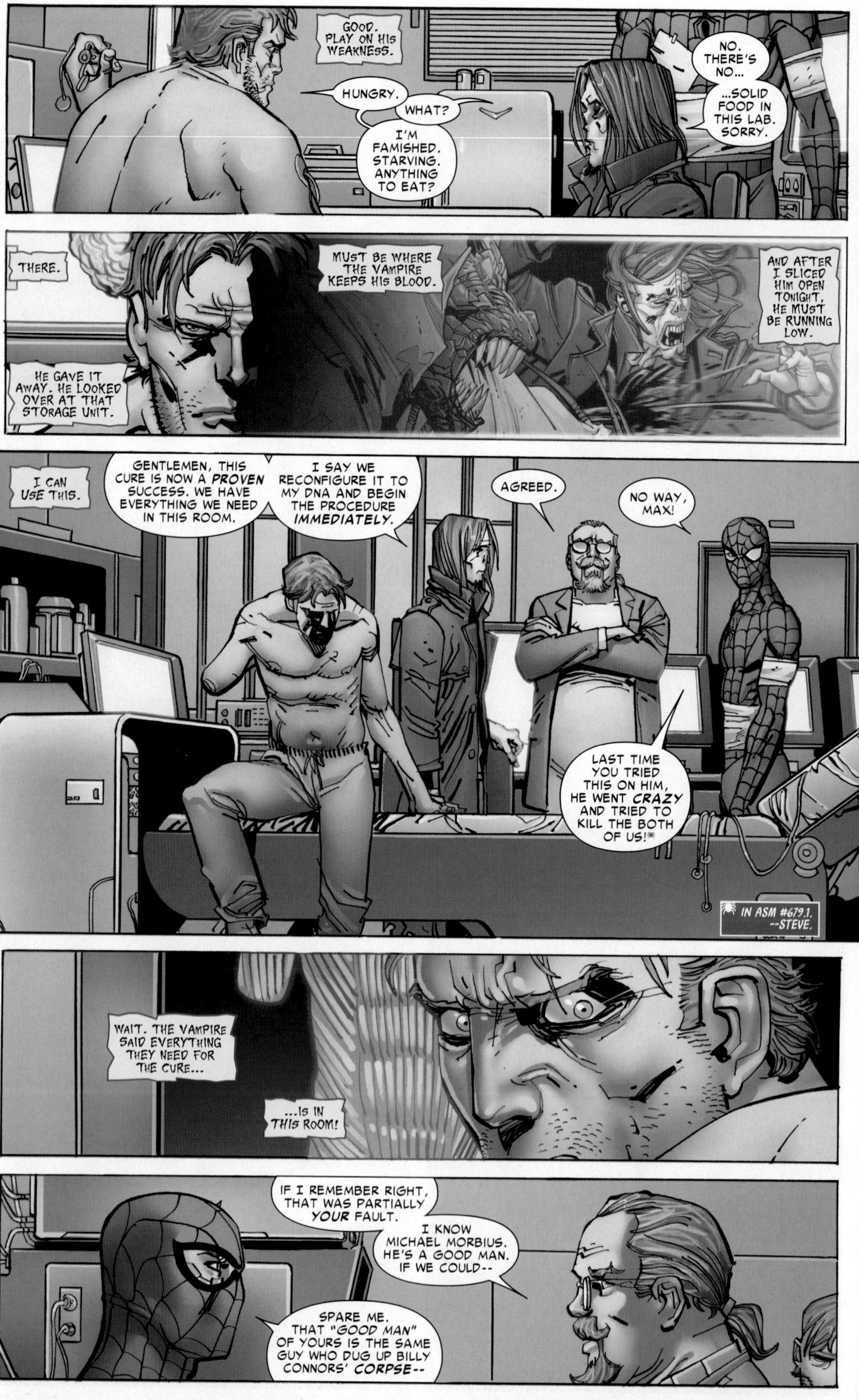
GOOD. PLAY ON HIS WEAKNESS.
HUNGRY.
WHAT?
I'M FAMISHED. STARVING. ANYTHING TO EAT?
NO. THERE'S NO...
...SOLID FOOD IN THIS LAB. SORRY.
THERE.
MUST BE WHERE THE VAMPIRE KEEPS HIS BLOOD.
AND AFTER I SLICED HIM OPEN TONIGHT, HE MUST BE RUNNING LOW.
HE GAVE IT AWAY. HE LOOKED OVER AT THAT STORAGE UNIT.
I CAN USE THIS.
GENTLEMEN, THIS CURE IS NOW A PROVEN SUCCESS. WE HAVE EVERYTHING WE NEED IN THIS ROOM.
I SAY WE RECONFIGURE IT TO MY DNA AND BEGIN THE PROCEDURE IMMEDIATELY.
AGREED.
NO WAY, MAX!
LAST TIME YOU TRIED THIS ON HIM, HE WENT CRAZY AND TRIED TO KILL THE BOTH OF US!*
*IN ASM #679.1. --STEVE.
WAIT. THE VAMPIRE SAID EVERYTHING THEY NEED FOR THE CURE...
...IS IN THIS ROOM!
IF I REMEMBER RIGHT, THAT WAS PARTIALLY YOUR FAULT.
I KNOW MICHAEL MORBIUS. HE'S A GOOD MAN. IF WE COULD--
SPARE ME. THAT "GOOD MAN" OF YOURS IS THE SAME GUY WHO DUG UP BILLY CONNORS' CORPSE--

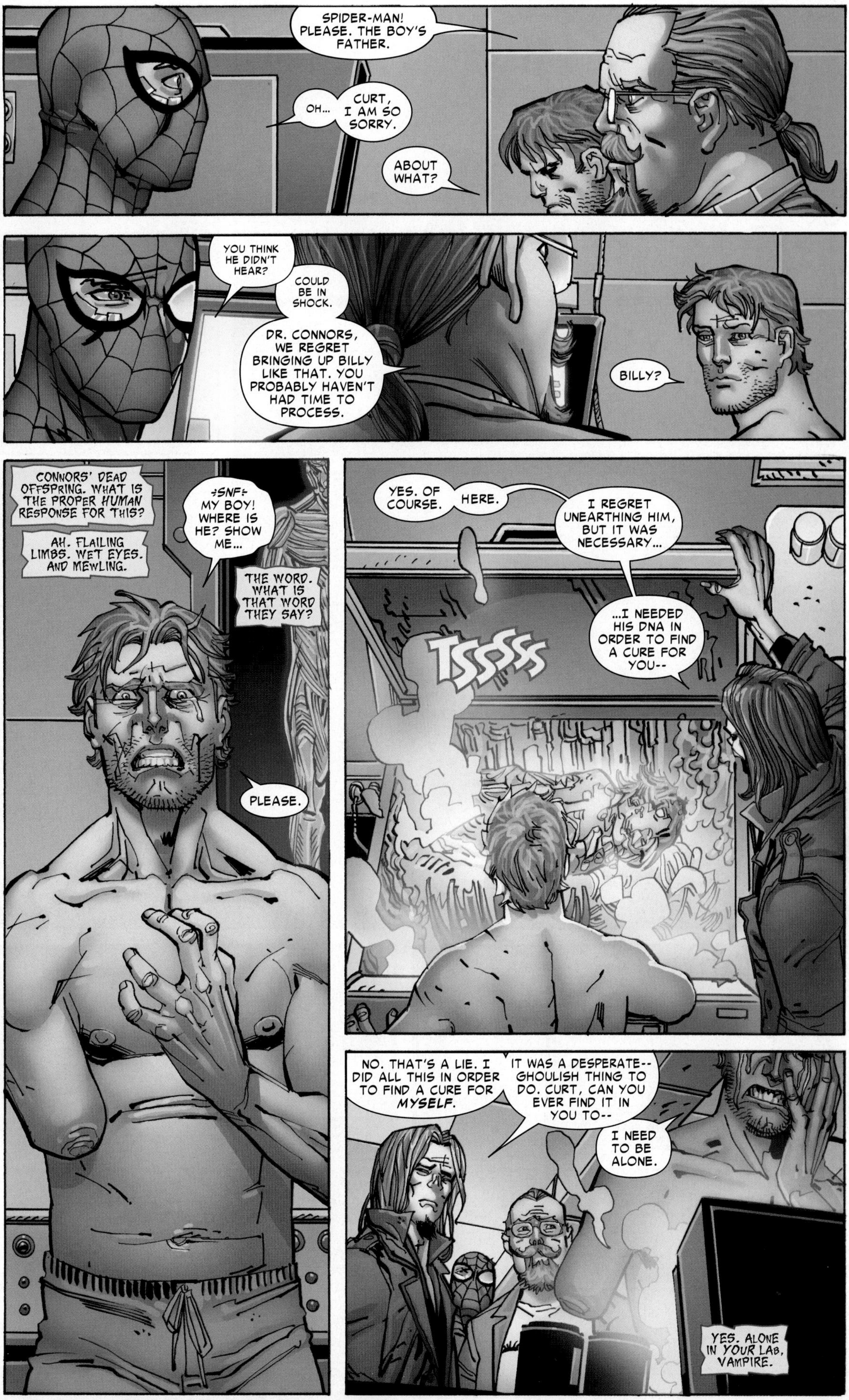

SPIDER-MAN! PLEASE. THE BOY'S FATHER.
OH...
CURT, I AM SO SORRY.
ABOUT WHAT?
YOU THINK HE DIDN'T HEAR?
COULD BE IN SHOCK.
DR. CONNORS, WE REGRET BRINGING UP BILLY LIKE THAT. YOU PROBABLY HAVEN'T HAD TIME TO PROCESS.
BILLY?
CONNORS' DEAD OFFSPRING. WHAT IS THE PROPER HUMAN RESPONSE FOR THIS?
AH. FLAILING LIMBS. WET EYES. AND MEWLING.
SNF MY BOY! WHERE IS HE? SHOW ME...
THE WORD. WHAT IS THAT WORD THEY SAY?
PLEASE.
YES. OF COURSE.
HERE.
I REGRET UNEARTHING HIM, BUT IT WAS NECESSARY...
...I NEEDED HIS DNA IN ORDER TO FIND A CURE FOR YOU--
TSSSS
NO. THAT'S A LIE. I DID ALL THIS IN ORDER TO FIND A CURE FOR MYSELF.
IT WAS A DESPERATE-- GHOULISH THING TO DO. CURT, CAN YOU EVER FIND IT IN YOU TO--
I NEED TO BE ALONE.
YES. ALONE IN YOUR LAB, VAMPIRE.

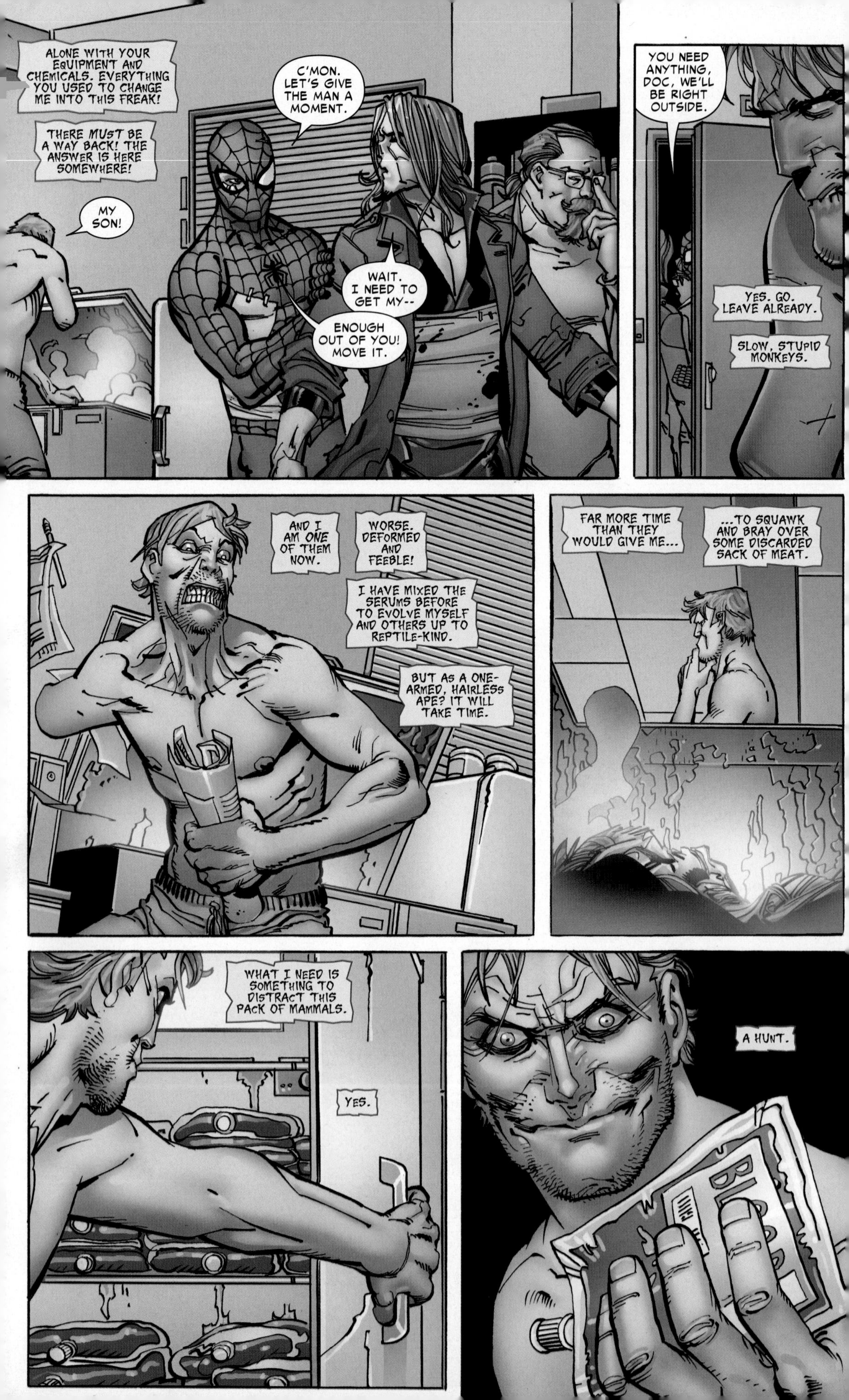
ALONE WITH YOUR EQUIPMENT AND CHEMICALS. EVERYTHING YOU USED TO CHANGE ME INTO THIS FREAK!
THERE MUST BE A WAY BACK! THE ANSWER IS HERE SOMEWHERE!
MY SON!
C'MON. LET'S GIVE THE MAN A MOMENT.
WAIT. I NEED TO GET MY--
ENOUGH OUT OF YOU! MOVE IT.
YOU NEED ANYTHING, DOC, WE'LL BE RIGHT OUTSIDE.
YES. GO. LEAVE ALREADY.
SLOW, STUPID MONKEYS.
AND I AM ONE OF THEM NOW.
WORSE. DEFORMED AND FEEBLE!
I HAVE MIXED THE SERUMS BEFORE TO EVOLVE MYSELF AND OTHERS UP TO REPTILE-KIND.
BUT AS A ONE-ARMED, HAIRLESS APE? IT WILL TAKE TIME.
FAR MORE TIME THAN THEY WOULD GIVE ME...
...TO SQUAWK AND BRAY OVER SOME DISCARDED SACK OF MEAT.
WHAT I NEED IS SOMETHING TO DISTRACT THIS PACK OF MAMMALS.
YES.
A HUNT.

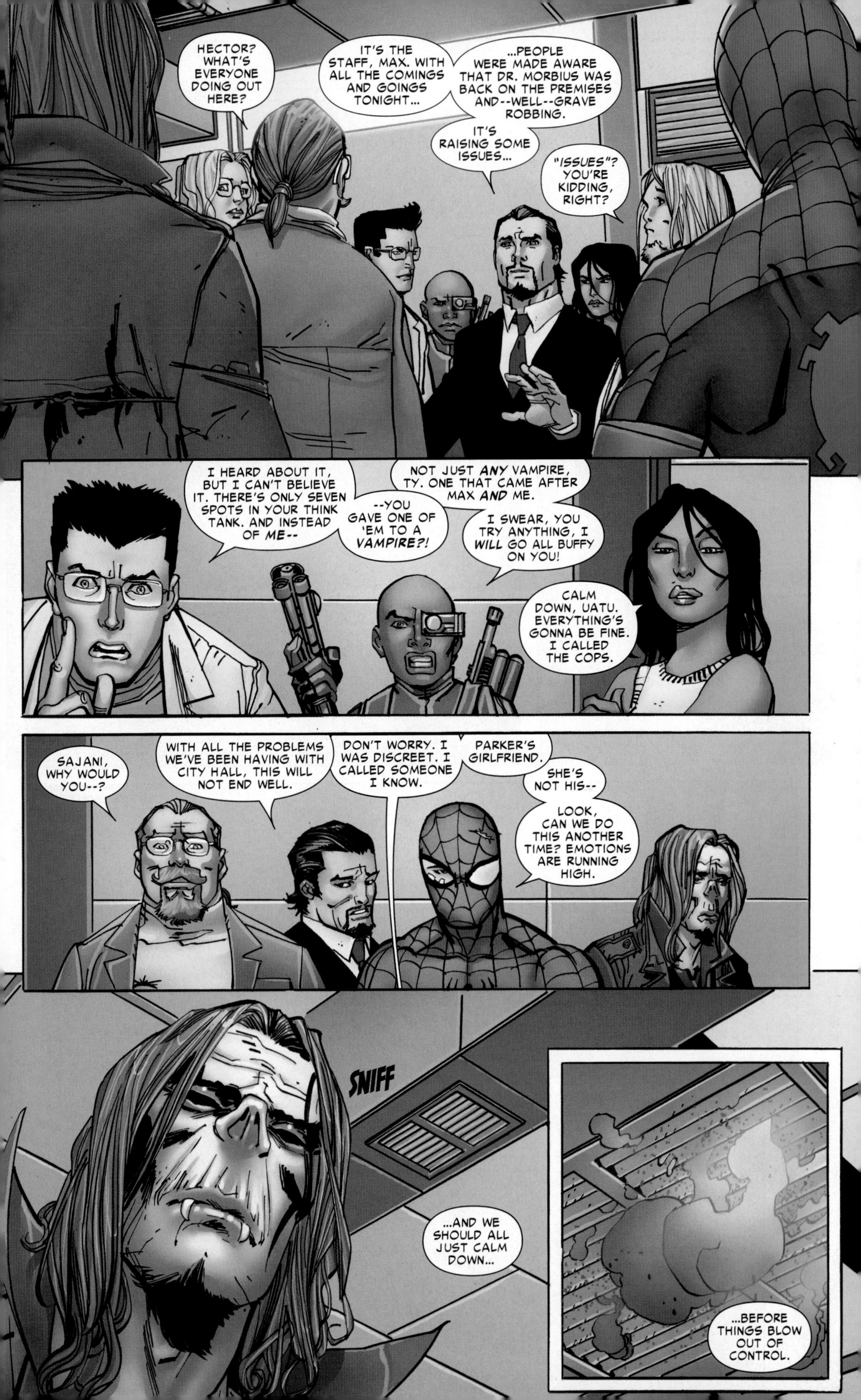
HECTOR? WHAT'S EVERYONE DOING OUT HERE?
IT'S THE STAFF, MAX. WITH ALL THE COMINGS AND GOINGS TONIGHT...
...PEOPLE WERE MADE AWARE THAT DR. MORBIUS WAS BACK ON THE PREMISES AND--WELL--GRAVE ROBBING.
IT'S RAISING SOME ISSUES...
"ISSUES"? YOU'RE KIDDING, RIGHT?
I HEARD ABOUT IT, BUT I CAN'T BELIEVE IT. THERE'S ONLY SEVEN SPOTS IN YOUR THINK TANK. AND INSTEAD OF ME--
--YOU GAVE ONE OF 'EM TO A VAMPIRE?!
NOT JUST ANY VAMPIRE, TY. ONE THAT CAME AFTER MAX AND ME.
I SWEAR, YOU TRY ANYTHING, I WILL GO ALL BUFFY ON YOU!
CALM DOWN, UATU. EVERYTHING'S GONNA BE FINE. I CALLED THE COPS.
SAJANI, WHY WOULD YOU--?
WITH ALL THE PROBLEMS WE'VE BEEN HAVING WITH CITY HALL, THIS WILL NOT END WELL.
DON'T WORRY. I WAS DISCREET. I CALLED SOMEONE I KNOW.
PARKER'S GIRLFRIEND.
SHE'S NOT HIS--
LOOK, CAN WE DO THIS ANOTHER TIME? EMOTIONS ARE RUNNING HIGH.
SNIFF
...AND WE SHOULD ALL JUST CALM DOWN...
...BEFORE THINGS BLOW OUT OF CONTROL.

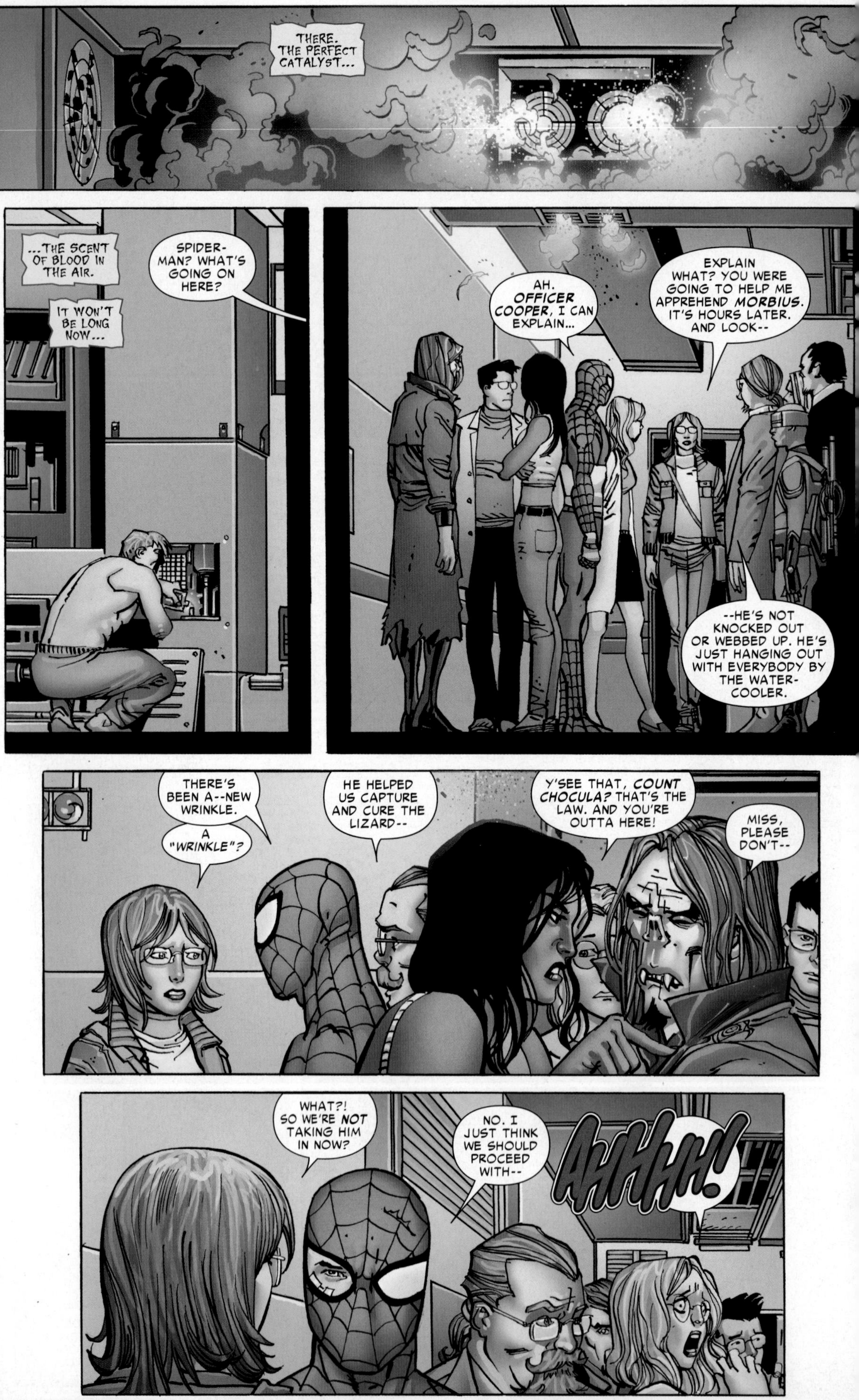

THERE. THE PERFECT CATALYST...
...THE SCENT OF BLOOD IN THE AIR.
IT WON'T BE LONG NOW...
SPIDER-MAN? WHAT'S GOING ON HERE?
AH. OFFICER COOPER, I CAN EXPLAIN...
EXPLAIN WHAT? YOU WERE GOING TO HELP ME APPREHEND MORBIUS. IT'S HOURS LATER. AND LOOK--
--HE'S NOT KNOCKED OUT OR WEBBED UP. HE'S JUST HANGING OUT WITH EVERYBODY BY THE WATER-COOLER.
THERE'S BEEN A--NEW WRINKLE.
A "WRINKLE"?
HE HELPED US CAPTURE AND CURE THE LIZARD--
Y'SEE THAT, COUNT CHOCULA? THAT'S THE LAW. AND YOU'RE OUTTA HERE!
MISS, PLEASE DON'T--
WHAT?! SO WE'RE NOT TAKING HIM IN NOW?
NO. I JUST THINK WE SHOULD PROCEED WITH--
AHHHH!

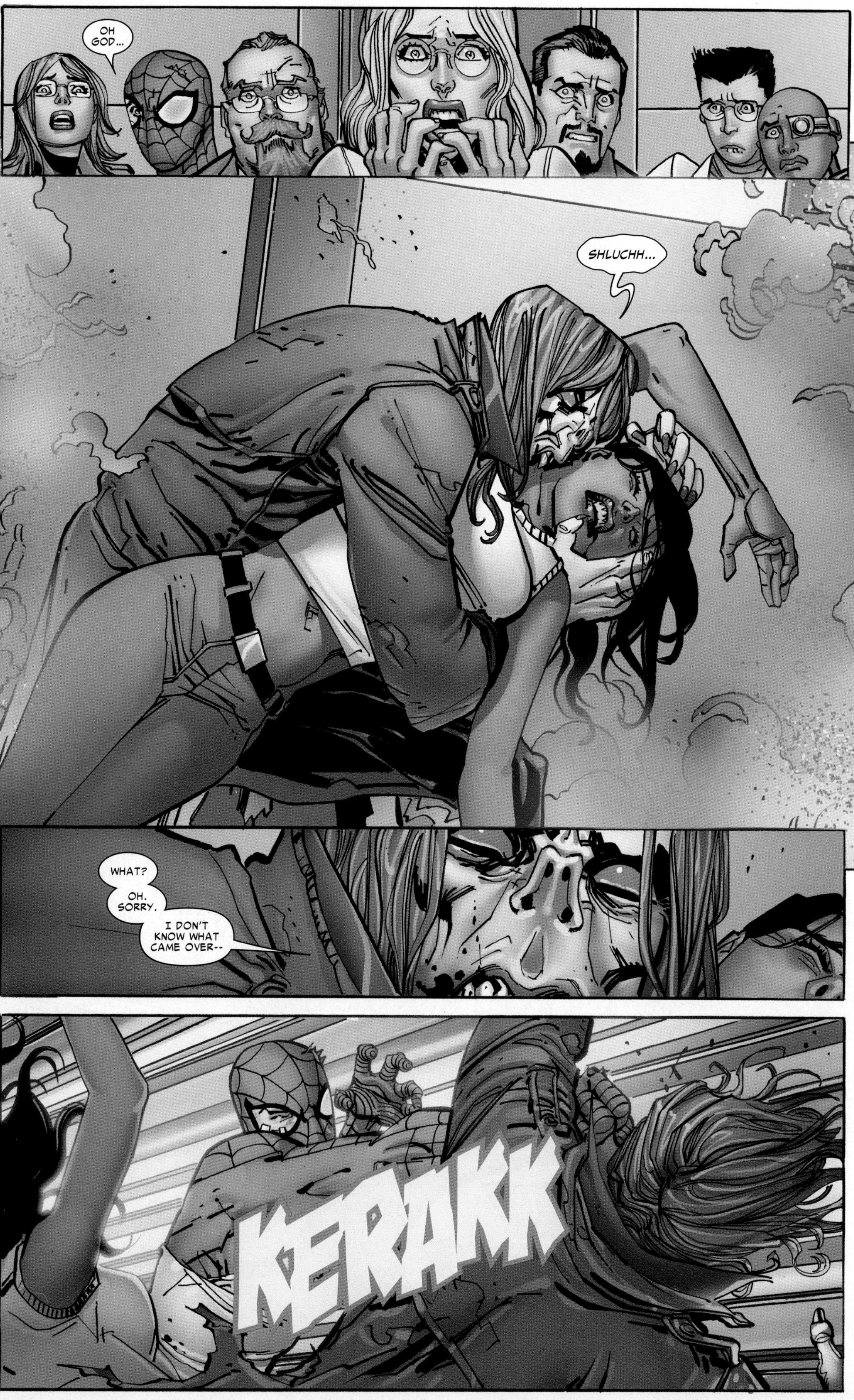
OH GOD...
SHLUCHH...
WHAT?
OH. SORRY.
I DON'T KNOW WHAT CAME OVER--
KERAKK

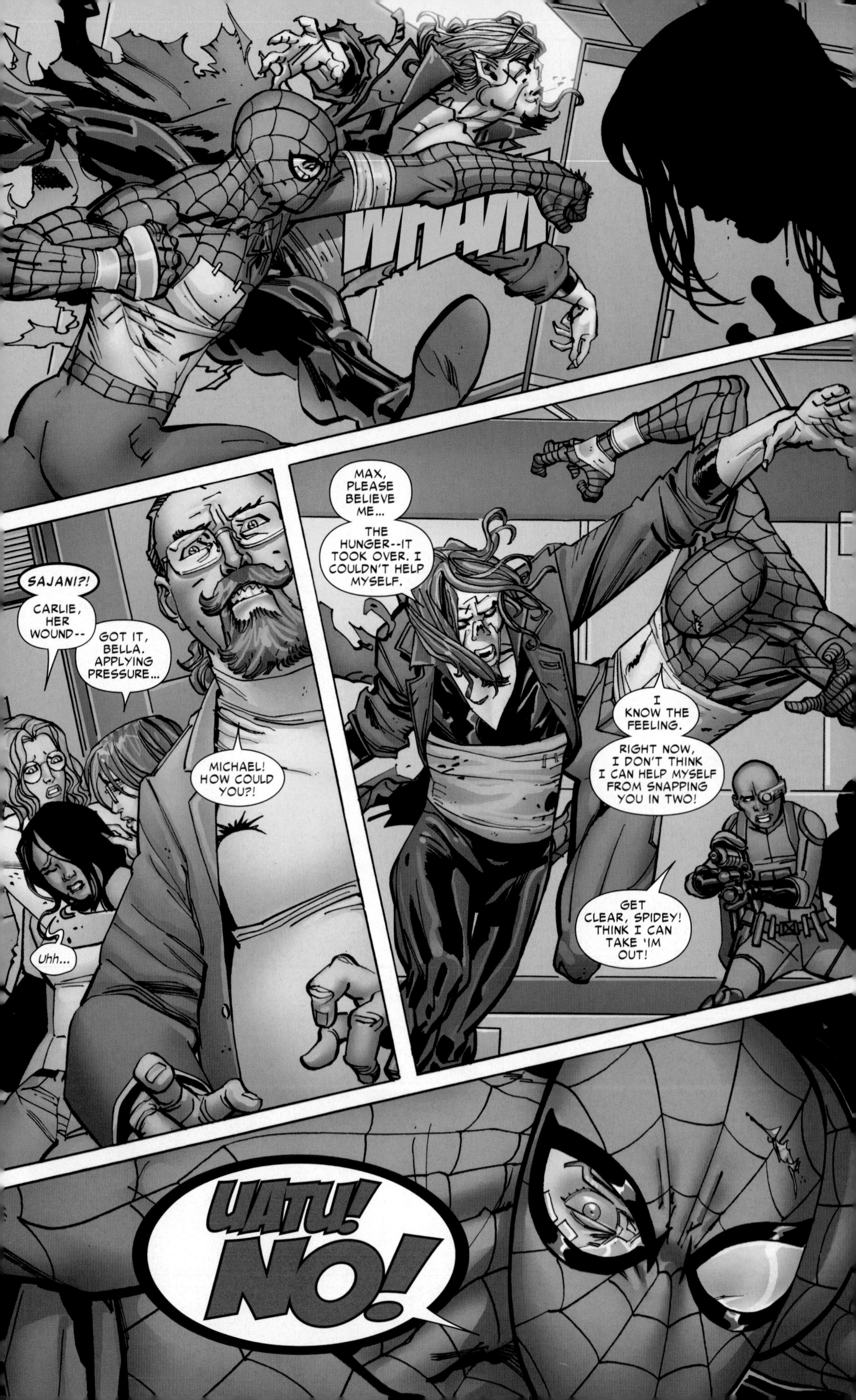
WHAM!
SAJANI?!
CARLIE, HER WOUND--
GOT IT, BELLA. APPLYING PRESSURE...
MICHAEL! HOW COULD YOU?!
Uhh...
MAX, PLEASE BELIEVE ME...
THE HUNGER--IT TOOK OVER. I COULDN'T HELP MYSELF.
I KNOW THE FEELING.
RIGHT NOW, I DON'T THINK I CAN HELP MYSELF FROM SNAPPING YOU IN TWO!
GET CLEAR, SPIDEY! THINK I CAN TAKE 'IM OUT!
UATU! NO!

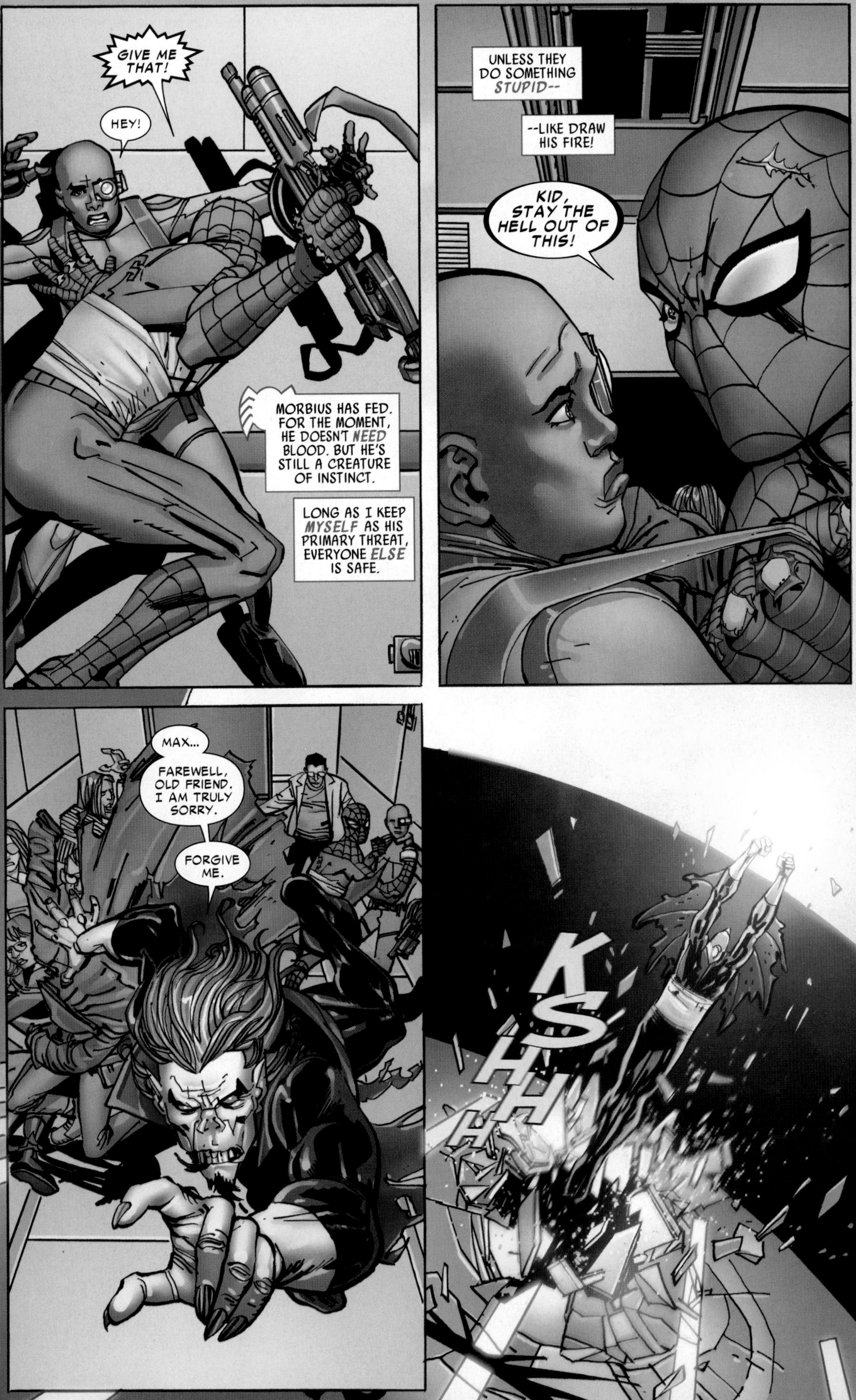

GIVE ME THAT!
HEY!
MORBIUS HAS FED. FOR THE MOMENT, HE DOESN'T NEED BLOOD. BUT HE'S STILL A CREATURE OF INSTINCT.
LONG AS I KEEP MYSELF AS HIS PRIMARY THREAT, EVERYONE ELSE IS SAFE.
UNLESS THEY DO SOMETHING STUPID--
--LIKE DRAW HIS FIRE!
KID, STAY THE HELL OUT OF THIS!
MAX...
FAREWELL, OLD FRIEND. I AM TRULY SORRY.
FORGIVE ME.
KSHHHH

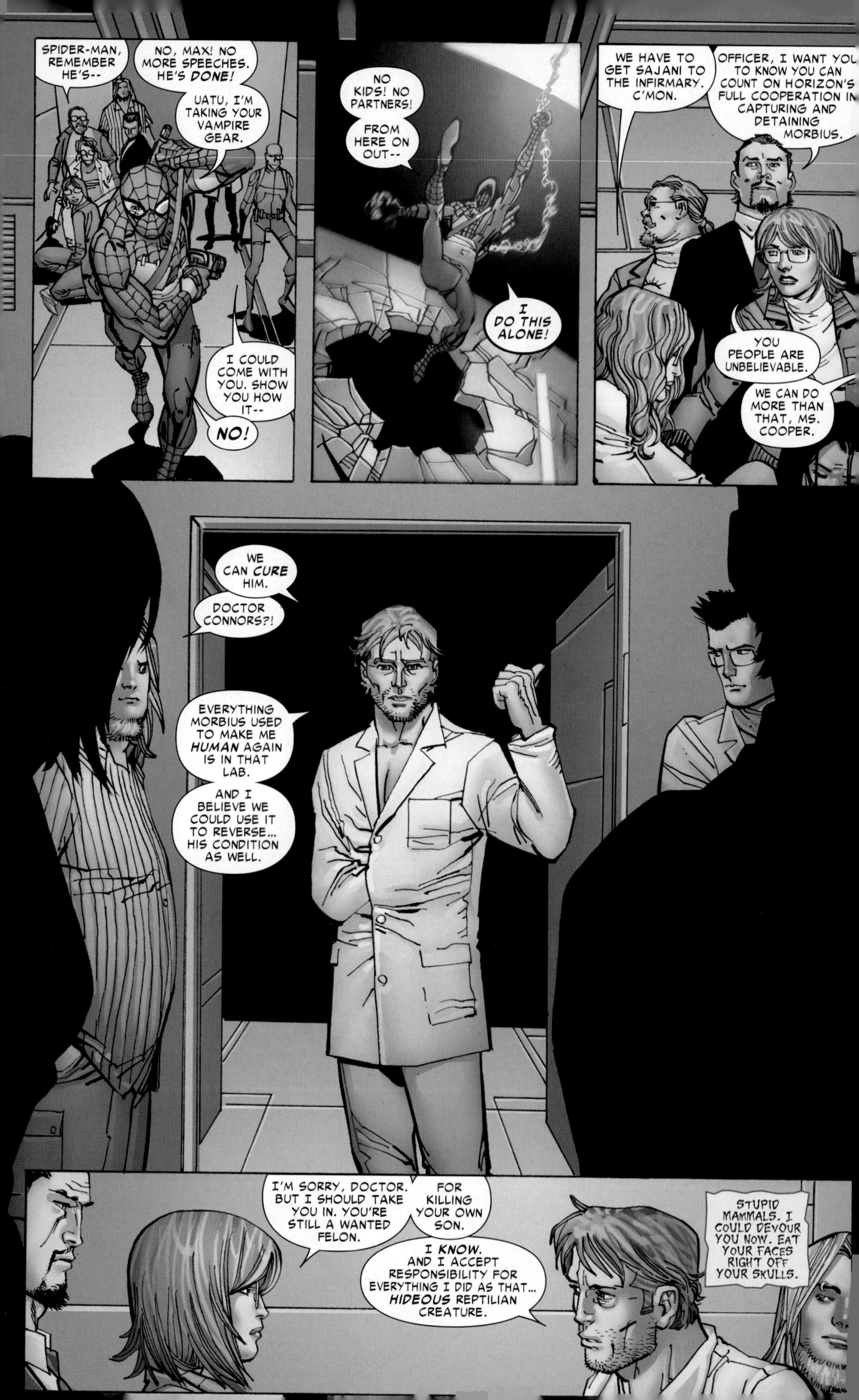
SPIDER-MAN, REMEMBER HE'S--
NO, MAX! NO MORE SPEECHES. HE'S DONE!
UATU, I'M TAKING YOUR VAMPIRE GEAR.
I COULD COME WITH YOU. SHOW YOU HOW IT--
NO!
NO KIDS! NO PARTNERS!
FROM HERE ON OUT--
I DO THIS ALONE!
WE HAVE TO GET SAJANI TO THE INFIRMARY. C'MON.
OFFICER, I WANT YOU TO KNOW YOU CAN COUNT ON HORIZON'S FULL COOPERATION IN CAPTURING AND DETAINING MORBIUS.
YOU PEOPLE ARE UNBELIEVABLE.
WE CAN DO MORE THAN THAT, MS. COOPER.
WE CAN CURE HIM.
DOCTOR CONNORS?!
EVERYTHING MORBIUS USED TO MAKE ME HUMAN AGAIN IS IN THAT LAB.
AND I BELIEVE WE COULD USE IT TO REVERSE... HIS CONDITION AS WELL.
I'M SORRY, DOCTOR. BUT I SHOULD TAKE YOU IN. YOU'RE STILL A WANTED FELON.
FOR KILLING YOUR OWN SON.
I KNOW. AND I ACCEPT RESPONSIBILITY FOR EVERYTHING I DID AS THAT... HIDEOUS REPTILIAN CREATURE.
STUPID MAMMALS. I COULD DEVOUR YOU NOW. EAT YOUR FACES RIGHT OFF YOUR SKULLS.

BUT I AM THE ONLY ONE HERE WHO KNOWS HOW THIS "CURE" IS MADE. I WORKED ON IT ONCE...

...IN AN ATTEMPT TO CHANGE MYSELF, MORBIUS, AND EVEN A MUTATED SPIDER-MAN BACK TO...NORMAL.*

WAYYYY BACK IN ASM #101. --NINETEEN SEVENTY-STEVE.

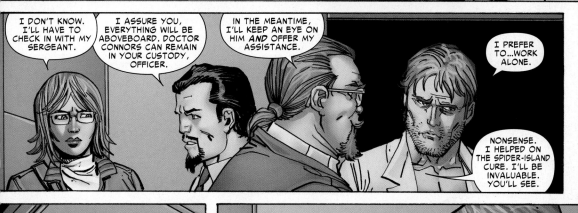

I DON'T KNOW. I'LL HAVE TO CHECK IN WITH MY SERGEANT.

I ASSURE YOU, EVERYTHING WILL BE ABOVEBOARD. DOCTOR CONNORS CAN REMAIN IN YOUR CUSTODY, OFFICER.

IN THE MEANTIME, I'LL KEEP AN EYE ON HIM AND OFFER MY ASSISTANCE.

I PREFER TO...WORK ALONE.

NONSENSE. I HELPED ON THE SPIDER-ISLAND CURE. I'LL BE INVALUABLE. YOU'LL SEE.

YEAH! AND I CAN CHIP IN TOO.

VAMPIRES, MONSTERS, AND STUFF LIKE THIS IS MY SPECIALTY.

GNNN. NO. I HAVE NO TIME TO WASTE...

...WITH ANNOYING CHILDREN RUNNING AROUND UNDER--

DOCTOR CONNORS?

BILLY...

UM...DOCTOR CONNORS? YOU OKAY?

I-I'M FINE. EXCUSE ME. I HAVE TO GO TO WORK NOW. ON THE CURE.

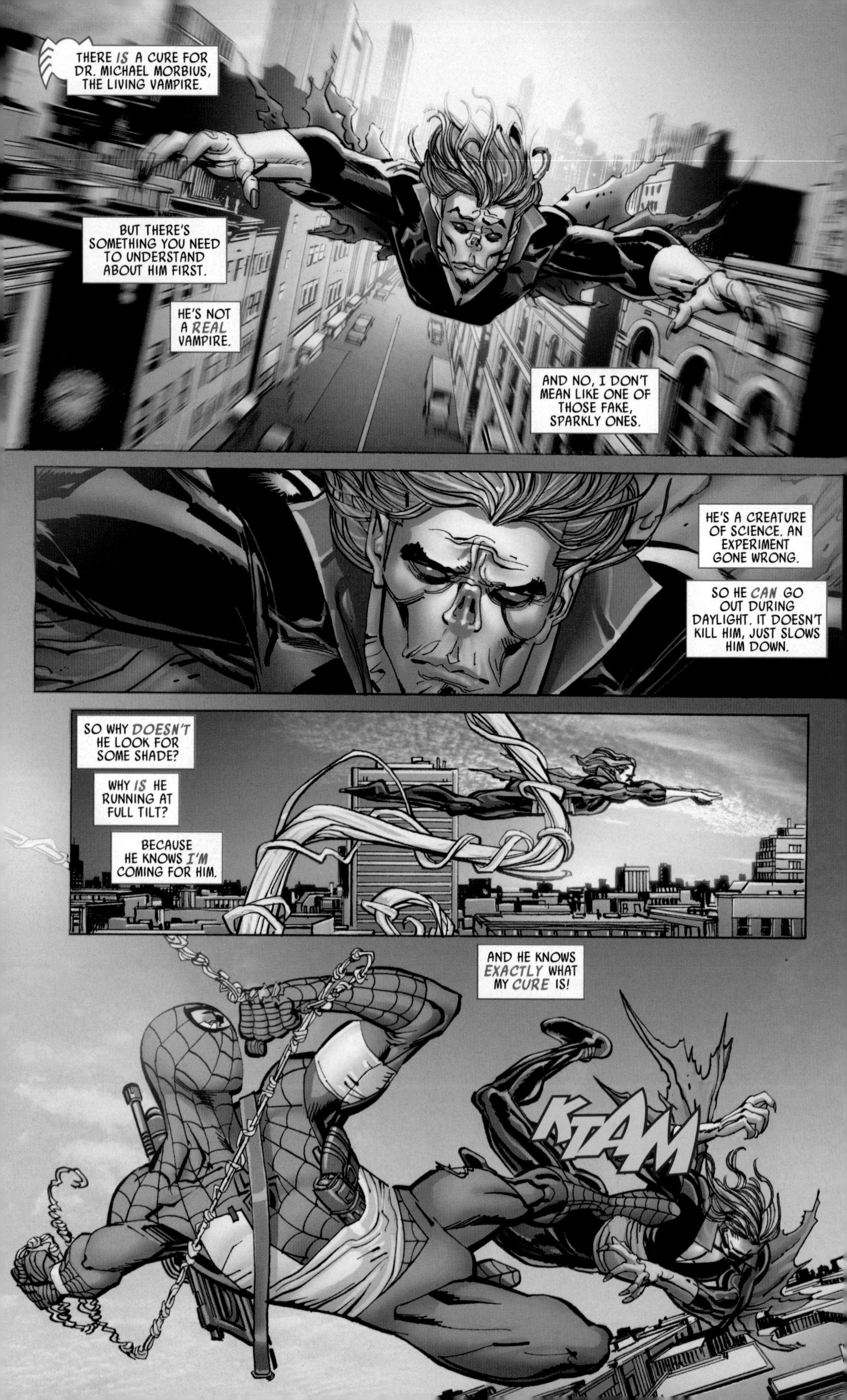
THERE IS A CURE FOR DR. MICHAEL MORBIUS, THE LIVING VAMPIRE.
BUT THERE'S SOMETHING YOU NEED TO UNDERSTAND ABOUT HIM FIRST.
HE'S NOT A REAL VAMPIRE.
AND NO, I DON'T MEAN LIKE ONE OF THOSE FAKE, SPARKLY ONES.
HE'S A CREATURE OF SCIENCE. AN EXPERIMENT GONE WRONG.
SO HE CAN GO OUT DURING DAYLIGHT. IT DOESN'T KILL HIM, JUST SLOWS HIM DOWN.
SO WHY DOESN'T HE LOOK FOR SOME SHADE?
WHY IS HE RUNNING AT FULL TILT?
BECAUSE HE KNOWS I'M COMING FOR HIM.
AND HE KNOWS EXACTLY WHAT MY CURE IS!
KTAM

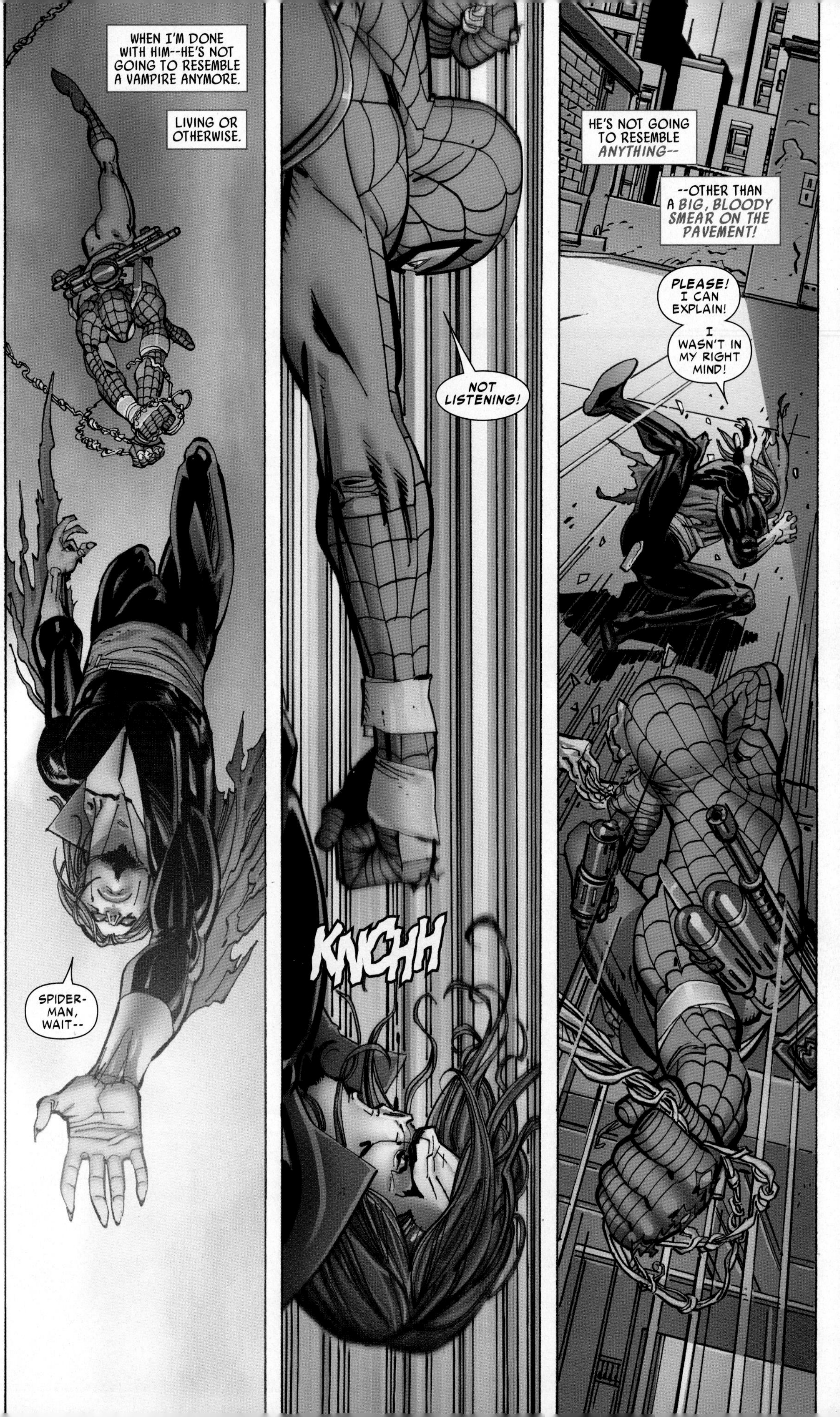
WHEN I'M DONE WITH HIM--HE'S NOT GOING TO RESEMBLE A VAMPIRE ANYMORE.
LIVING OR OTHERWISE.
SPIDER-MAN, WAIT--
NOT LISTENING!
KNCHH
HE'S NOT GOING TO RESEMBLE ANYTHING--
--OTHER THAN A BIG, BLOODY SMEAR ON THE PAVEMENT!
PLEASE! I CAN EXPLAIN!
I WASN'T IN MY RIGHT MIND!

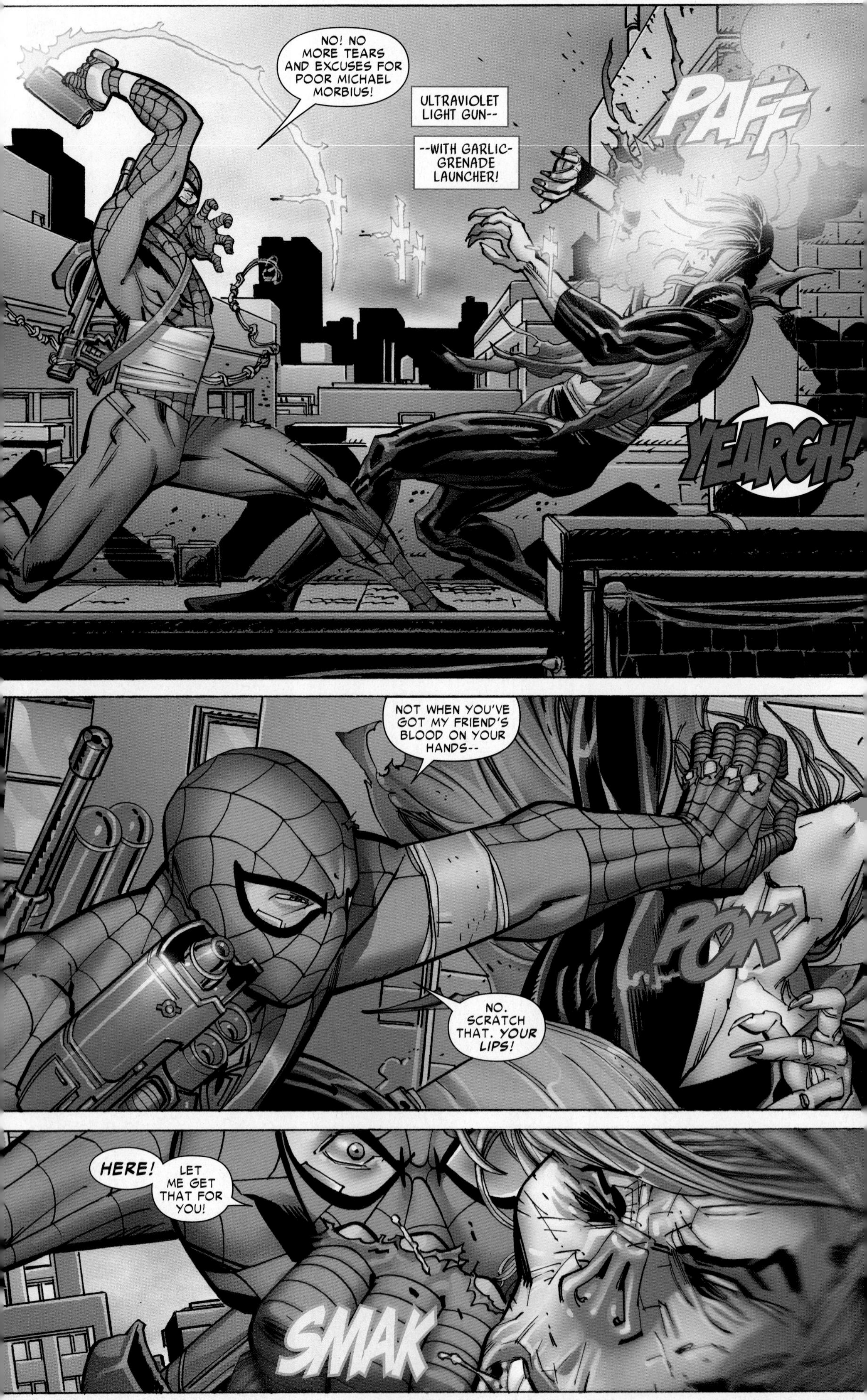

NO! NO MORE TEARS AND EXCUSES FOR POOR MICHAEL MORBIUS!
ULTRAVIOLET LIGHT GUN--
--WITH GARLIC-GRENADE LAUNCHER!
PAFF
YEARGH!
NOT WHEN YOU'VE GOT MY FRIEND'S BLOOD ON YOUR HANDS--
POK
NO. SCRATCH THAT. YOUR LIPS!
HERE!
LET ME GET THAT FOR YOU!
SMAK

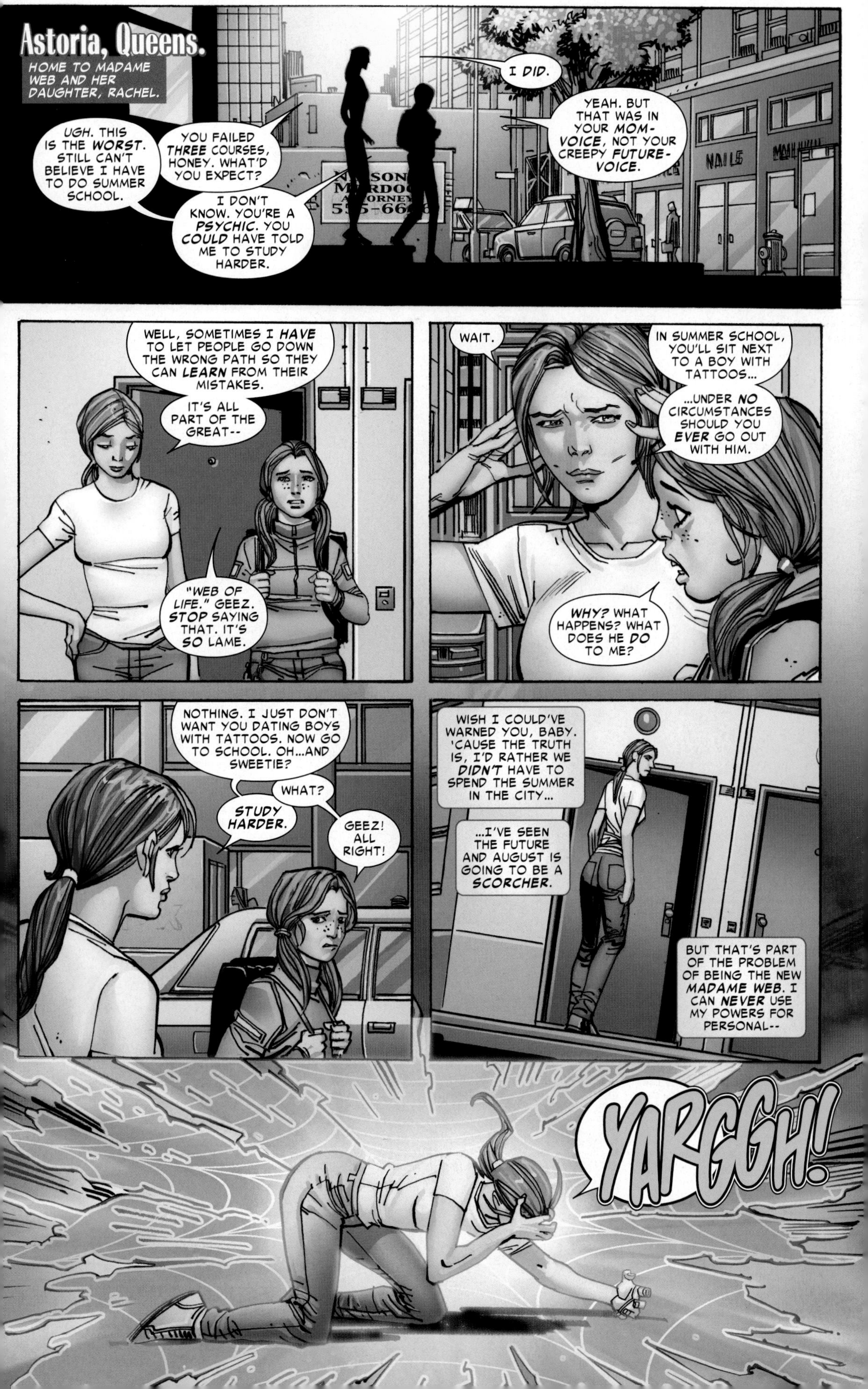

Astoria, Queens.
HOME TO MADAME WEB AND HER DAUGHTER, RACHEL.
UGH. THIS IS THE WORST. STILL CAN'T BELIEVE I HAVE TO DO SUMMER SCHOOL.
YOU FAILED THREE COURSES, HONEY. WHAT'D YOU EXPECT?
I DON'T KNOW. YOU'RE A PSYCHIC. YOU COULD HAVE TOLD ME TO STUDY HARDER.
I DID.
YEAH. BUT THAT WAS IN YOUR MOM-VOICE, NOT YOUR CREEPY FUTURE-VOICE.
WELL, SOMETIMES I HAVE TO LET PEOPLE GO DOWN THE WRONG PATH SO THEY CAN LEARN FROM THEIR MISTAKES.
IT'S ALL PART OF THE GREAT--
"WEB OF LIFE." GEEZ. STOP SAYING THAT. IT'S SO LAME.
WAIT.
IN SUMMER SCHOOL, YOU'LL SIT NEXT TO A BOY WITH TATTOOS...
...UNDER NO CIRCUMSTANCES SHOULD YOU EVER GO OUT WITH HIM.
WHY? WHAT HAPPENS? WHAT DOES HE DO TO ME?
NOTHING. I JUST DON'T WANT YOU DATING BOYS WITH TATTOOS. NOW GO TO SCHOOL. OH...AND SWEETIE?
WHAT?
STUDY HARDER.
GEEZ! ALL RIGHT!
WISH I COULD'VE WARNED YOU, BABY. 'CAUSE THE TRUTH IS, I'D RATHER WE DIDN'T HAVE TO SPEND THE SUMMER IN THE CITY...
...I'VE SEEN THE FUTURE AND AUGUST IS GOING TO BE A SCORCHER.
BUT THAT'S PART OF THE PROBLEM OF BEING THE NEW MADAME WEB. I CAN NEVER USE MY POWERS FOR PERSONAL--
YARGGH!

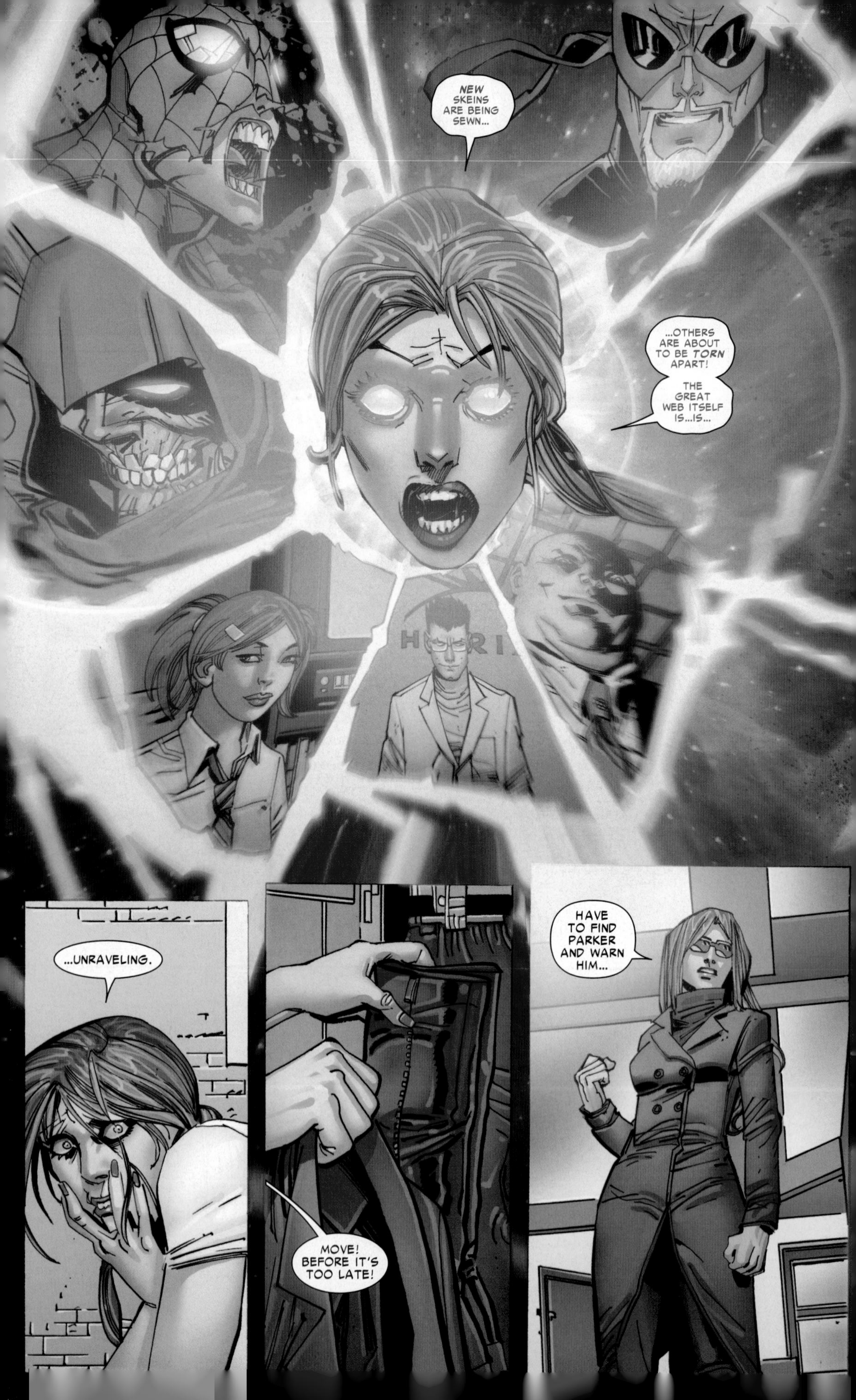
NEW SKEINS ARE BEING SEWN...
...OTHERS ARE ABOUT TO BE TORN APART!
THE GREAT WEB ITSELF IS...IS...
...UNRAVELING.
MOVE! BEFORE IT'S TOO LATE!
HAVE TO FIND PARKER AND WARN HIM...

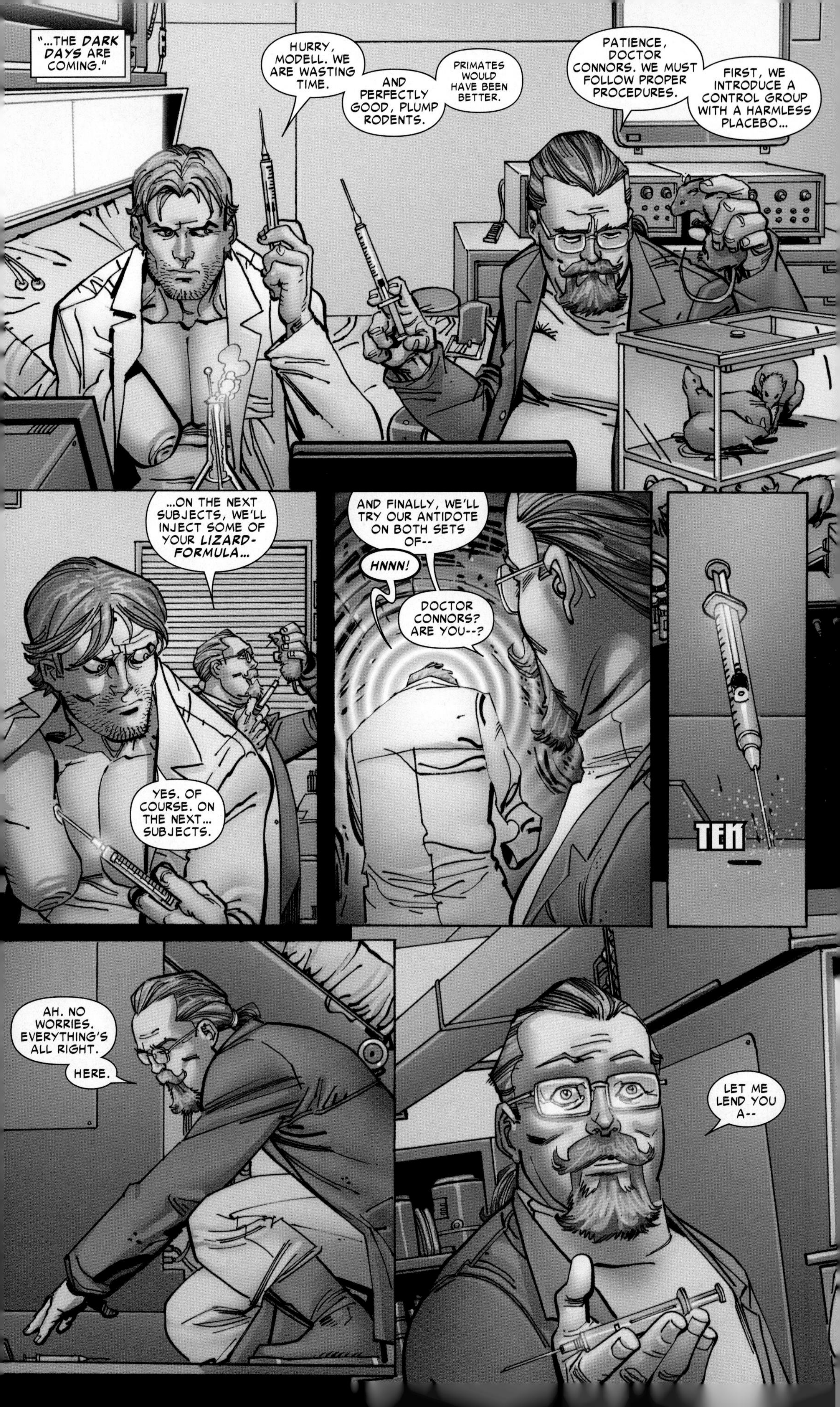
"...THE DARK DAYS ARE COMING."
HURRY, MODELL. WE ARE WASTING TIME.
AND PERFECTLY GOOD, PLUMP RODENTS.
PRIMATES WOULD HAVE BEEN BETTER.
PATIENCE, DOCTOR CONNORS. WE MUST FOLLOW PROPER PROCEDURES.
FIRST, WE INTRODUCE A CONTROL GROUP WITH A HARMLESS PLACEBO...
...ON THE NEXT SUBJECTS, WE'LL INJECT SOME OF YOUR LIZARD-FORMULA...
YES. OF COURSE. ON THE NEXT... SUBJECTS.
AND FINALLY, WE'LL TRY OUR ANTIDOTE ON BOTH SETS OF--
HNNN!
DOCTOR CONNORS? ARE YOU--?
TEK
AH. NO WORRIES. EVERYTHING'S ALL RIGHT.
HERE.
LET ME LEND YOU A--

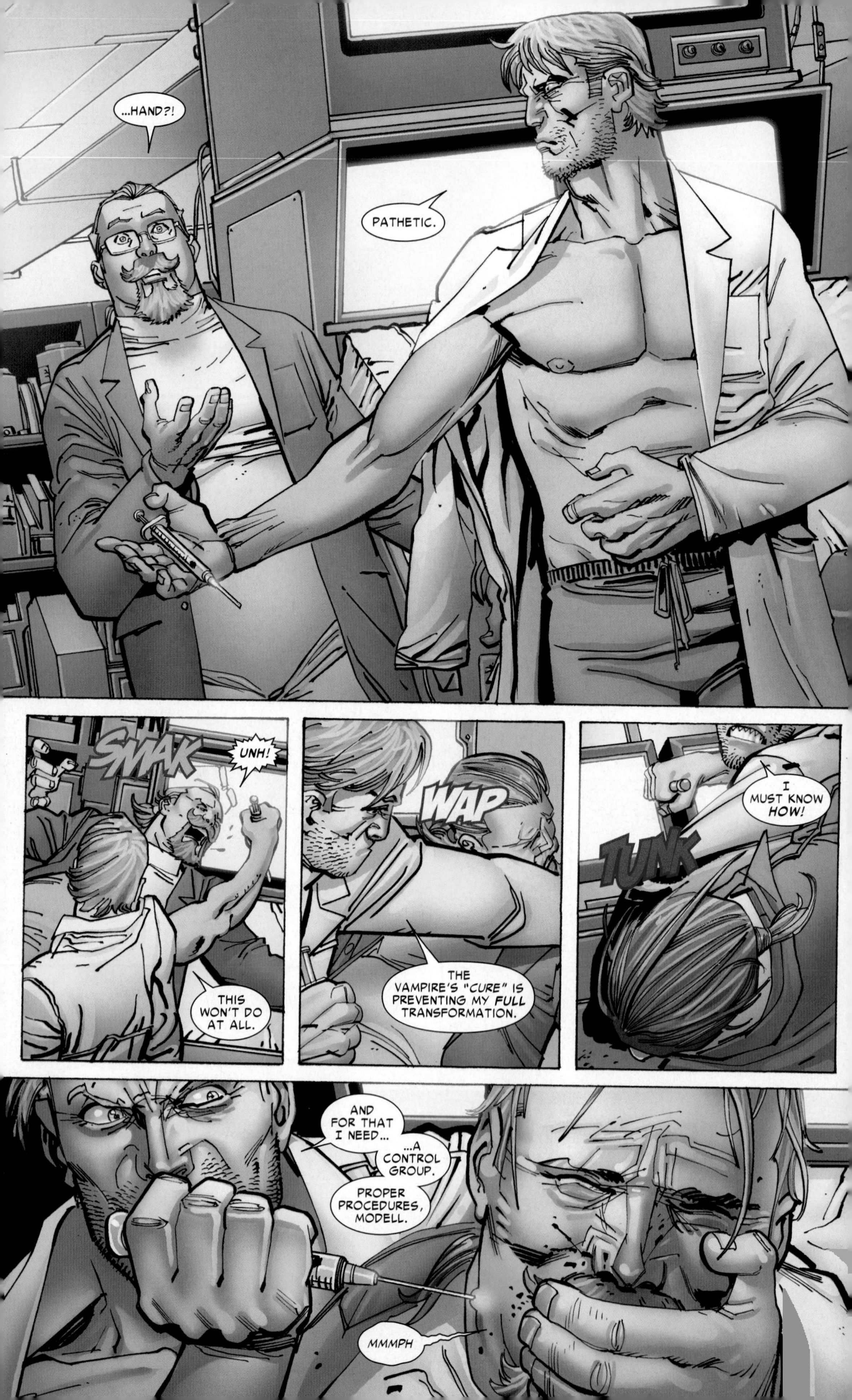
...HAND?!
PATHETIC.
SMAK
UNH!
THIS WON'T DO AT ALL.
WAP
THE VAMPIRE'S "CURE" IS PREVENTING MY FULL TRANSFORMATION.
I MUST KNOW HOW!
TUNK
AND FOR THAT I NEED...
...A CONTROL GROUP.
PROPER PROCEDURES, MODELL.
MMMPH

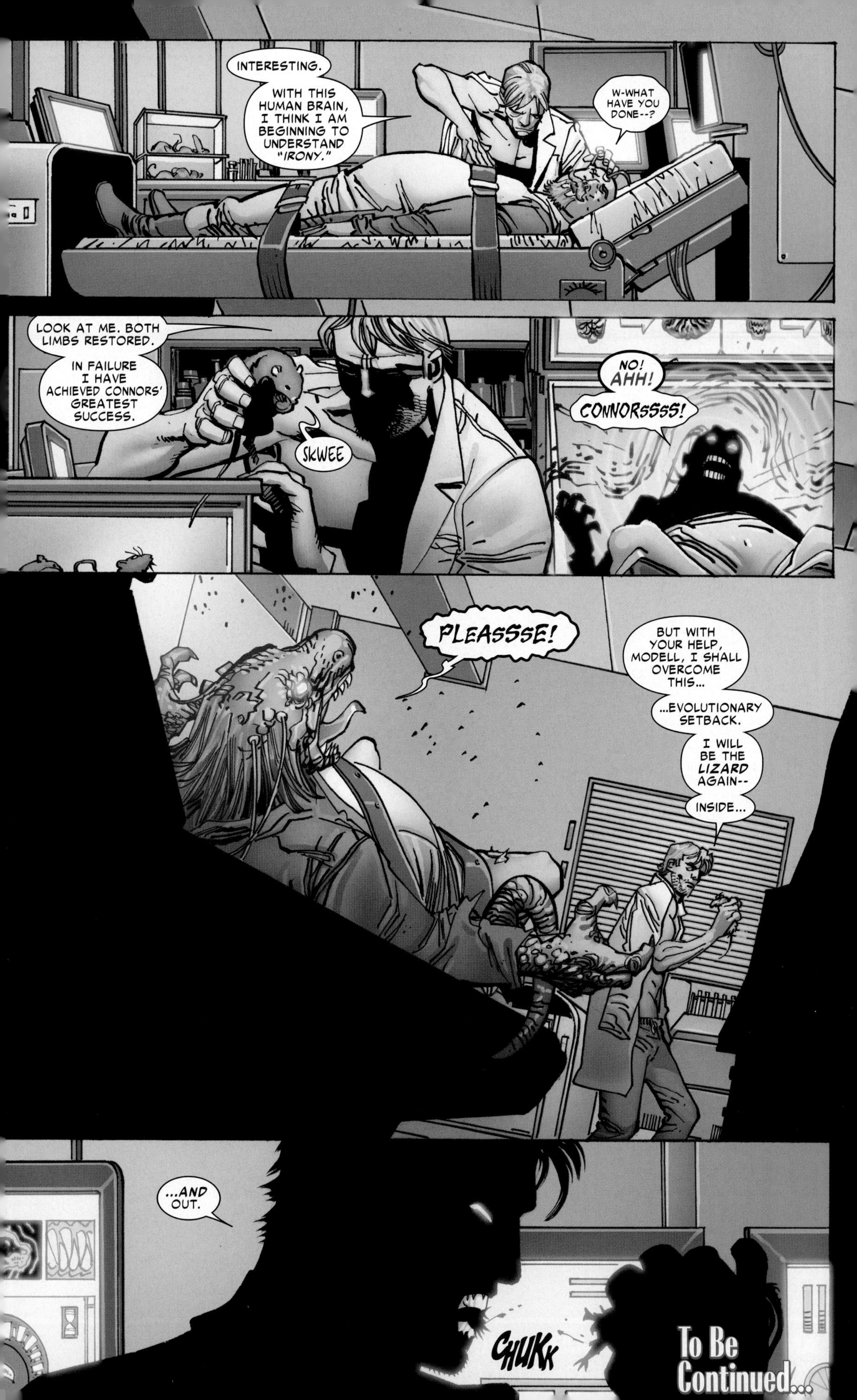
INTERESTING.
WITH THIS HUMAN BRAIN, I THINK I AM BEGINNING TO UNDERSTAND "IRONY."
W-WHAT HAVE YOU DONE--?
LOOK AT ME. BOTH LIMBS RESTORED.
IN FAILURE I HAVE ACHIEVED CONNORS' GREATEST SUCCESS.
SKWEE
NO! AHH!
CONNORSSSS!
PLEASSSE!
BUT WITH YOUR HELP, MODELL, I SHALL OVERCOME THIS...
...EVOLUTIONARY SETBACK.
I WILL BE THE LIZARD AGAIN--
INSIDE...
...AND OUT.
CHUKK
To Be Continued...

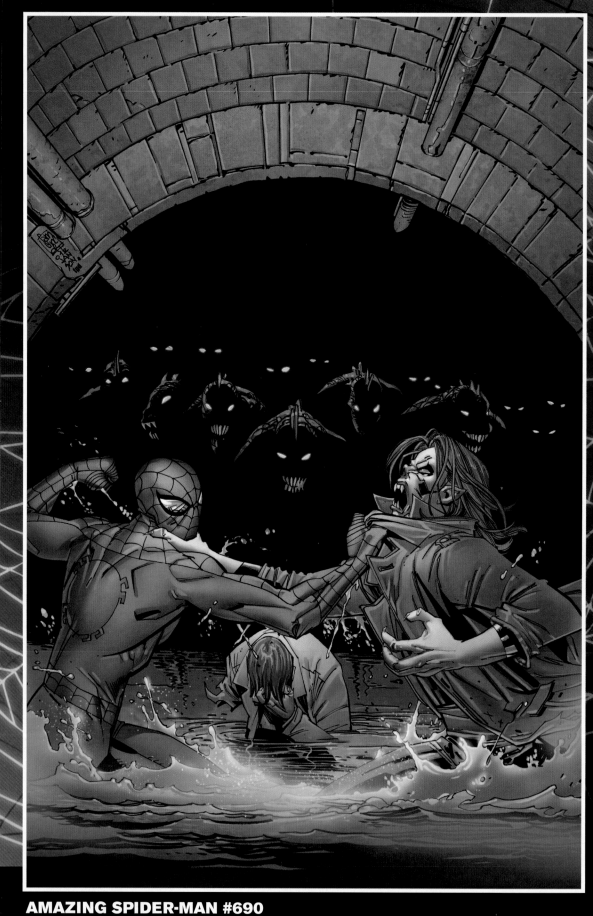

AMAZING SPIDER-MAN #690
COVER BY GIUSEPPE CAMUNCOLI, KLAUS JANSON & FRANK D'ARMATA

Lab #6.
HORIZON LABS. SOUTH STREET SEAPORT.

I'VE REACHED A DEAD END. MY CURRENT FORMULA HAS FAILED TO RETURN ME TO MY NATURAL STATE.

I REMAIN A LOWLY...HOMO SAPIEN.

WORSE...

...I AM NOW A PERFECT SPECIMEN.

TOO PERFECT.

ZZZEE

CURT CONNORS IS A ONE-ARMED CRIPPLE.

ZWWAW

IF I AM TO CONTINUE TO WALK UPRIGHT AMONGST THESE HAIRLESS APES...

...THEY CANNOT KNOW WHAT I AM UP TO UNTIL IT'S TOO LATE.

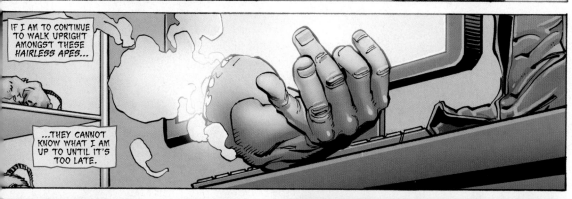

NOW I MUST GO.

SCAVENGE.

GATHER UP MORE CHEMICALS, EQUIPMENT...

HURRR...

...AND TEST SUBJECTS.

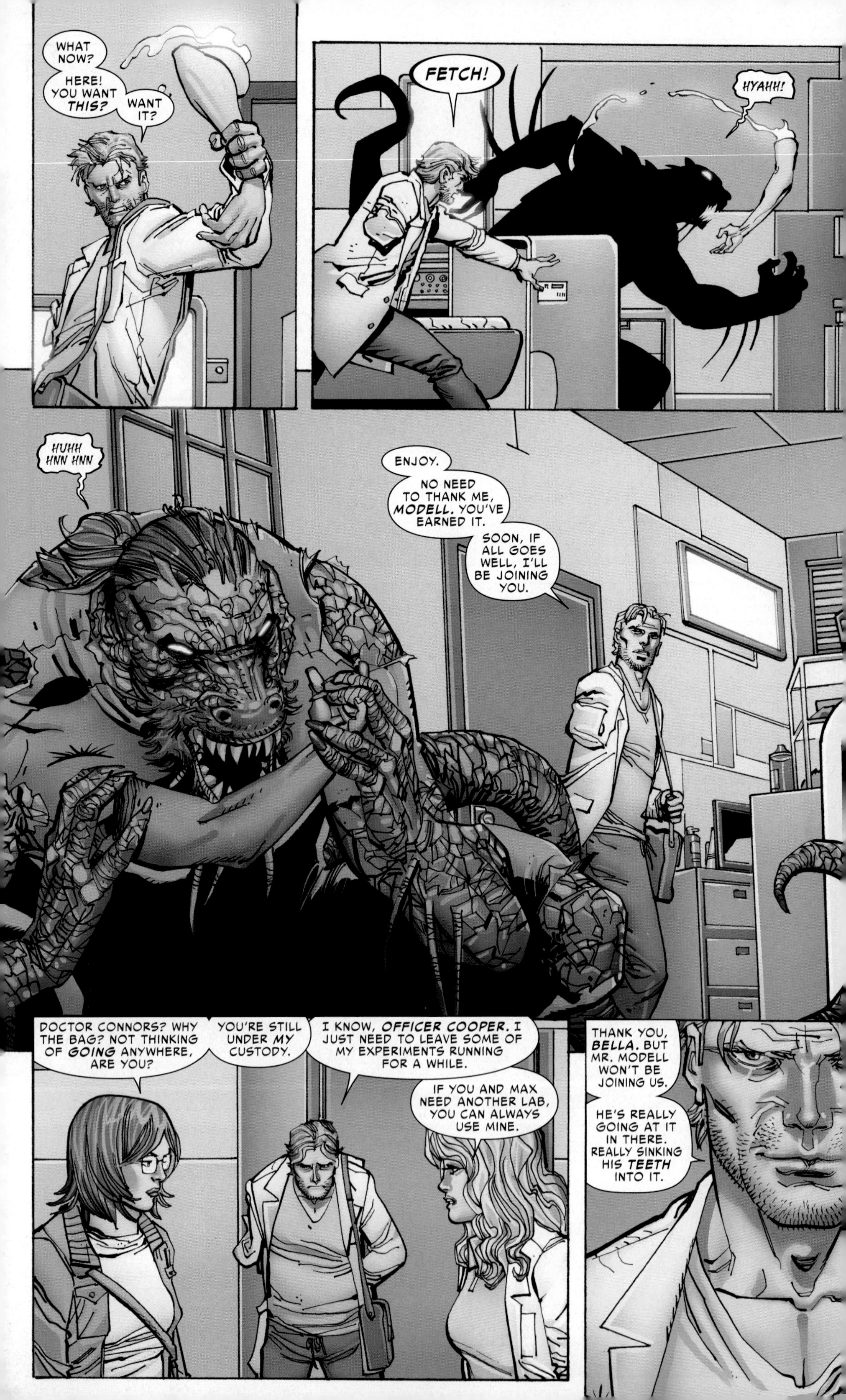
WHAT NOW?
HERE! YOU WANT THIS?
WANT IT?
FETCH!
HYAHH!
HUHH HNN HNN
ENJOY.
NO NEED TO THANK ME, MODELL. YOU'VE EARNED IT.
SOON, IF ALL GOES WELL, I'LL BE JOINING YOU.
DOCTOR CONNORS? WHY THE BAG? NOT THINKING OF GOING ANYWHERE, ARE YOU?
YOU'RE STILL UNDER MY CUSTODY.
I KNOW, OFFICER COOPER. I JUST NEED TO LEAVE SOME OF MY EXPERIMENTS RUNNING FOR A WHILE.
IF YOU AND MAX NEED ANOTHER LAB, YOU CAN ALWAYS USE MINE.
THANK YOU, BELLA. BUT MR. MODELL WON'T BE JOINING US.
HE'S REALLY GOING AT IT IN THERE. REALLY SINKING HIS TEETH INTO IT.

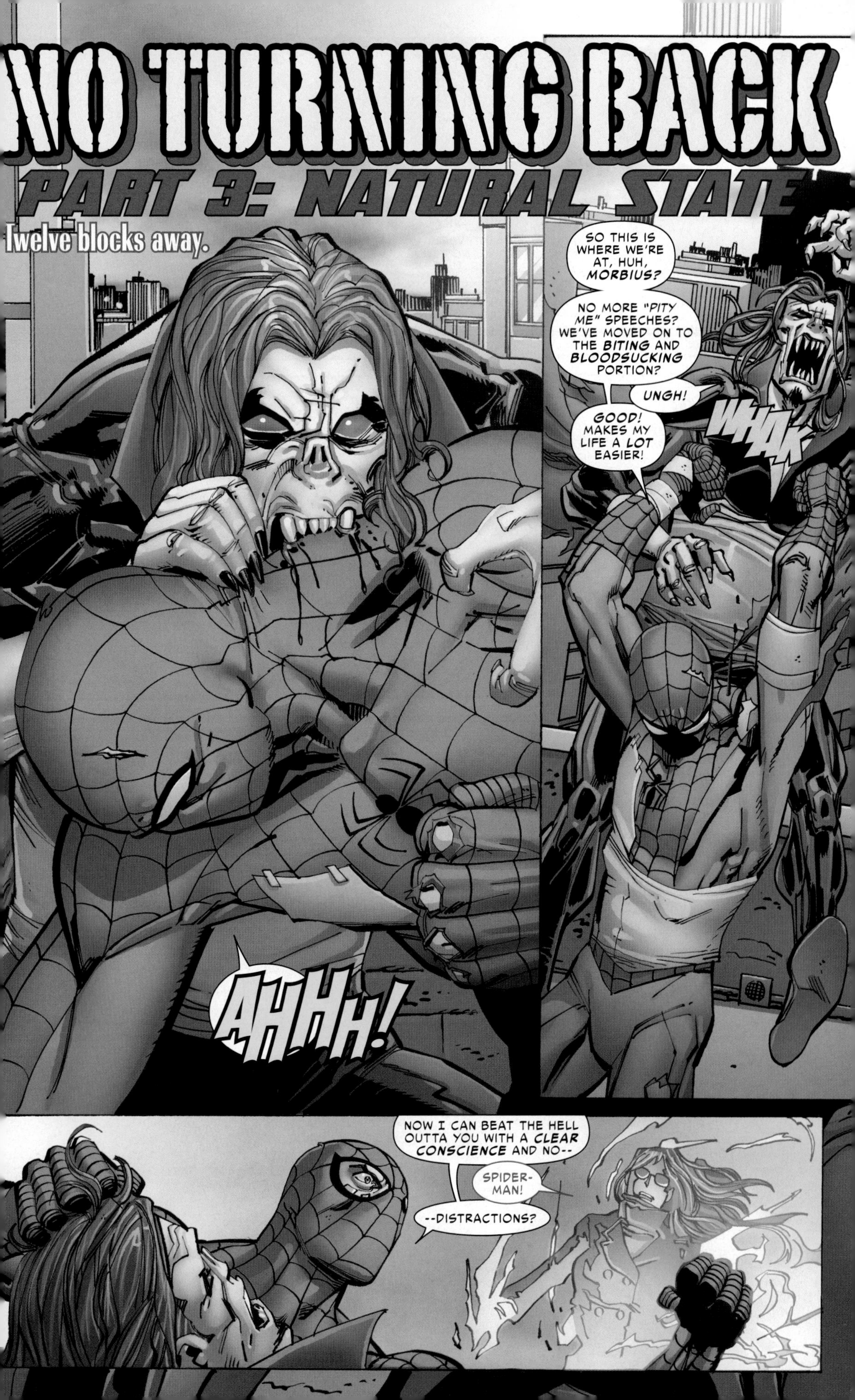
NO TURNING BACK
PART 3: NATURAL STATE
Twelve blocks away.
AHHH!
SO THIS IS WHERE WE'RE AT, HUH, MORBIUS?
NO MORE "PITY ME" SPEECHES? WE'VE MOVED ON TO THE BITING AND BLOODSUCKING PORTION?
UNGH!
WHAK
GOOD! MAKES MY LIFE A LOT EASIER!
NOW I CAN BEAT THE HELL OUTTA YOU WITH A CLEAR CONSCIENCE AND NO--
SPIDER-MAN!
--DISTRACTIONS?

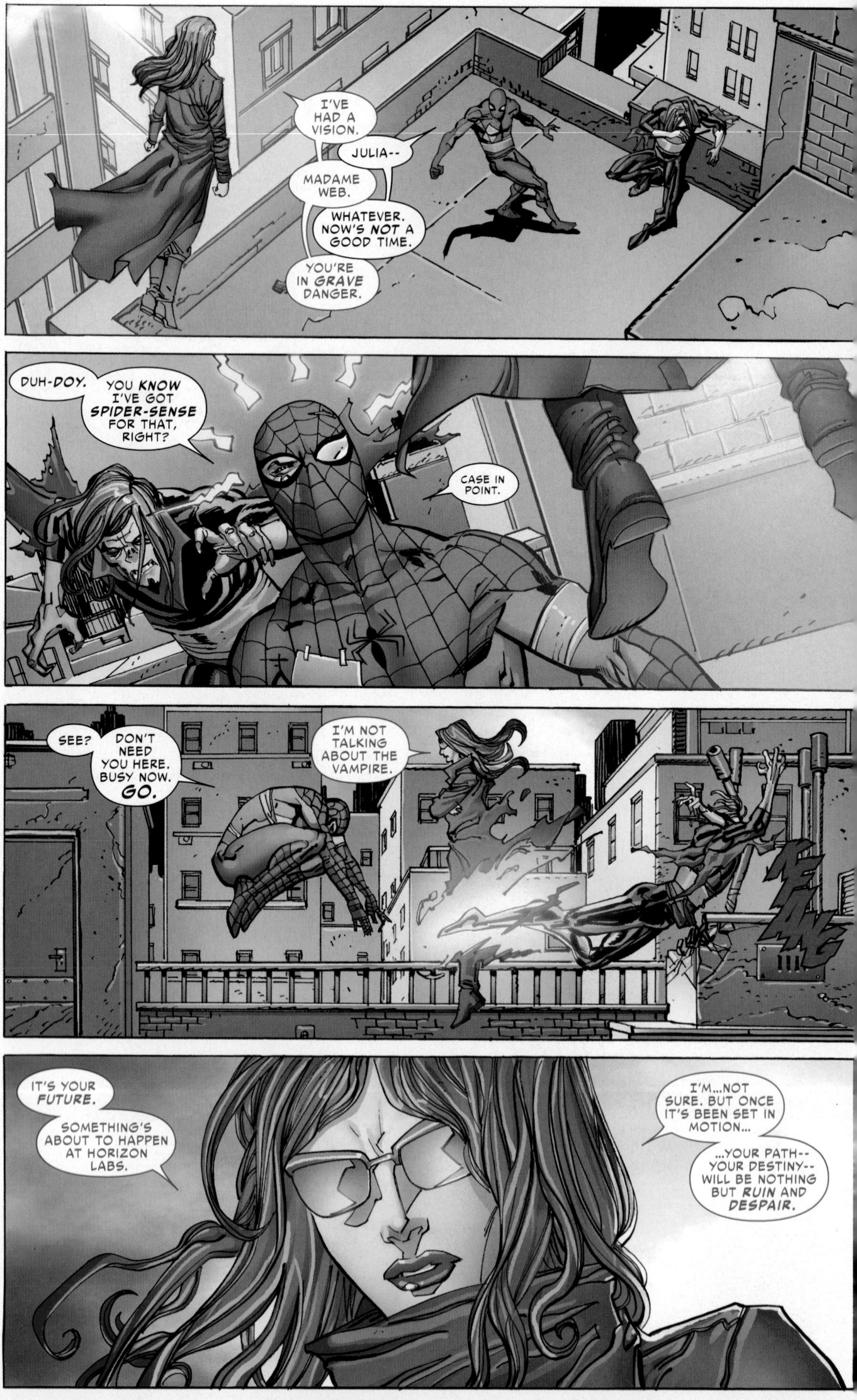

I'VE HAD A VISION.
JULIA--
MADAME WEB.
WHATEVER. NOW'S NOT A GOOD TIME.
YOU'RE IN GRAVE DANGER.
DUH-DOY.
YOU KNOW I'VE GOT SPIDER-SENSE FOR THAT, RIGHT?
CASE IN POINT.
SEE?
DON'T NEED YOU HERE. BUSY NOW. GO.
I'M NOT TALKING ABOUT THE VAMPIRE.
IT'S YOUR FUTURE.
SOMETHING'S ABOUT TO HAPPEN AT HORIZON LABS.
I'M...NOT SURE. BUT ONCE IT'S BEEN SET IN MOTION...
...YOUR PATH--YOUR DESTINY--WILL BE NOTHING BUT RUIN AND DESPAIR.

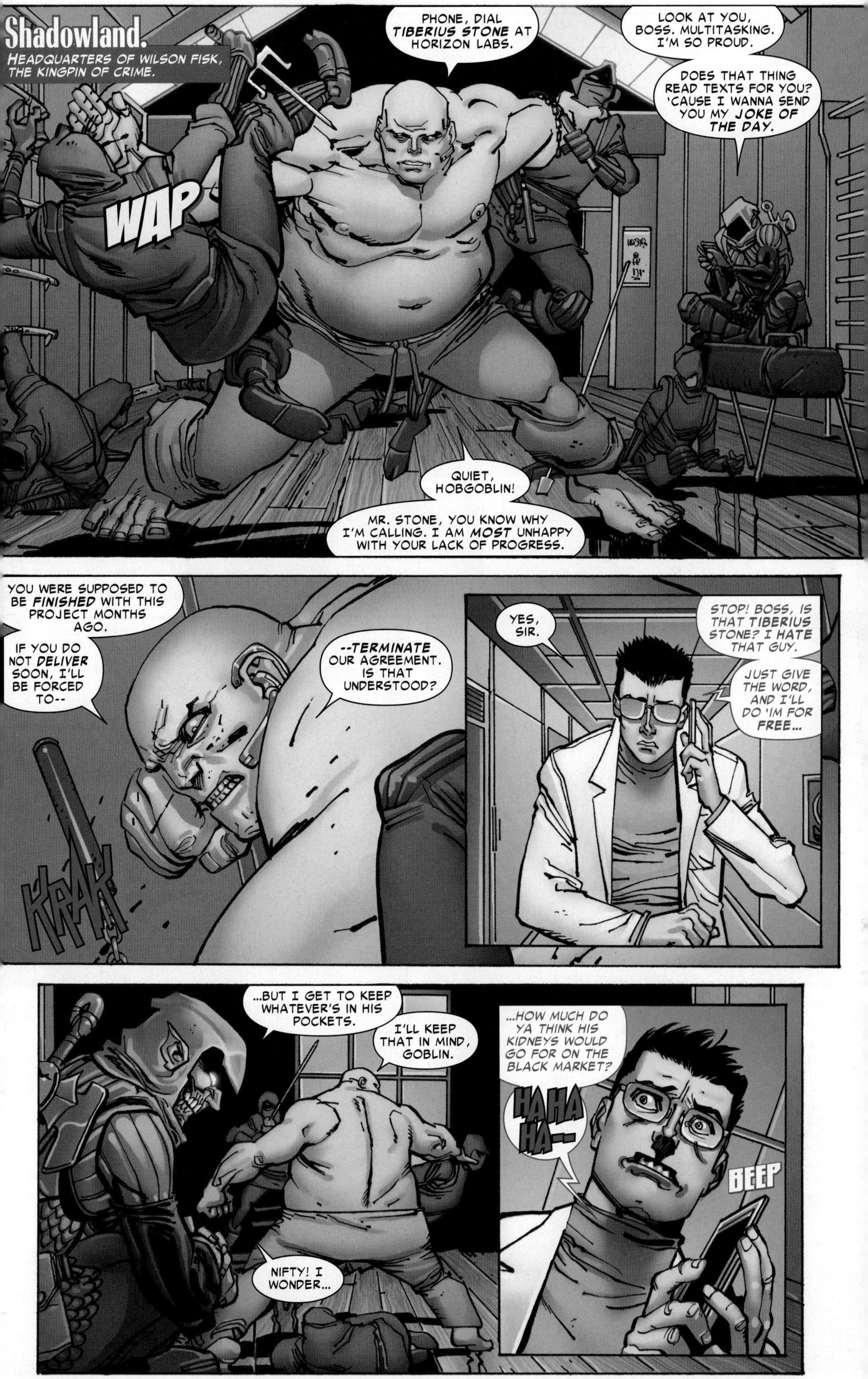
Shadowland.
Headquarters of Wilson Fisk, the Kingpin of Crime.
PHONE, DIAL TIBERIUS STONE AT HORIZON LABS.
LOOK AT YOU, BOSS. MULTITASKING. I'M SO PROUD.
DOES THAT THING READ TEXTS FOR YOU? 'CAUSE I WANNA SEND YOU MY JOKE OF THE DAY.
WAP
QUIET, HOBGOBLIN!
MR. STONE, YOU KNOW WHY I'M CALLING. I AM MOST UNHAPPY WITH YOUR LACK OF PROGRESS.
YOU WERE SUPPOSED TO BE FINISHED WITH THIS PROJECT MONTHS AGO.
IF YOU DO NOT DELIVER SOON, I'LL BE FORCED TO--
--TERMINATE OUR AGREEMENT. IS THAT UNDERSTOOD?
KRAK
YES, SIR.
STOP! BOSS, IS THAT TIBERIUS STONE? I HATE THAT GUY.
JUST GIVE THE WORD, AND I'LL DO 'IM FOR FREE...
...BUT I GET TO KEEP WHATEVER'S IN HIS POCKETS.
I'LL KEEP THAT IN MIND, GOBLIN.
NIFTY! I WONDER...
...HOW MUCH DO YA THINK HIS KIDNEYS WOULD GO FOR ON THE BLACK MARKET?
HAHAHA--
BEEP

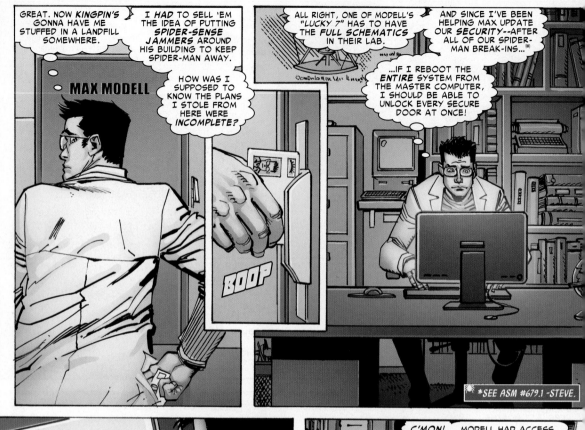

GREAT. NOW *KINGPIN'S* GONNA HAVE ME STUFFED IN A LANDFILL SOMEWHERE.

I *HAD* TO SELL 'EM THE IDEA OF PUTTING *SPIDER-SENSE JAMMERS* AROUND HIS BUILDING TO KEEP SPIDER-MAN AWAY.

MAX MODELL

HOW WAS I SUPPOSED TO KNOW THE PLANS I STOLE FROM HERE WERE *INCOMPLETE?*

ALL RIGHT, ONE OF MODELL'S "LUCKY 7" HAS TO HAVE THE *FULL SCHEMATICS* IN THEIR LAB.

AND SINCE I'VE BEEN HELPING MAX UPDATE OUR *SECURITY*--AFTER ALL OF OUR SPIDER-MAN BREAK-INS...*

...IF I REBOOT THE *ENTIRE* SYSTEM FROM THE MASTER COMPUTER, I SHOULD BE ABLE TO UNLOCK EVERY SECURE DOOR AT ONCE!

BOOP

*SEE ASM #679.1 -STEVE.

FILE UPLOADING 2%

SECURITY SYSTEM REBOOTING

AH! THIS'S TAKING TOO LONG! MY *LIFE'S* ON THE LINE HERE!

C'MON!

MODELL HAD ACCESS TO THOSE PLANS! MAYBE *HE* HAS A SET SOMEWHERE!

JUST HAVE TO TEAR THIS PLACE APART UNTIL I--

FOUND IT! ON THE FIRST GO.

MAN, AM I LUCKY TODAY OR WHAT?!

TO THINK WHAT I *ALMOST* WENT THROUGH FOR THIS.

FILE UPLOADING

SECURITY SYSTEM REBOOTING

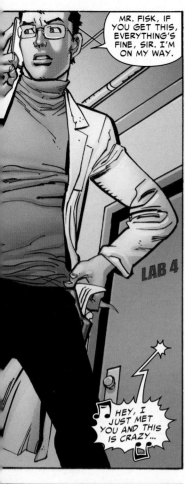

MR. FISK, IF YOU GET THIS, EVERYTHING'S FINE, SIR. I'M ON MY WAY.

LAB 4

♪ HEY, I JUST MET YOU AND THIS IS CRAZY... ♪

♪ ...BUT HERE'S MY NUMBER, SO CALL ME MAYBE? ♪

HERE'S YOUR PROBLEM RIGHT HERE, DOC.

THIS COMPOUND IS BLOCKING A NUMBER OF RECEPTORS.

WHAT? I WAS DISTRACTED. THAT RHYTHMIC SOUND...

OH. SORRY. I LIKE LISTENING TO MUSIC WHILE I WORK.

PEACE

TAP TAP

MUSIC? I'VE NEVER HEARD...

...THIS KIND OF MUSIC BEFORE.

NOT WITH HUMAN EARS. AND A MAMMAL BRAIN.

ADDING THIS ENZYME MIGHT DO THE TRICK.

GOOD. WE SHOULD TEST IT OUT. RIGHT AWAY.

WHERE ARE YOUR LAB ANIMALS?

DON'T HAVE ANY. I DON'T REALLY BELIEVE IN ANIMAL TESTING.

A PITY, MS. FISHBACH.

♪ IT'S HARD TO LOOK RIGHT AT YOU BABY, BUT HERE'S MY NUMBER, SO CALL ME, MAYBE? ♪

"SPIDER-MAN, PLEASE. IF YOU DON'T HEAD BACK TO HORIZON RIGHT NOW..."

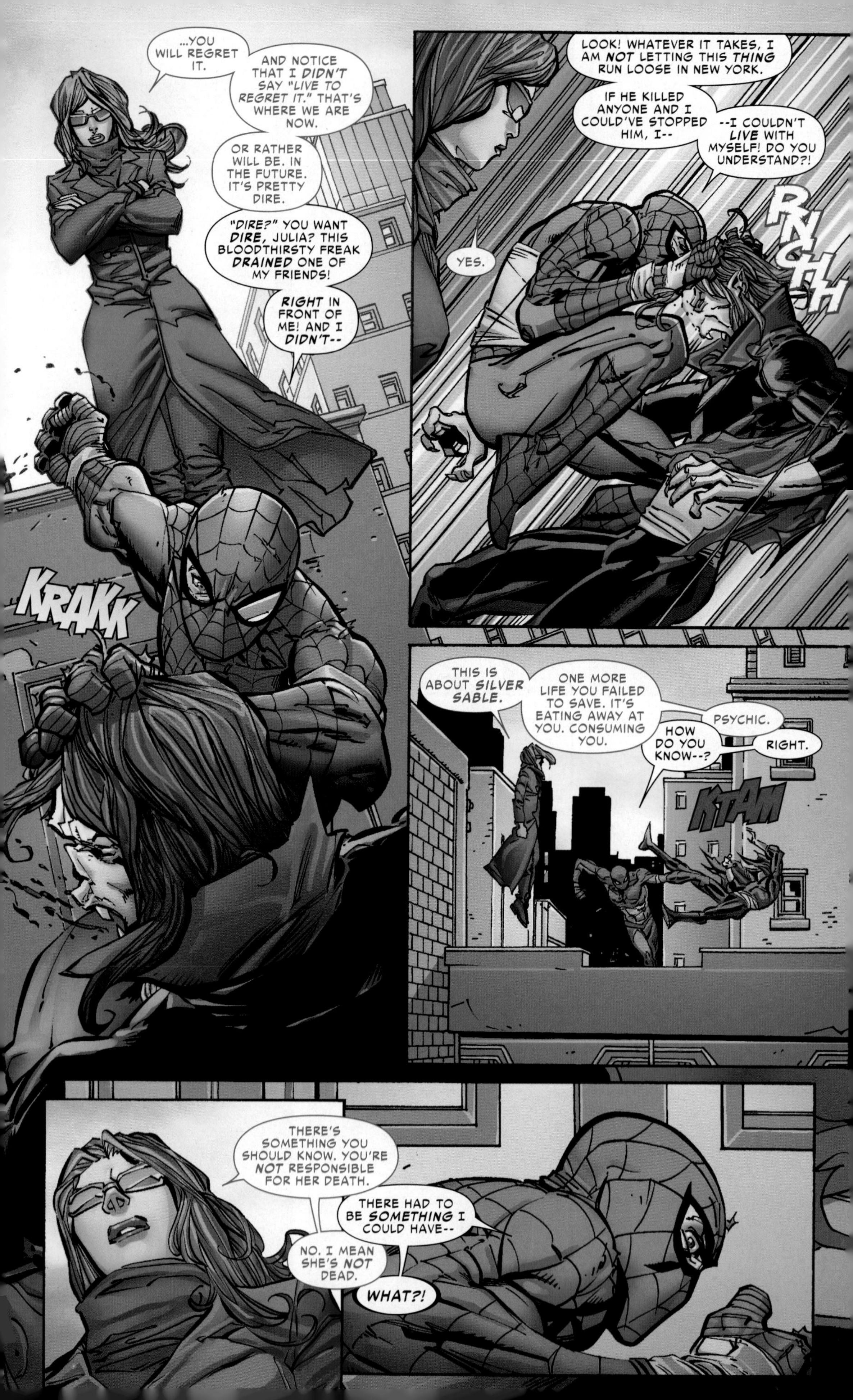
...YOU WILL REGRET IT.
AND NOTICE THAT I *DIDN'T* SAY "*LIVE TO REGRET IT.*" THAT'S WHERE WE ARE NOW.
OR RATHER WILL BE. IN THE FUTURE. IT'S PRETTY DIRE.
"*DIRE?*" YOU WANT ***DIRE,*** JULIA? THIS BLOODTHIRSTY FREAK ***DRAINED*** ONE OF MY FRIENDS!
RIGHT IN FRONT OF ME! AND I ***DIDN'T***--
KRAKK
LOOK! WHATEVER IT TAKES, I AM ***NOT*** LETTING THIS ***THING*** RUN LOOSE IN NEW YORK.
IF HE KILLED ANYONE AND I COULD'VE STOPPED HIM, I--
--I COULDN'T ***LIVE*** WITH MYSELF! DO YOU UNDERSTAND?!
RNCHH
YES.
THIS IS ABOUT ***SILVER SABLE.***
ONE MORE LIFE YOU FAILED TO SAVE. IT'S EATING AWAY AT YOU. CONSUMING YOU.
HOW DO YOU KNOW--?
PSYCHIC.
RIGHT.
KTAM
THERE'S SOMETHING YOU SHOULD KNOW. YOU'RE ***NOT*** RESPONSIBLE FOR HER DEATH.
THERE HAD TO BE ***SOMETHING*** I COULD HAVE--
NO. I MEAN SHE'S ***NOT*** DEAD.
WHAT?!

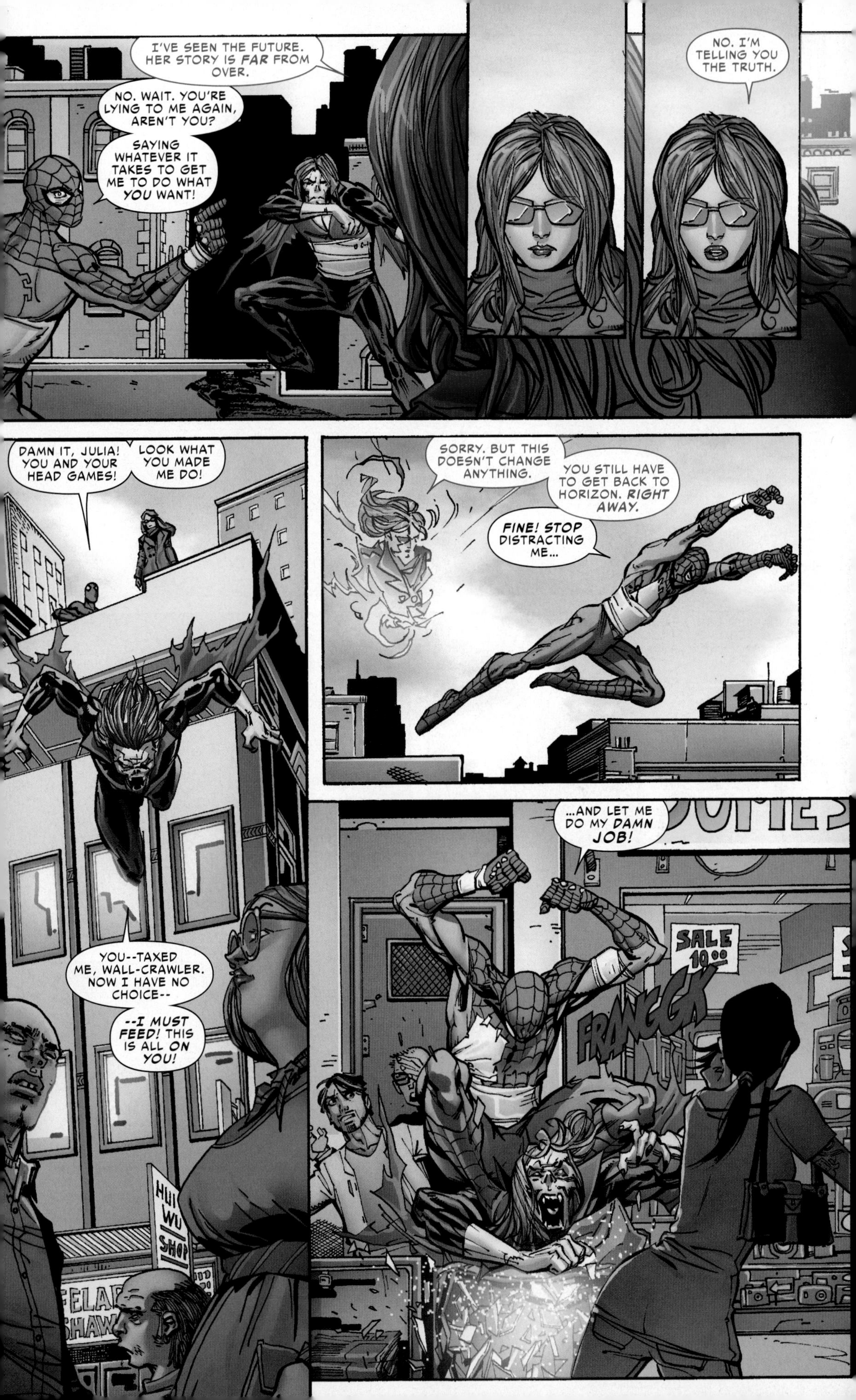
I'VE SEEN THE FUTURE. HER STORY IS FAR FROM OVER.
NO. WAIT. YOU'RE LYING TO ME AGAIN, AREN'T YOU?
SAYING WHATEVER IT TAKES TO GET ME TO DO WHAT YOU WANT!
NO. I'M TELLING YOU THE TRUTH.
DAMN IT, JULIA! YOU AND YOUR HEAD GAMES!
LOOK WHAT YOU MADE ME DO!
YOU--TAXED ME, WALL-CRAWLER. NOW I HAVE NO CHOICE--
--I MUST FEED! THIS IS ALL ON YOU!
SORRY. BUT THIS DOESN'T CHANGE ANYTHING.
YOU STILL HAVE TO GET BACK TO HORIZON. RIGHT AWAY.
FINE! STOP DISTRACTING ME...
...AND LET ME DO MY DAMN JOB!
SALE 10.00
FRANGGK
HUI WU SHOP

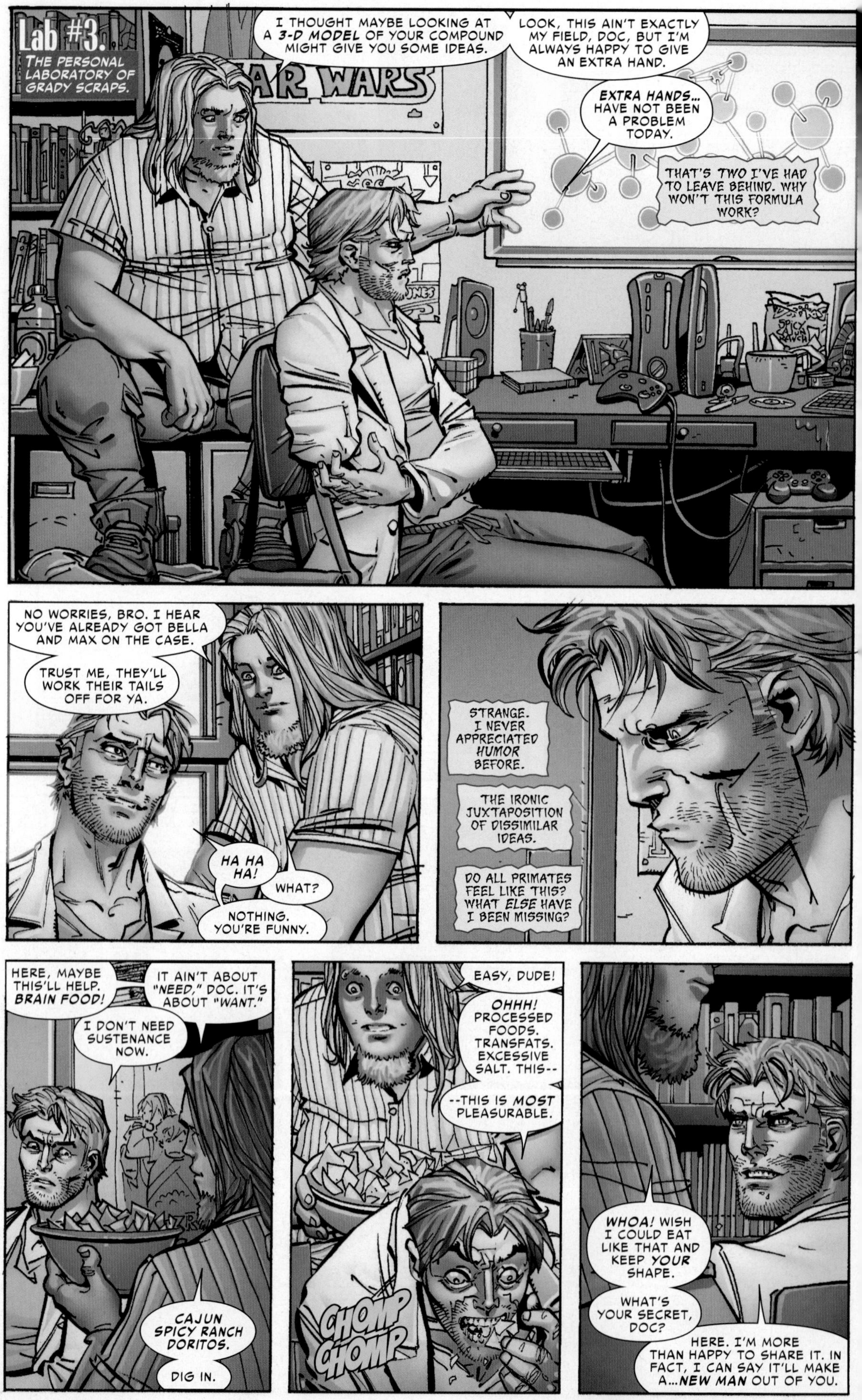
Lab #3.
THE PERSONAL LABORATORY OF GRADY SCRAPS.
I THOUGHT MAYBE LOOKING AT A 3-D MODEL OF YOUR COMPOUND MIGHT GIVE YOU SOME IDEAS.
LOOK, THIS AIN'T EXACTLY MY FIELD, DOC, BUT I'M ALWAYS HAPPY TO GIVE AN EXTRA HAND.
EXTRA HANDS... HAVE NOT BEEN A PROBLEM TODAY.
THAT'S TWO I'VE HAD TO LEAVE BEHIND. WHY WON'T THIS FORMULA WORK?
STAR WARS
SPICY CAJUN RANCH
NO WORRIES, BRO. I HEAR YOU'VE ALREADY GOT BELLA AND MAX ON THE CASE.
TRUST ME, THEY'LL WORK THEIR TAILS OFF FOR YA.
HA HA HA!
WHAT?
NOTHING. YOU'RE FUNNY.
STRANGE. I NEVER APPRECIATED HUMOR BEFORE.
THE IRONIC JUXTAPOSITION OF DISSIMILAR IDEAS.
DO ALL PRIMATES FEEL LIKE THIS? WHAT ELSE HAVE I BEEN MISSING?
HERE, MAYBE THIS'LL HELP. BRAIN FOOD!
I DON'T NEED SUSTENANCE NOW.
IT AIN'T ABOUT "NEED," DOC. IT'S ABOUT "WANT."
CAJUN SPICY RANCH DORITOS.
DIG IN.
EASY, DUDE!
OHHH! PROCESSED FOODS. TRANSFATS. EXCESSIVE SALT. THIS--
--THIS IS MOST PLEASURABLE.
CHOMP CHOMP
WHOA! WISH I COULD EAT LIKE THAT AND KEEP YOUR SHAPE.
WHAT'S YOUR SECRET, DOC?
HERE. I'M MORE THAN HAPPY TO SHARE IT. IN FACT, I CAN SAY IT'LL MAKE A...NEW MAN OUT OF YOU.

GET 'IM, WEB-HEAD!

THIS IS CAR FOURTEEN. WE'VE GOT A *CAPE ALTERCATION* IN PROGRESS. SPIDER-MAN'S *ASSAULTING* ANOTHER COSTUMED INDIVIDUAL. PROCEEDING WITH CAUTION--

NO! OFFICERS, STAY BACK!

AND YOU--STAY DOWN!

THWOK

SPIDER-MAN, PLEASE! I CAN'T CONTROL THE HUNGER! I'M NOT IN MY RIGHT--

THWIP

ENOUGH OUT OF YOU!

SAVE IT FOR THE SHRINKS AT *RYKERS!* I'M DONE WITH YOU, MORBIUS. OR DON'T YOU GET IT?

YOU'RE *NOT* SOME POOR, TORTURED SOUL TO ME. NOT ANYMORE.

FROM HERE OUT, YOU'RE JUST ANOTHER *LOSER* I'M LEAVING WEBBED UP AND HANGING FOR THE COPS.

9 RANK

ALL RIGHT, YOU KNOW THE DRILL. THE WEBBING TAKES AN HOUR TO DISSOLVE.

SEND FOR A SUPERHUMAN CONTAINMENT VEHICLE.

AND YOU'LL NEED ABOUT THREE PINTS OF *BLOOD* TO KEEP HIM *FED* BUT NOT ENOUGH TO--

HOLD ON! WHAT GIVES YOU THE AUTHORITY TO--

SPIDER-MAN. LICENSED *AVENGER.*

MAKE THE CALL.

AVENGERS
OFFICIAL IDENTIFICATION

SECURITY CLEARANCE
ALPHA

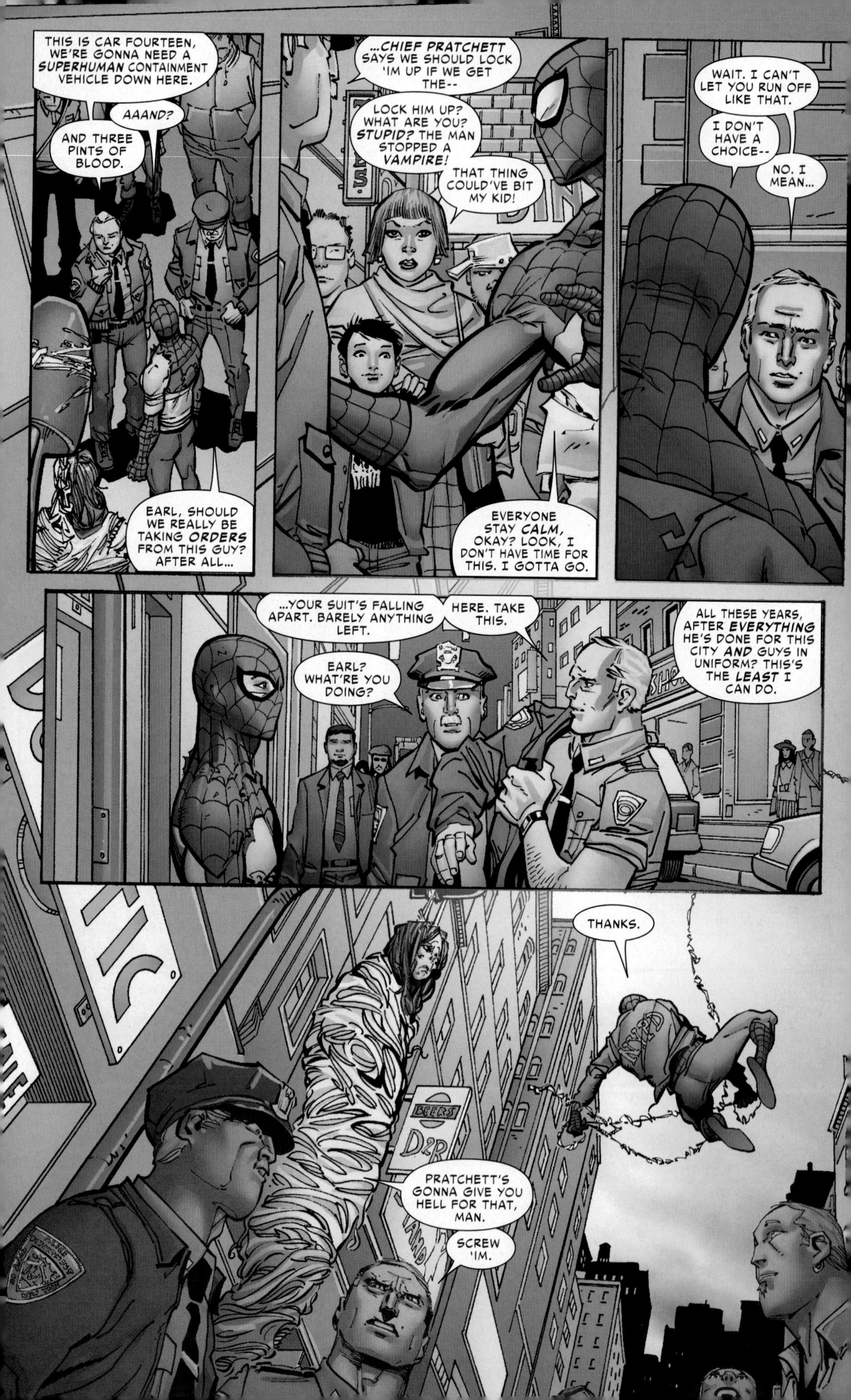
THIS IS CAR FOURTEEN, WE'RE GONNA NEED A SUPERHUMAN CONTAINMENT VEHICLE DOWN HERE.
AAAND?
AND THREE PINTS OF BLOOD.
EARL, SHOULD WE REALLY BE TAKING ORDERS FROM THIS GUY? AFTER ALL...
...CHIEF PRATCHETT SAYS WE SHOULD LOCK 'IM UP IF WE GET THE--
LOCK HIM UP? WHAT ARE YOU? STUPID? THE MAN STOPPED A VAMPIRE!
THAT THING COULD'VE BIT MY KID!
EVERYONE STAY CALM, OKAY? LOOK, I DON'T HAVE TIME FOR THIS. I GOTTA GO.
WAIT. I CAN'T LET YOU RUN OFF LIKE THAT.
I DON'T HAVE A CHOICE--
NO. I MEAN...
...YOUR SUIT'S FALLING APART. BARELY ANYTHING LEFT.
HERE. TAKE THIS.
EARL? WHAT'RE YOU DOING?
ALL THESE YEARS, AFTER EVERYTHING HE'S DONE FOR THIS CITY AND GUYS IN UNIFORM? THIS'S THE LEAST I CAN DO.
THANKS.
PRATCHETT'S GONNA GIVE YOU HELL FOR THAT, MAN.
SCREW 'IM.

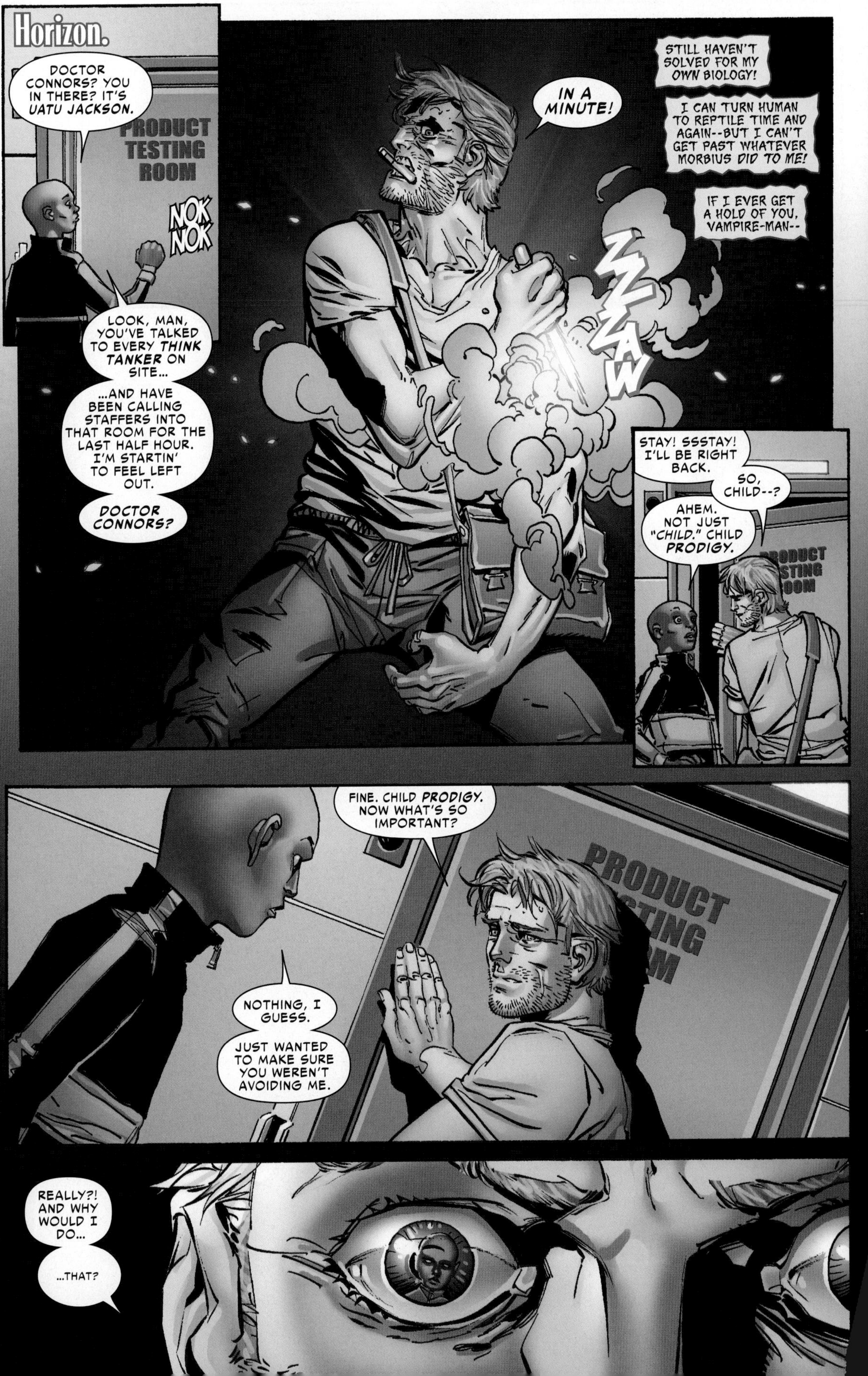
Horizon.
DOCTOR CONNORS? YOU IN THERE? IT'S UATU JACKSON.
PRODUCT TESTING ROOM
NOK NOK
IN A MINUTE!
STILL HAVEN'T SOLVED FOR MY OWN BIOLOGY!
I CAN TURN HUMAN TO REPTILE TIME AND AGAIN--BUT I CAN'T GET PAST WHATEVER MORBIUS DID TO ME!
IF I EVER GET A HOLD OF YOU, VAMPIRE-MAN--
ZZZAW
LOOK, MAN, YOU'VE TALKED TO EVERY THINK TANKER ON SITE...
...AND HAVE BEEN CALLING STAFFERS INTO THAT ROOM FOR THE LAST HALF HOUR. I'M STARTIN' TO FEEL LEFT OUT.
DOCTOR CONNORS?
STAY! SSSTAY! I'LL BE RIGHT BACK.
SO, CHILD--?
AHEM. NOT JUST "CHILD." CHILD PRODIGY.
FINE. CHILD PRODIGY. NOW WHAT'S SO IMPORTANT?
NOTHING, I GUESS.
JUST WANTED TO MAKE SURE YOU WEREN'T AVOIDING ME.
REALLY?! AND WHY WOULD I DO...
...THAT?

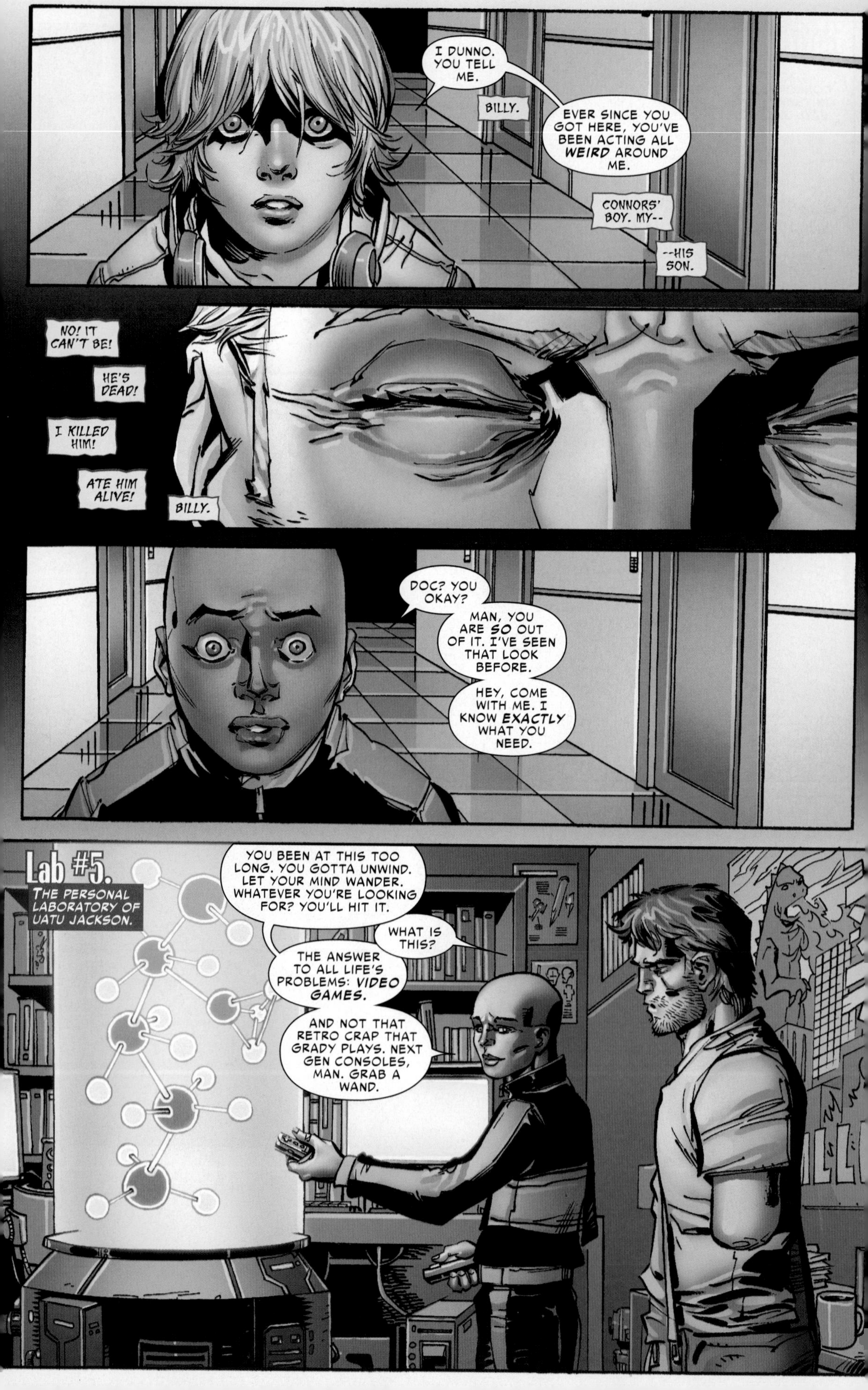
I DUNNO. YOU TELL ME.
BILLY.
EVER SINCE YOU GOT HERE, YOU'VE BEEN ACTING ALL WEIRD AROUND ME.
CONNORS' BOY. MY--
--HIS SON.
NO! IT CAN'T BE!
HE'S DEAD!
I KILLED HIM!
ATE HIM ALIVE!
BILLY.
DOC? YOU OKAY?
MAN, YOU ARE SO OUT OF IT. I'VE SEEN THAT LOOK BEFORE.
HEY, COME WITH ME. I KNOW EXACTLY WHAT YOU NEED.
Lab #5.
THE PERSONAL LABORATORY OF UATU JACKSON.
YOU BEEN AT THIS TOO LONG. YOU GOTTA UNWIND. LET YOUR MIND WANDER. WHATEVER YOU'RE LOOKING FOR? YOU'LL HIT IT.
WHAT IS THIS?
THE ANSWER TO ALL LIFE'S PROBLEMS: VIDEO GAMES.
AND NOT THAT RETRO CRAP THAT GRADY PLAYS. NEXT GEN CONSOLES, MAN. GRAB A WAND.

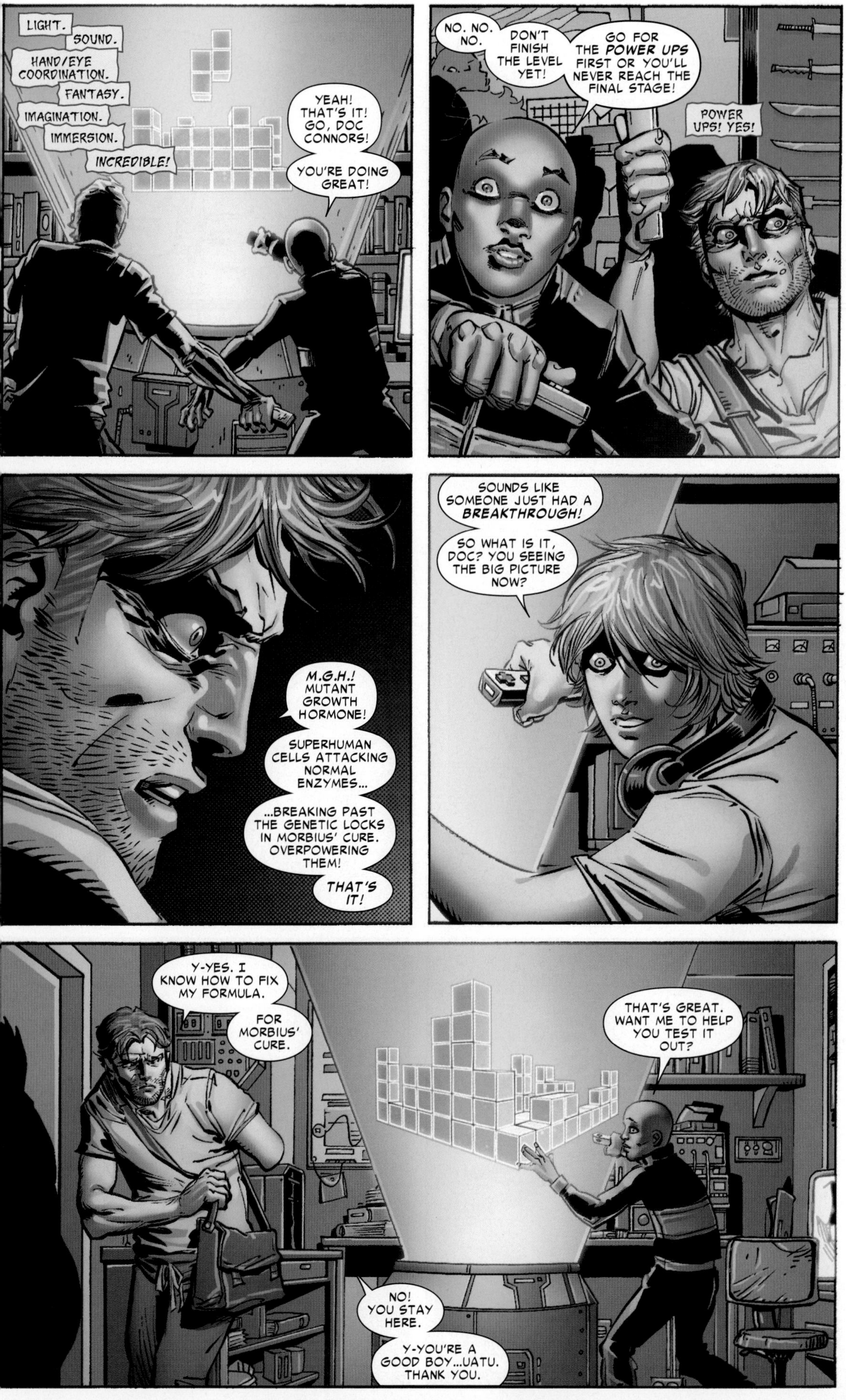
LIGHT.
SOUND.
HAND/EYE COORDINATION.
FANTASY.
IMAGINATION.
IMMERSION.
INCREDIBLE!
YEAH! THAT'S IT! GO, DOC CONNORS!
YOU'RE DOING GREAT!
NO. NO. NO.
DON'T FINISH THE LEVEL YET!
GO FOR THE POWER UPS FIRST OR YOU'LL NEVER REACH THE FINAL STAGE!
POWER UPS! YES!
M.G.H.! MUTANT GROWTH HORMONE!
SUPERHUMAN CELLS ATTACKING NORMAL ENZYMES...
...BREAKING PAST THE GENETIC LOCKS IN MORBIUS' CURE. OVERPOWERING THEM!
THAT'S IT!
SOUNDS LIKE SOMEONE JUST HAD A BREAKTHROUGH!
SO WHAT IS IT, DOC? YOU SEEING THE BIG PICTURE NOW?
Y-YES. I KNOW HOW TO FIX MY FORMULA.
FOR MORBIUS' CURE.
THAT'S GREAT. WANT ME TO HELP YOU TEST IT OUT?
NO! YOU STAY HERE.
Y-YOU'RE A GOOD BOY...UATU. THANK YOU.

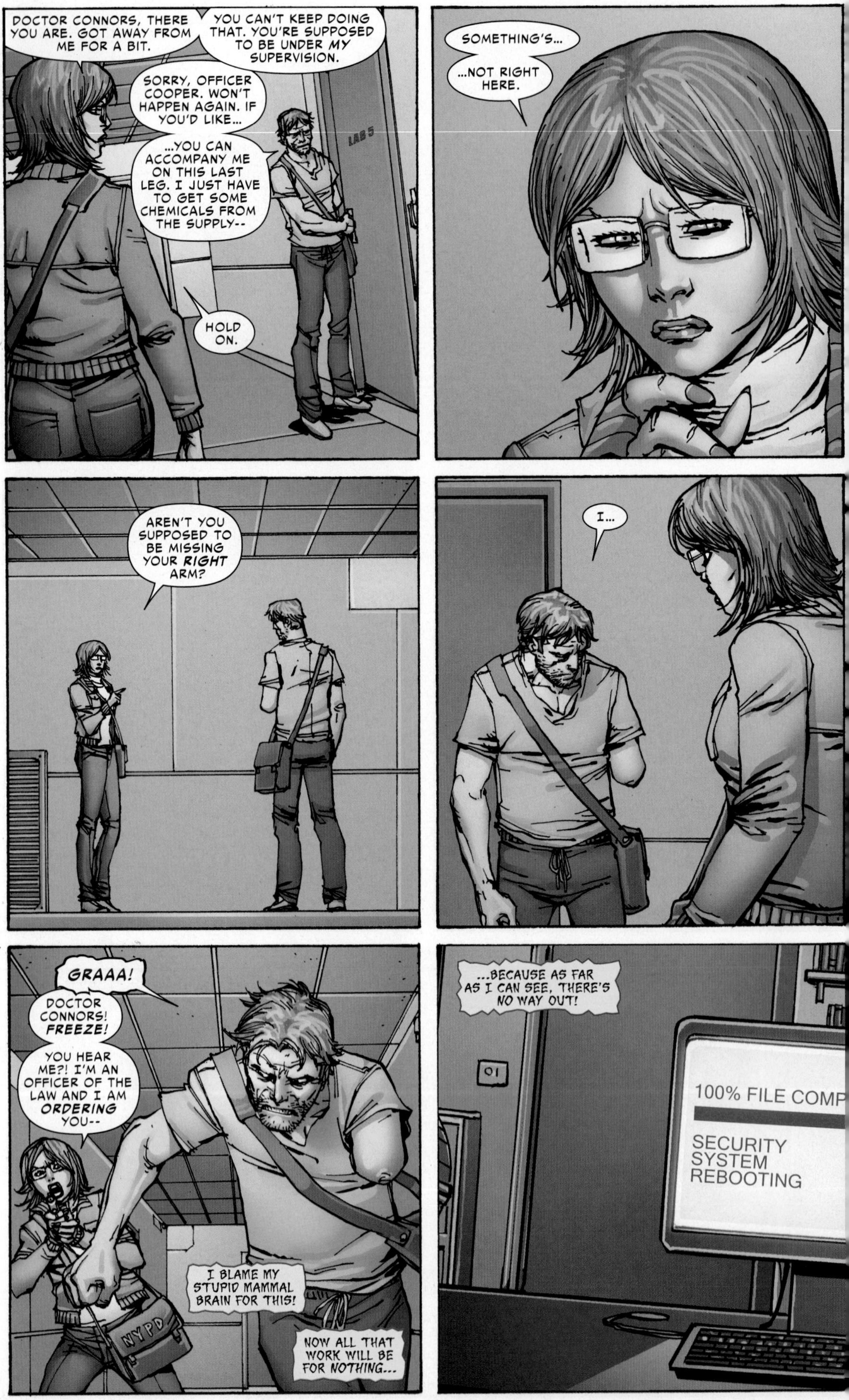
DOCTOR CONNORS, THERE YOU ARE. GOT AWAY FROM ME FOR A BIT.
YOU CAN'T KEEP DOING THAT. YOU'RE SUPPOSED TO BE UNDER *MY* SUPERVISION.
SORRY, OFFICER COOPER. WON'T HAPPEN AGAIN. IF YOU'D LIKE...
...YOU CAN ACCOMPANY ME ON THIS LAST LEG. I JUST HAVE TO GET SOME CHEMICALS FROM THE SUPPLY--
LAB 5
HOLD ON.
SOMETHING'S...
...NOT RIGHT HERE.
AREN'T YOU SUPPOSED TO BE MISSING YOUR *RIGHT* ARM?
I...
GRAAA!
DOCTOR CONNORS! *FREEZE!*
YOU HEAR ME?! I'M AN OFFICER OF THE LAW AND I AM *ORDERING* YOU--
I BLAME MY STUPID MAMMAL BRAIN FOR THIS!
NOW ALL THAT WORK WILL BE FOR *NOTHING*...
NYPD
...BECAUSE AS FAR AS I CAN SEE, THERE'S NO WAY OUT!
01
100% FILE COMP
SECURITY SYSTEM REBOOTING

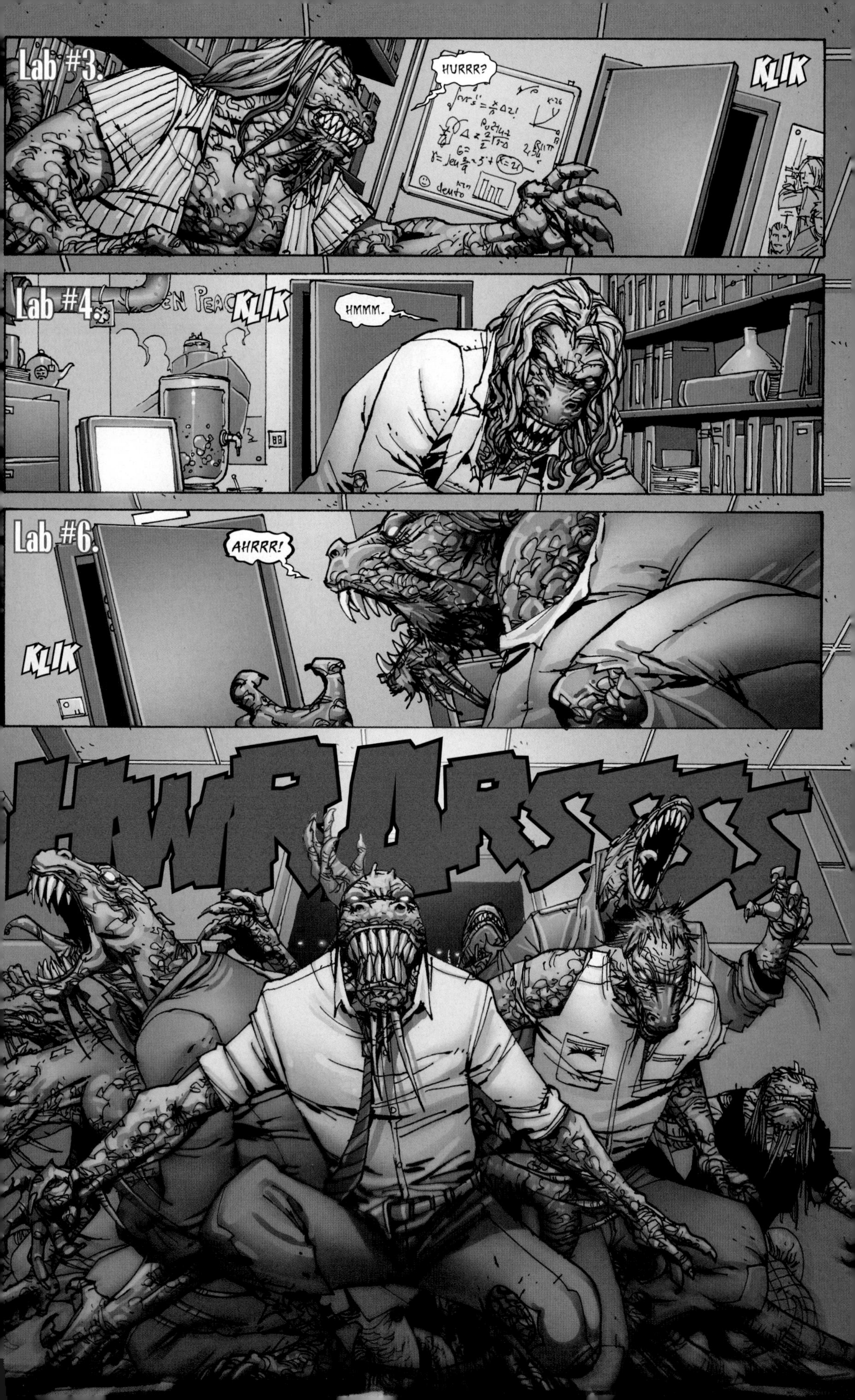
Lab #3.
HURRR?
KLIK
Lab #4.
KLIK
HMMM.
Lab #6.
AHRRR!
KLIK
HWRURSSS

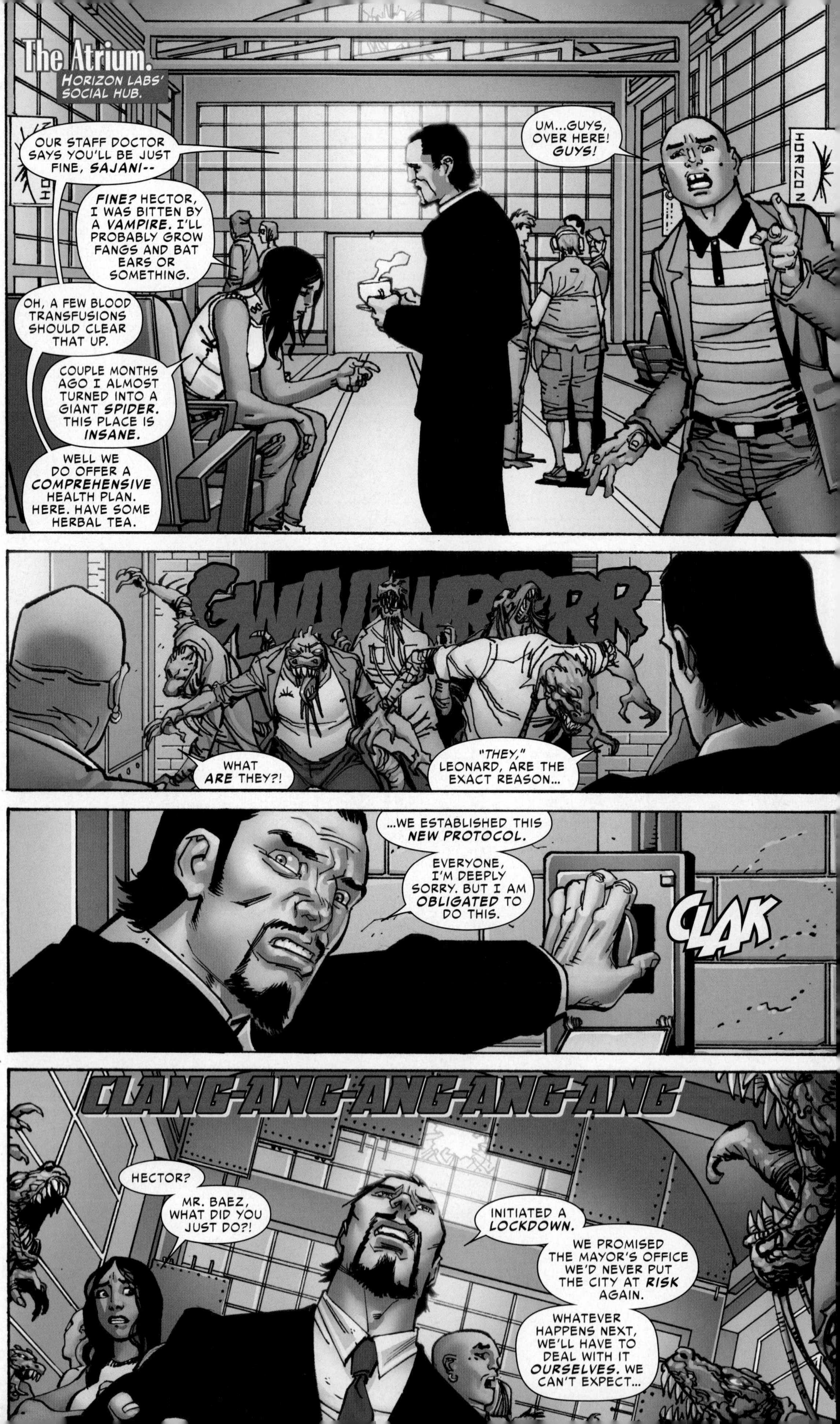

The Atrium.
HORIZON LABS' SOCIAL HUB.
OUR STAFF DOCTOR SAYS YOU'LL BE JUST FINE, SAJANI--
FINE? HECTOR, I WAS BITTEN BY A VAMPIRE. I'LL PROBABLY GROW FANGS AND BAT EARS OR SOMETHING.
OH, A FEW BLOOD TRANSFUSIONS SHOULD CLEAR THAT UP.
COUPLE MONTHS AGO I ALMOST TURNED INTO A GIANT SPIDER. THIS PLACE IS INSANE.
WELL WE DO OFFER A COMPREHENSIVE HEALTH PLAN. HERE. HAVE SOME HERBAL TEA.
UM...GUYS, OVER HERE! GUYS!
GWAAWRRRR
WHAT ARE THEY?!
"THEY," LEONARD, ARE THE EXACT REASON...
...WE ESTABLISHED THIS NEW PROTOCOL.
EVERYONE, I'M DEEPLY SORRY. BUT I AM OBLIGATED TO DO THIS.
CLAK
CLANG-ANG-ANG-ANG-ANG
HECTOR?
MR. BAEZ, WHAT DID YOU JUST DO?!
INITIATED A LOCKDOWN.
WE PROMISED THE MAYOR'S OFFICE WE'D NEVER PUT THE CITY AT RISK AGAIN.
WHATEVER HAPPENS NEXT, WE'LL HAVE TO DEAL WITH IT OURSELVES. WE CAN'T EXPECT...

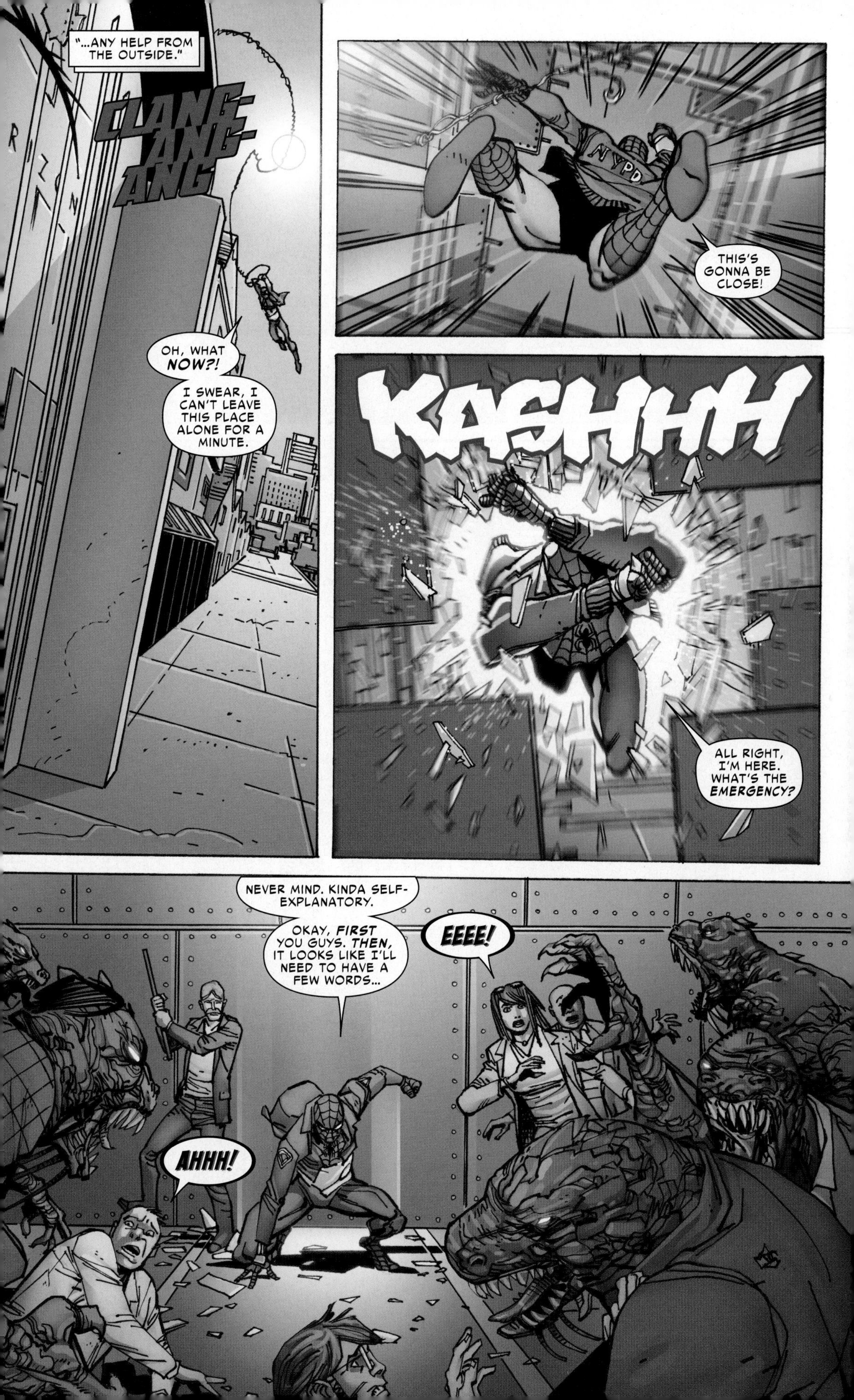
"...ANY HELP FROM THE OUTSIDE."
CLANG-ANG-ANG
THIS'S GONNA BE CLOSE!
OH, WHAT NOW?!
I SWEAR, I CAN'T LEAVE THIS PLACE ALONE FOR A MINUTE.
KASHHH
ALL RIGHT, I'M HERE. WHAT'S THE EMERGENCY?
NEVER MIND. KINDA SELF-EXPLANATORY.
OKAY, FIRST YOU GUYS. THEN, IT LOOKS LIKE I'LL NEED TO HAVE A FEW WORDS...
EEEE!
AHHH!

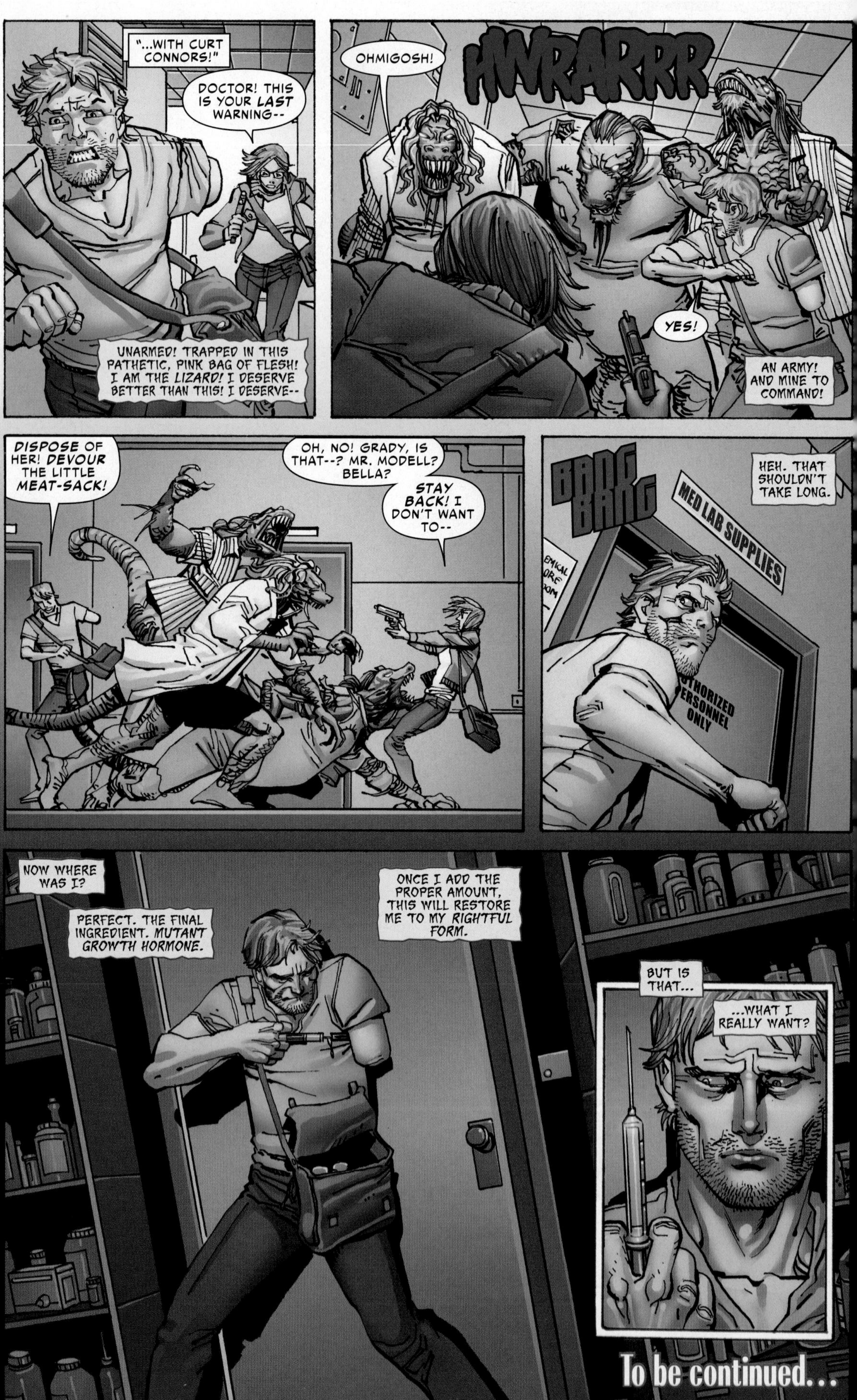
"...WITH CURT CONNORS!"
DOCTOR! THIS IS YOUR LAST WARNING--
UNARMED! TRAPPED IN THIS PATHETIC, PINK BAG OF FLESH! I AM THE LIZARD! I DESERVE BETTER THAN THIS! I DESERVE--
OHMIGOSH!
HWRARRR
YES!
AN ARMY! AND MINE TO COMMAND!
DISPOSE OF HER! DEVOUR THE LITTLE MEAT-SACK!
OH, NO! GRADY, IS THAT--? MR. MODELL? BELLA?
STAY BACK! I DON'T WANT TO--
BANG BANG
MED LAB SUPPLIES
HEH. THAT SHOULDN'T TAKE LONG.
UTHORIZED PERSONNEL ONLY
NOW WHERE WAS I?
PERFECT. THE FINAL INGREDIENT. MUTANT GROWTH HORMONE.
ONCE I ADD THE PROPER AMOUNT, THIS WILL RESTORE ME TO MY RIGHTFUL FORM.
BUT IS THAT...
...WHAT I REALLY WANT?
To be continued. . .

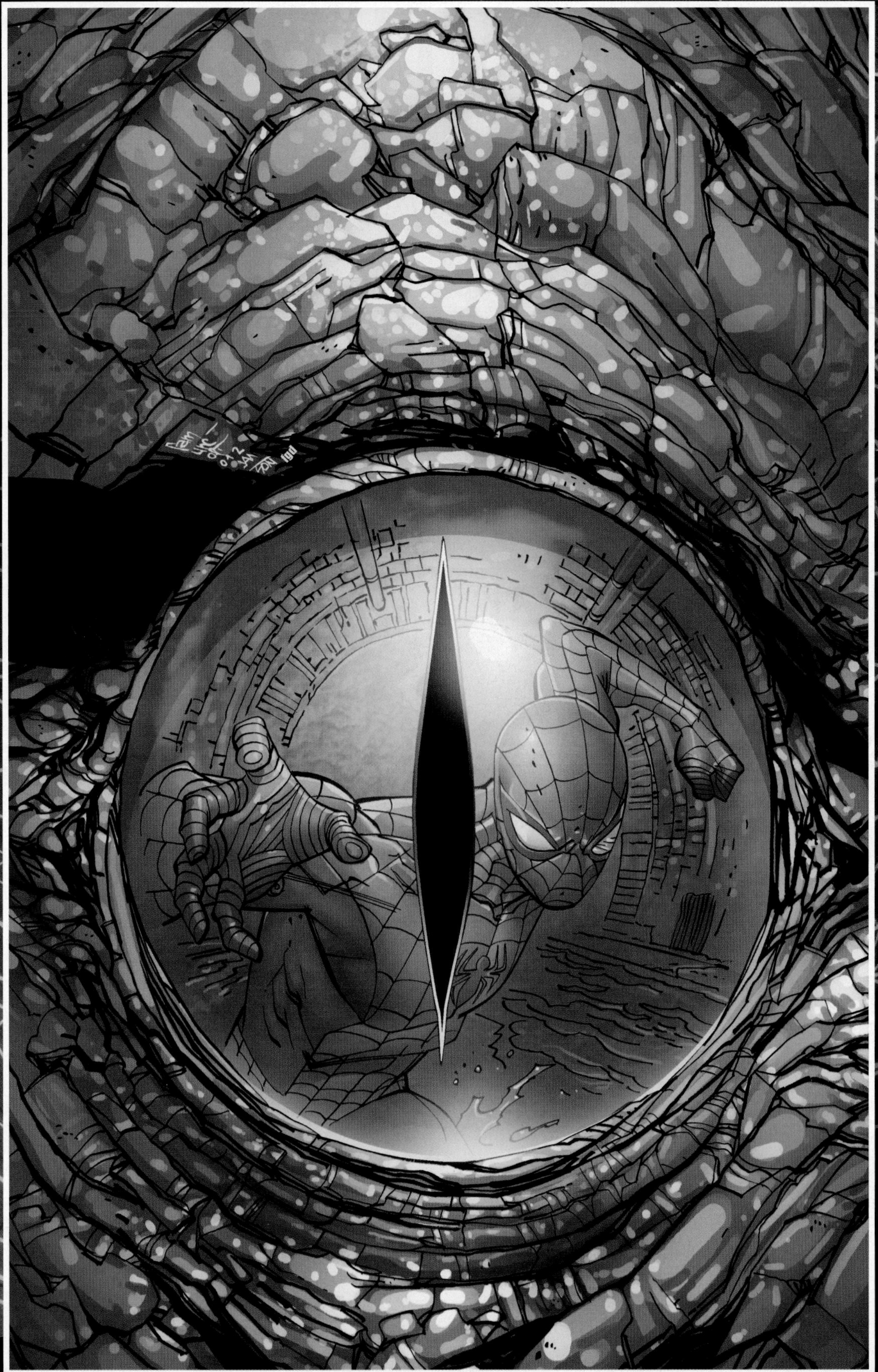

AMAZING SPIDER-MAN #691
COVER BY GIUSEPPE CAMUNCOLI, KLAUS JANSON & FRANK D'ARMATA

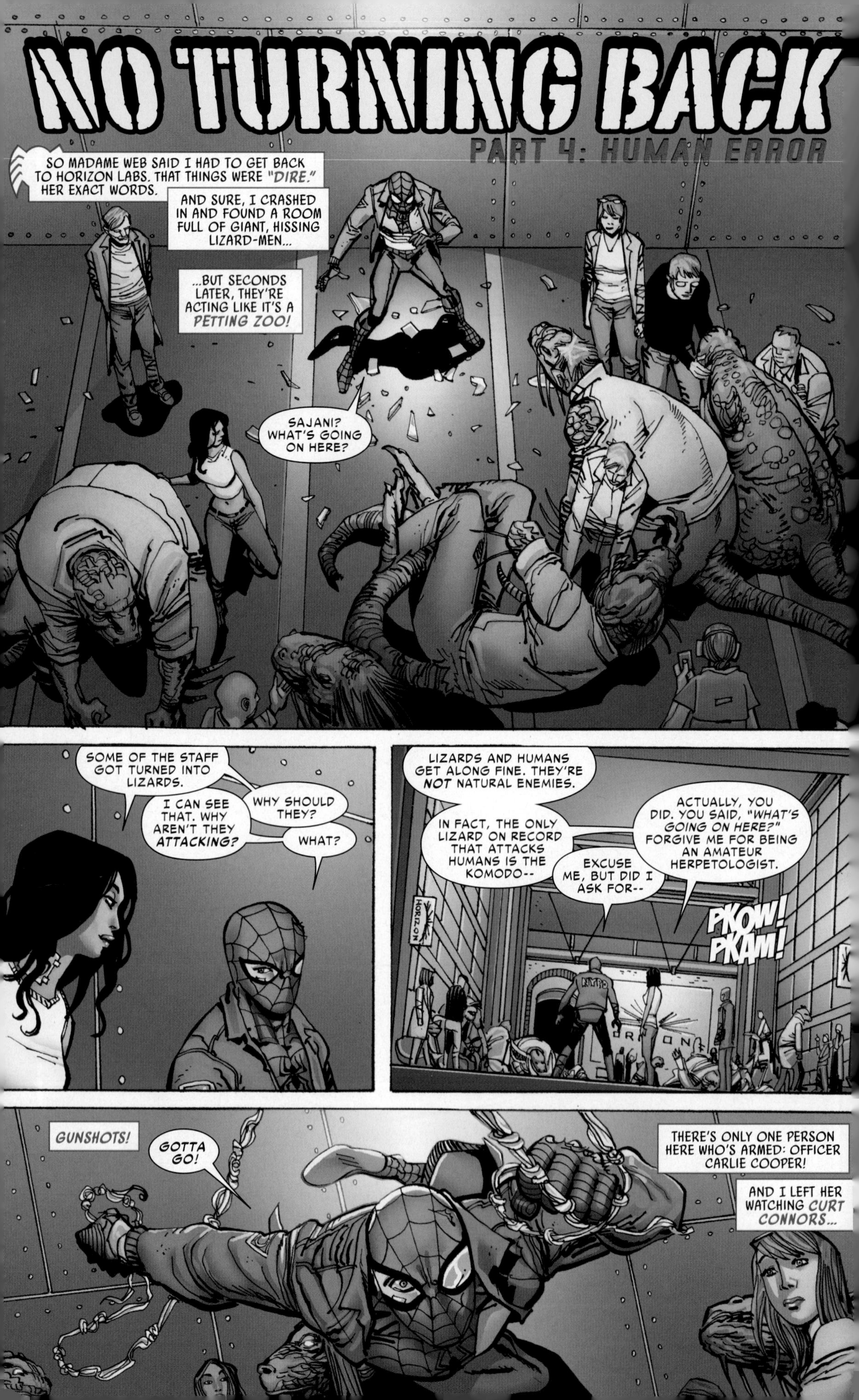
NO TURNING BACK
PART 4: HUMAN ERROR
SO MADAME WEB SAID I HAD TO GET BACK TO HORIZON LABS. THAT THINGS WERE "DIRE." HER EXACT WORDS.
AND SURE, I CRASHED IN AND FOUND A ROOM FULL OF GIANT, HISSING LIZARD-MEN...
...BUT SECONDS LATER, THEY'RE ACTING LIKE IT'S A PETTING ZOO!
SAJANI? WHAT'S GOING ON HERE?
SOME OF THE STAFF GOT TURNED INTO LIZARDS.
I CAN SEE THAT. WHY AREN'T THEY ATTACKING?
WHY SHOULD THEY?
WHAT?
LIZARDS AND HUMANS GET ALONG FINE. THEY'RE NOT NATURAL ENEMIES.
IN FACT, THE ONLY LIZARD ON RECORD THAT ATTACKS HUMANS IS THE KOMODO--
EXCUSE ME, BUT DID I ASK FOR--
ACTUALLY, YOU DID. YOU SAID, "WHAT'S GOING ON HERE?" FORGIVE ME FOR BEING AN AMATEUR HERPETOLOGIST.
HORIZON
NYPD
PKOW! PKAM!
GUNSHOTS!
GOTTA GO!
THERE'S ONLY ONE PERSON HERE WHO'S ARMED: OFFICER CARLIE COOPER!
AND I LEFT HER WATCHING CURT CONNORS...

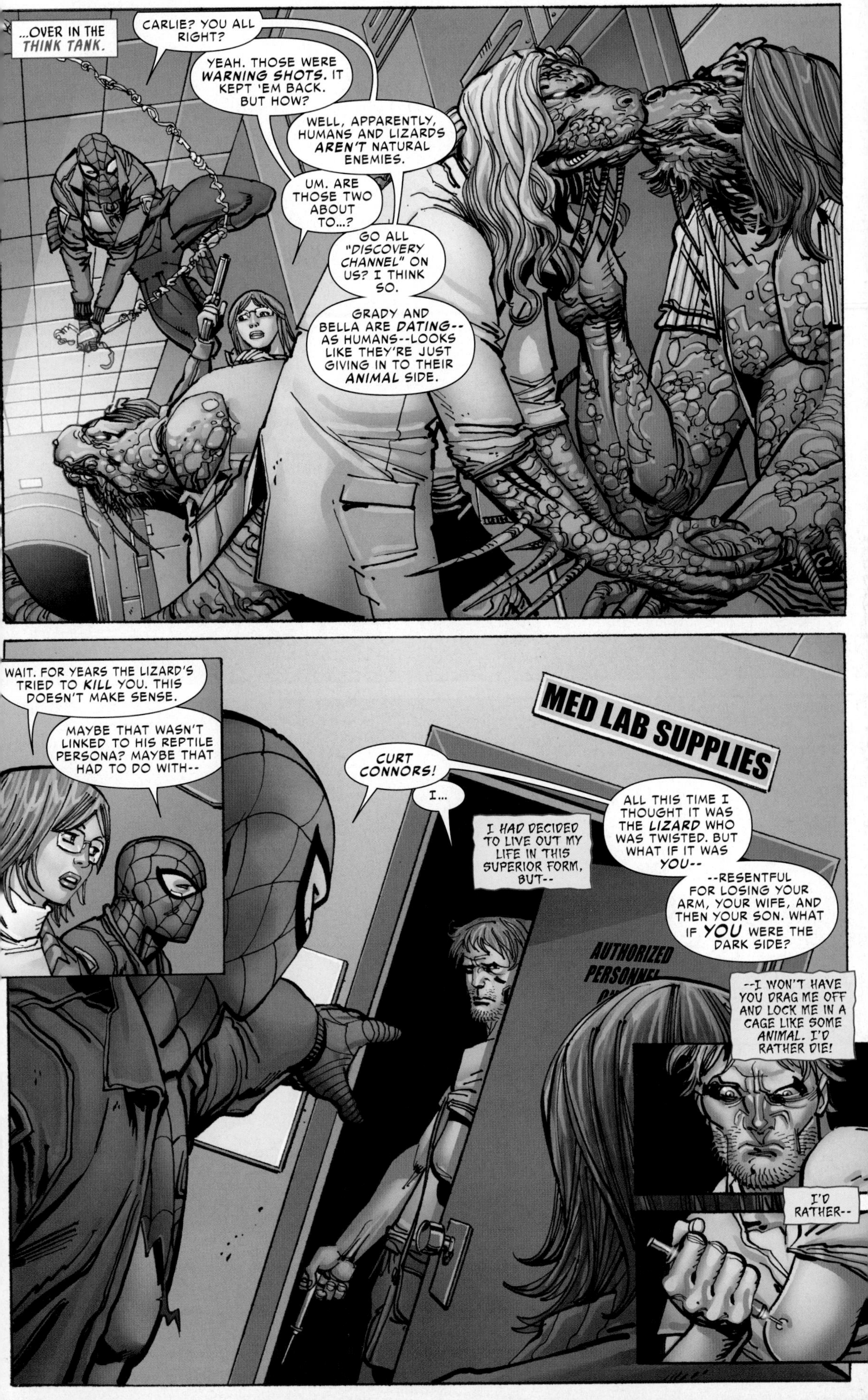

...OVER IN THE THINK TANK.
CARLIE? YOU ALL RIGHT?
YEAH. THOSE WERE WARNING SHOTS. IT KEPT 'EM BACK. BUT HOW?
WELL, APPARENTLY, HUMANS AND LIZARDS AREN'T NATURAL ENEMIES.
UM. ARE THOSE TWO ABOUT TO...?
GO ALL "DISCOVERY CHANNEL" ON US? I THINK SO.
GRADY AND BELLA ARE DATING--AS HUMANS--LOOKS LIKE THEY'RE JUST GIVING IN TO THEIR ANIMAL SIDE.
WAIT. FOR YEARS THE LIZARD'S TRIED TO KILL YOU. THIS DOESN'T MAKE SENSE.
MAYBE THAT WASN'T LINKED TO HIS REPTILE PERSONA? MAYBE THAT HAD TO DO WITH--
MED LAB SUPPLIES
CURT CONNORS!
I...
I HAD DECIDED TO LIVE OUT MY LIFE IN THIS SUPERIOR FORM, BUT--
ALL THIS TIME I THOUGHT IT WAS THE LIZARD WHO WAS TWISTED. BUT WHAT IF IT WAS YOU--
--RESENTFUL FOR LOSING YOUR ARM, YOUR WIFE, AND THEN YOUR SON. WHAT IF YOU WERE THE DARK SIDE?
AUTHORIZED PERSONNEL
--I WON'T HAVE YOU DRAG ME OFF AND LOCK ME IN A CAGE LIKE SOME ANIMAL. I'D RATHER DIE!
I'D RATHER--

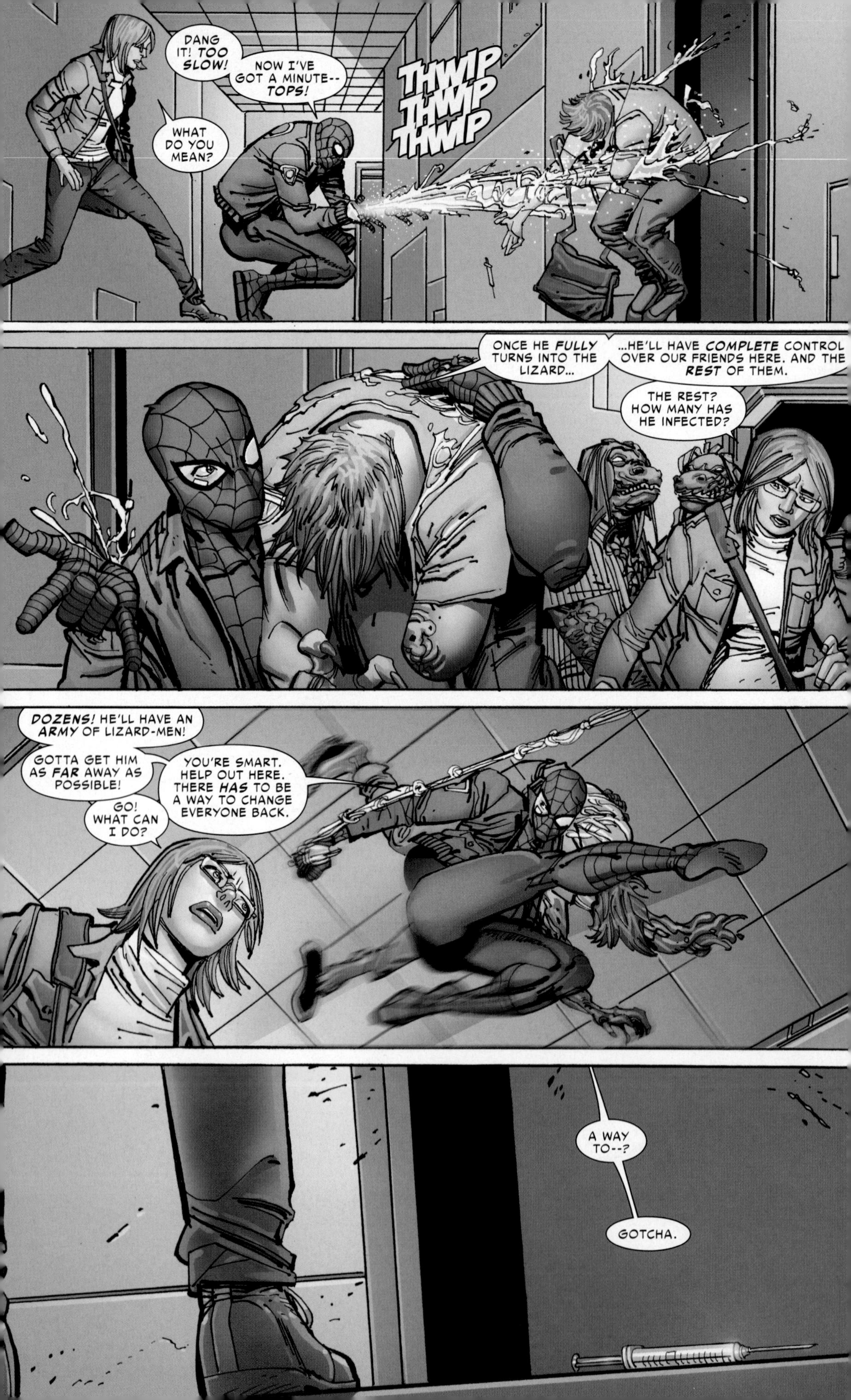
DANG IT! TOO SLOW!
WHAT DO YOU MEAN?
NOW I'VE GOT A MINUTE-- TOPS!
THWIP THWIP THWIP
ONCE HE FULLY TURNS INTO THE LIZARD...
...HE'LL HAVE COMPLETE CONTROL OVER OUR FRIENDS HERE. AND THE REST OF THEM.
THE REST? HOW MANY HAS HE INFECTED?
DOZENS! HE'LL HAVE AN ARMY OF LIZARD-MEN!
GOTTA GET HIM AS FAR AWAY AS POSSIBLE!
GO! WHAT CAN I DO?
YOU'RE SMART. HELP OUT HERE. THERE HAS TO BE A WAY TO CHANGE EVERYONE BACK.
A WAY TO--?
GOTCHA.

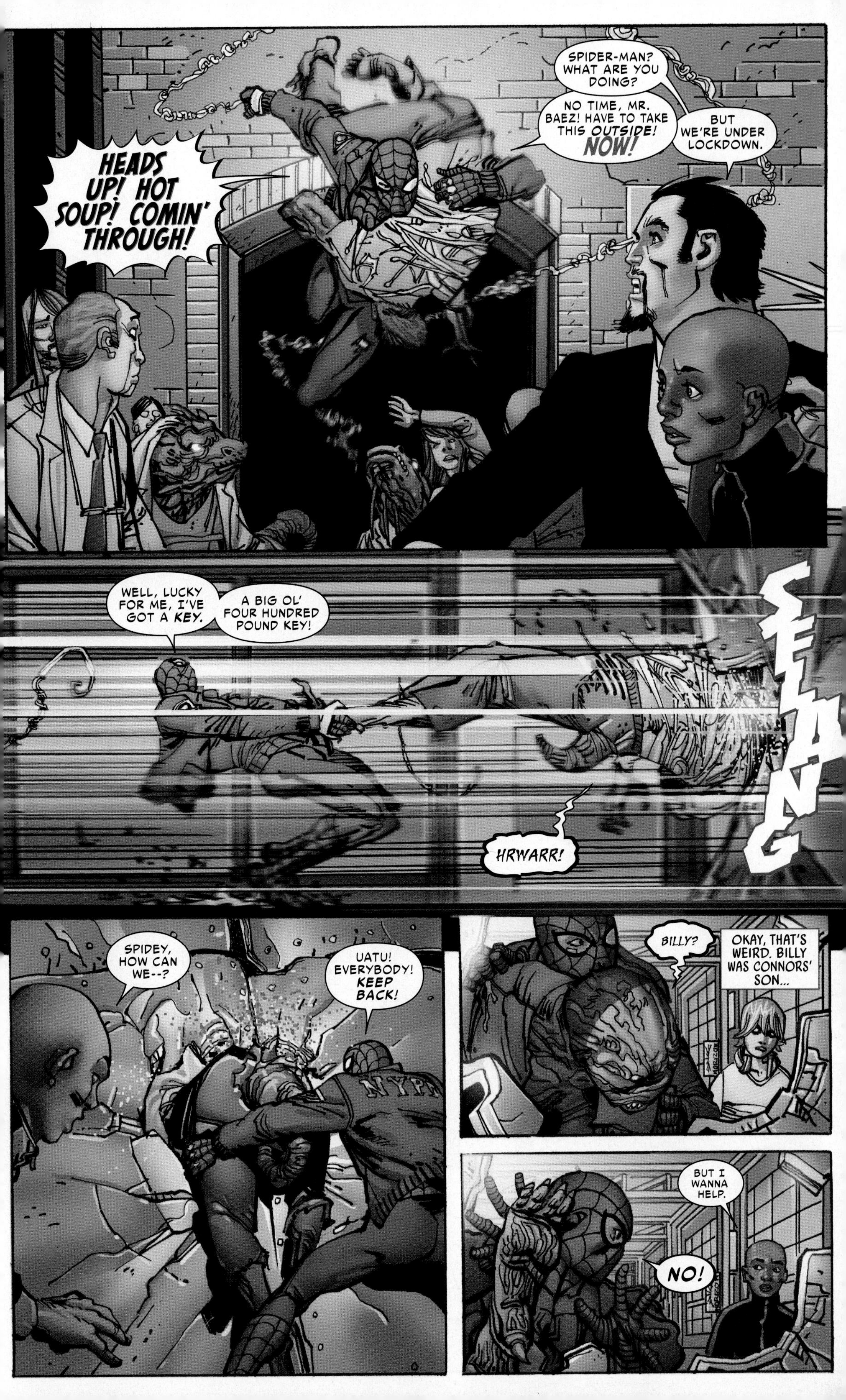
HEADS UP! HOT SOUP! COMIN' THROUGH!
SPIDER-MAN? WHAT ARE YOU DOING?
NO TIME, MR. BAEZ! HAVE TO TAKE THIS OUTSIDE! NOW!
BUT WE'RE UNDER LOCKDOWN.
WELL, LUCKY FOR ME, I'VE GOT A KEY.
A BIG OL' FOUR HUNDRED POUND KEY!
HRWARR!
SPIDEY, HOW CAN WE--?
UATU! EVERYBODY! KEEP BACK!
NYPD
BILLY?
OKAY, THAT'S WEIRD. BILLY WAS CONNORS' SON...
BUT I WANNA HELP.
NO!

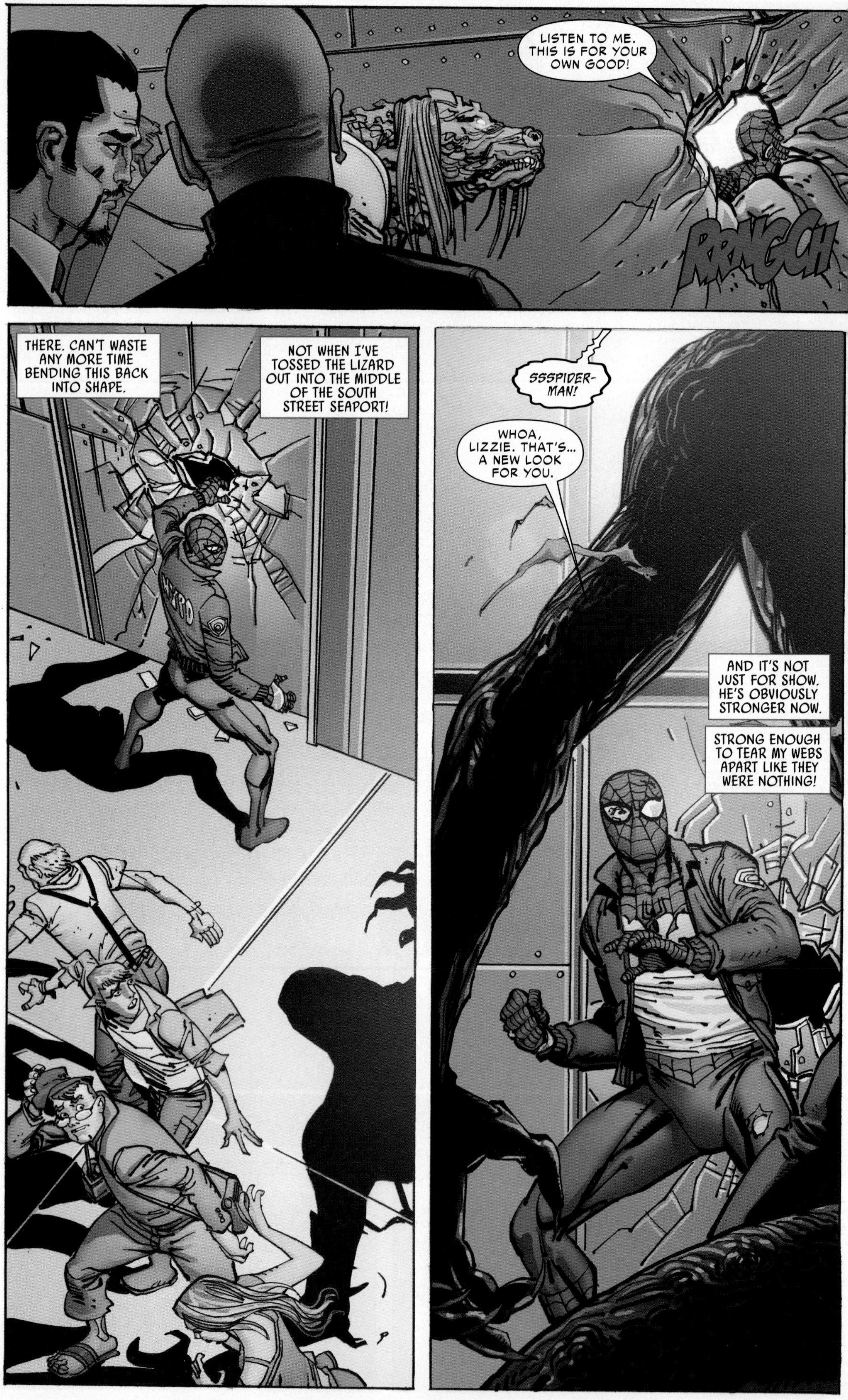
LISTEN TO ME. THIS IS FOR YOUR OWN GOOD!
RRNGCH
THERE. CAN'T WASTE ANY MORE TIME BENDING THIS BACK INTO SHAPE.
NOT WHEN I'VE TOSSED THE LIZARD OUT INTO THE MIDDLE OF THE SOUTH STREET SEAPORT!
SSSPIDER-MAN!
WHOA, LIZZIE. THAT'S... A NEW LOOK FOR YOU.
AND IT'S NOT JUST FOR SHOW. HE'S OBVIOUSLY STRONGER NOW.
STRONG ENOUGH TO TEAR MY WEBS APART LIKE THEY WERE NOTHING!

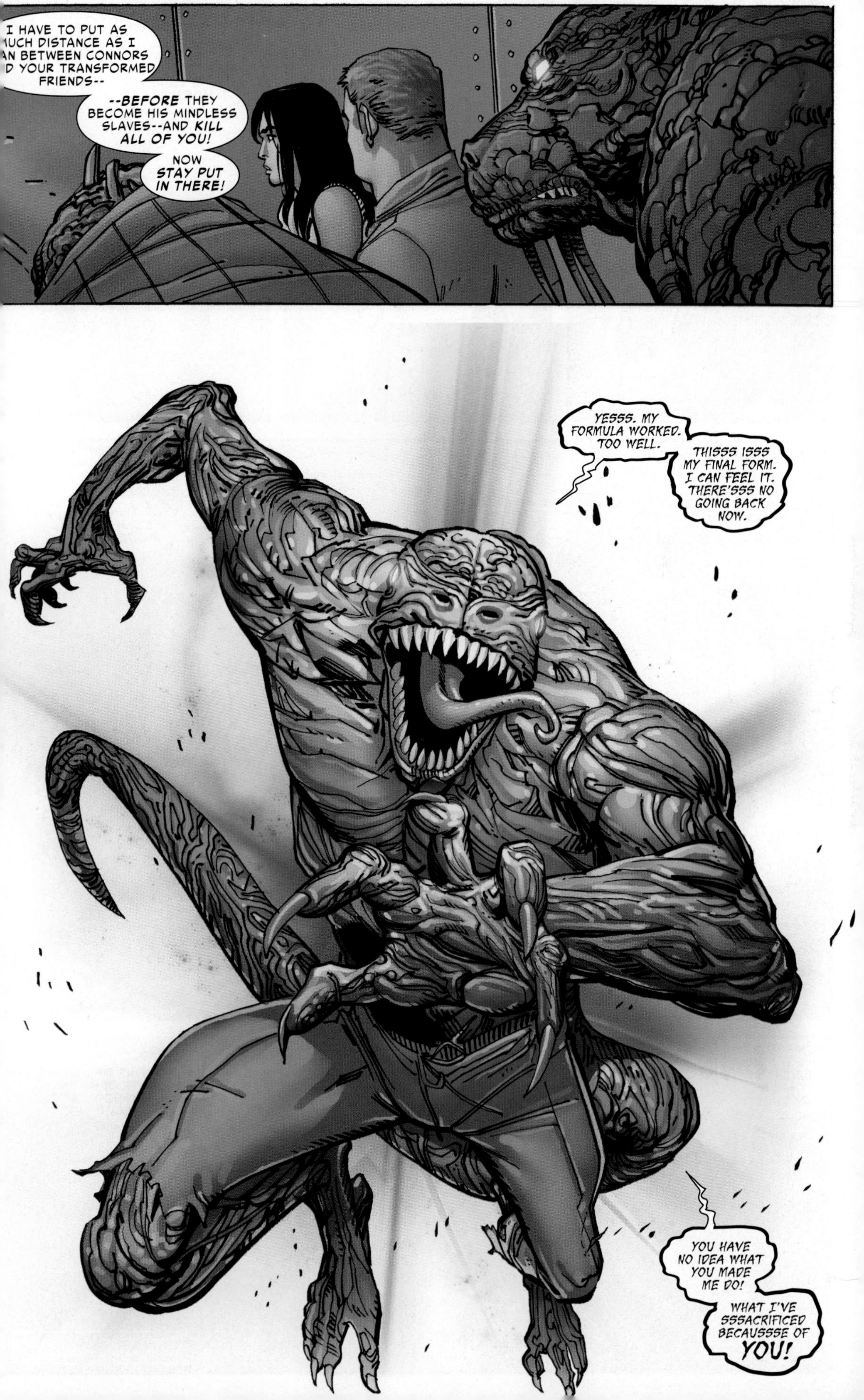
I HAVE TO PUT AS UCH DISTANCE AS I AN BETWEEN CONNORS D YOUR TRANSFORMED FRIENDS--
--BEFORE THEY BECOME HIS MINDLESS SLAVES--AND KILL ALL OF YOU!
NOW STAY PUT IN THERE!
YESSS. MY FORMULA WORKED. TOO WELL.
THISSS ISSS MY FINAL FORM. I CAN FEEL IT. THERE'SSS NO GOING BACK NOW.
YOU HAVE NO IDEA WHAT YOU MADE ME DO!
WHAT I'VE SSSACRIFICED BECAUSSSE OF YOU!

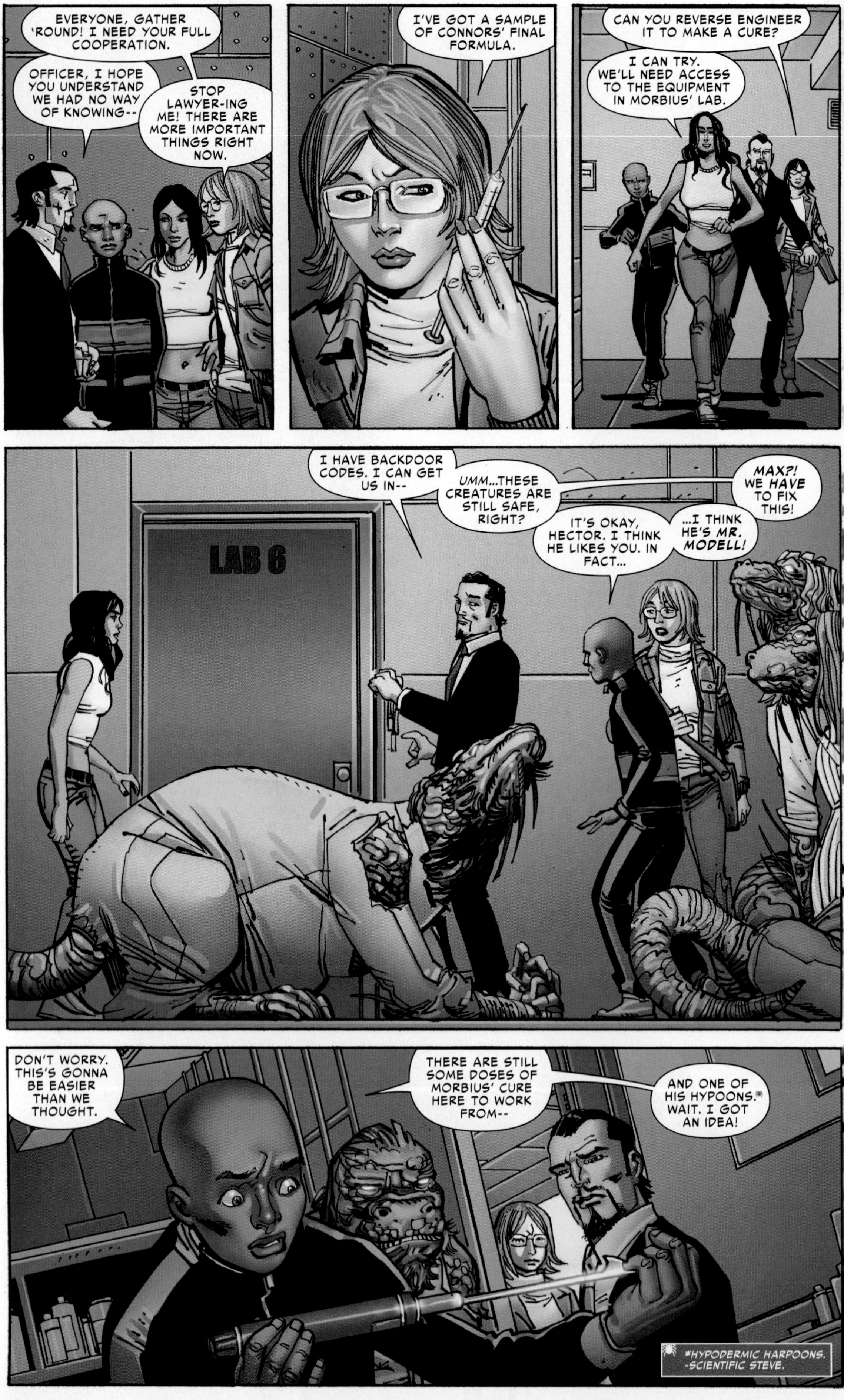
EVERYONE, GATHER 'ROUND! I NEED YOUR FULL COOPERATION.
OFFICER, I HOPE YOU UNDERSTAND WE HAD NO WAY OF KNOWING--
STOP LAWYER-ING ME! THERE ARE MORE IMPORTANT THINGS RIGHT NOW.
I'VE GOT A SAMPLE OF CONNORS' FINAL FORMULA.
CAN YOU REVERSE ENGINEER IT TO MAKE A CURE?
I CAN TRY. WE'LL NEED ACCESS TO THE EQUIPMENT IN MORBIUS' LAB.
I HAVE BACKDOOR CODES. I CAN GET US IN--
UMM...THESE CREATURES ARE STILL SAFE, RIGHT?
MAX?! WE HAVE TO FIX THIS!
IT'S OKAY, HECTOR. I THINK HE LIKES YOU. IN FACT...
...I THINK HE'S MR. MODELL!
LAB 6
DON'T WORRY. THIS'S GONNA BE EASIER THAN WE THOUGHT.
THERE ARE STILL SOME DOSES OF MORBIUS' CURE HERE TO WORK FROM--
AND ONE OF HIS HYPOONS.* WAIT. I GOT AN IDEA!
*HYPODERMIC HARPOONS. -SCIENTIFIC STEVE.

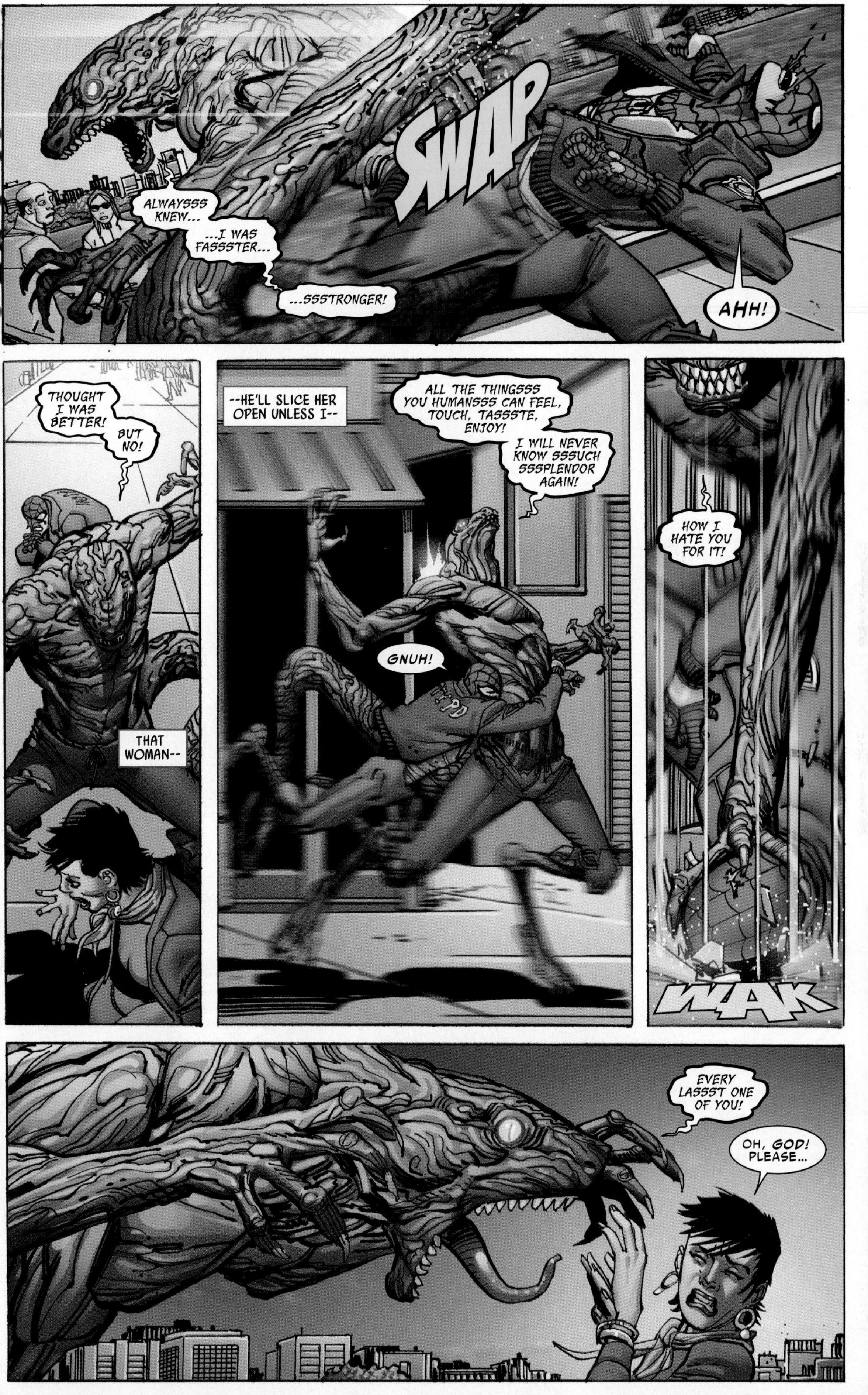
SWAP
ALWAYSSS KNEW...
...I WAS FASSSTER...
...SSSTRONGER!
AHH!
THOUGHT I WAS BETTER!
BUT NO!
THAT WOMAN--
--HE'LL SLICE HER OPEN UNLESS I--
ALL THE THINGSSS YOU HUMANSSS CAN FEEL, TOUCH, TASSSTE, ENJOY!
I WILL NEVER KNOW SSSUCH SSSPLENDOR AGAIN!
GNUH!
HOW I HATE YOU FOR IT!
WAK
EVERY LASSST ONE OF YOU!
OH, GOD! PLEASE...

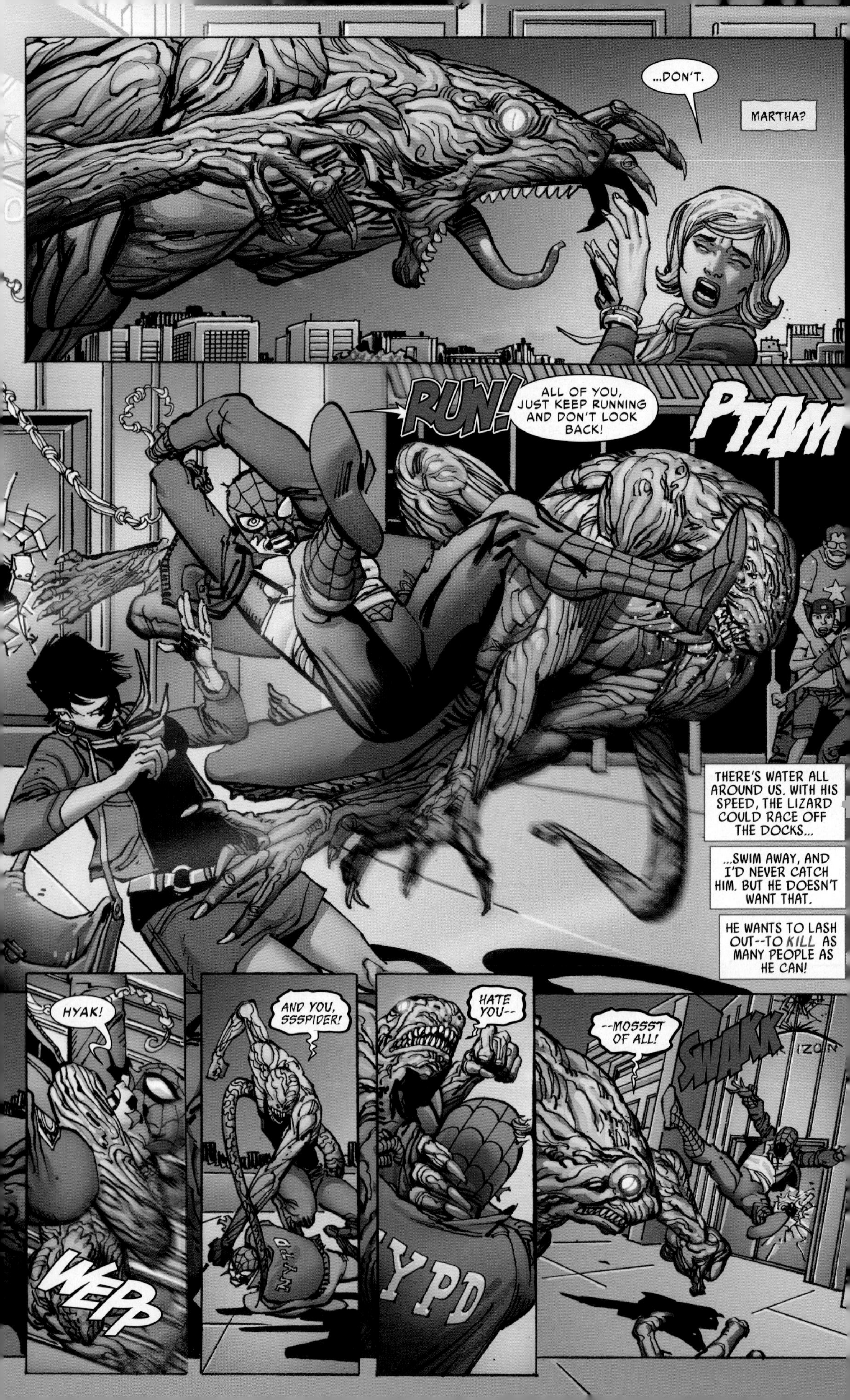

...DON'T.
MARTHA?
RUN!
ALL OF YOU, JUST KEEP RUNNING AND DON'T LOOK BACK!
PTAM
THERE'S WATER ALL AROUND US. WITH HIS SPEED, THE LIZARD COULD RACE OFF THE DOCKS...
...SWIM AWAY, AND I'D NEVER CATCH HIM. BUT HE DOESN'T WANT THAT.
HE WANTS TO LASH OUT--TO KILL AS MANY PEOPLE AS HE CAN!
HYAK!
WEPP
AND YOU, SSSPIDER!
HATE YOU--
--MOSSST OF ALL!
SWAKK
NYPD
YPD

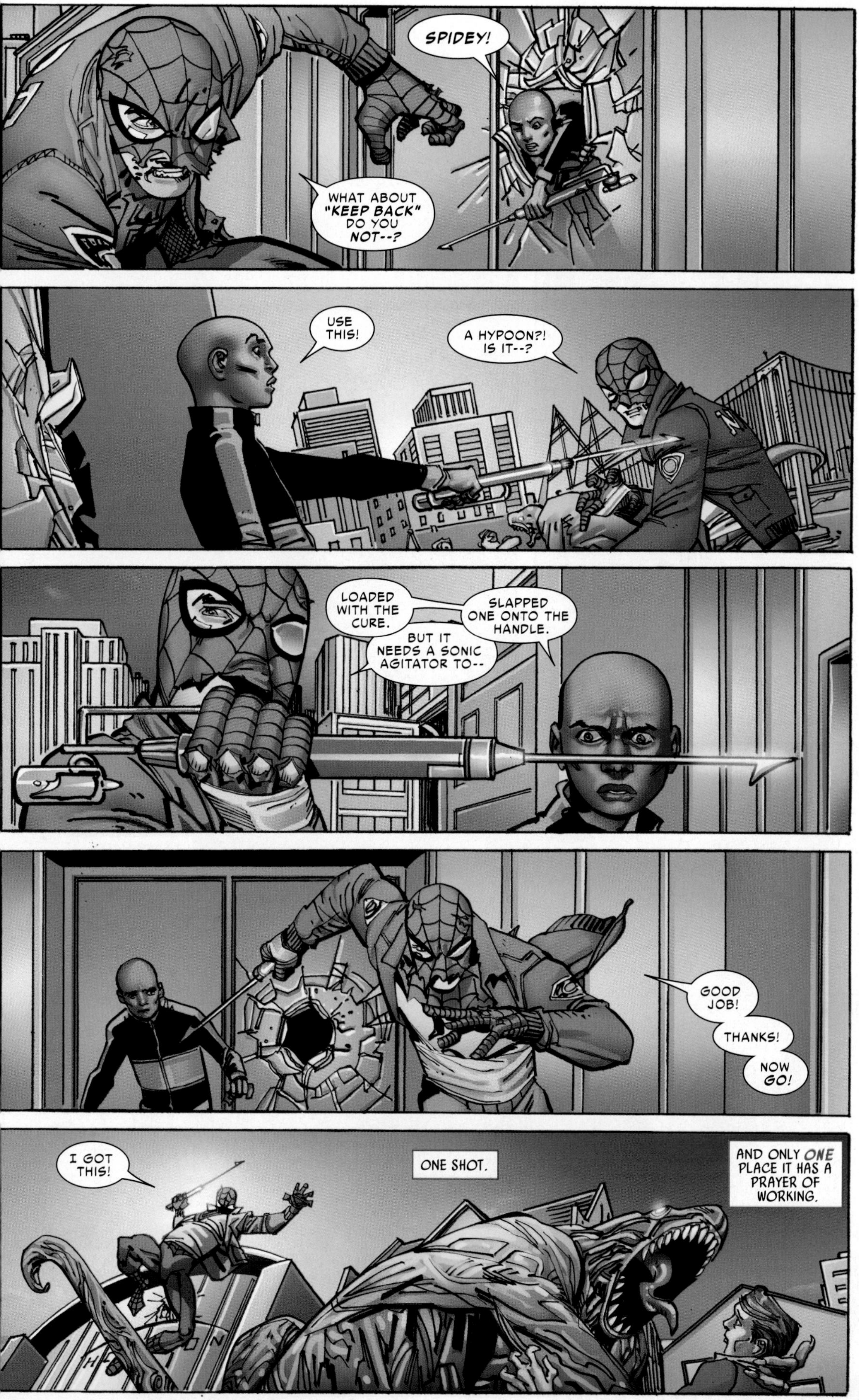
SPIDEY!
WHAT ABOUT "KEEP BACK" DO YOU NOT--?
USE THIS!
A HYPOON?! IS IT--?
LOADED WITH THE CURE.
SLAPPED ONE ONTO THE HANDLE.
BUT IT NEEDS A SONIC AGITATOR TO--
GOOD JOB!
THANKS!
NOW GO!
I GOT THIS!
ONE SHOT.
AND ONLY ONE PLACE IT HAS A PRAYER OF WORKING.

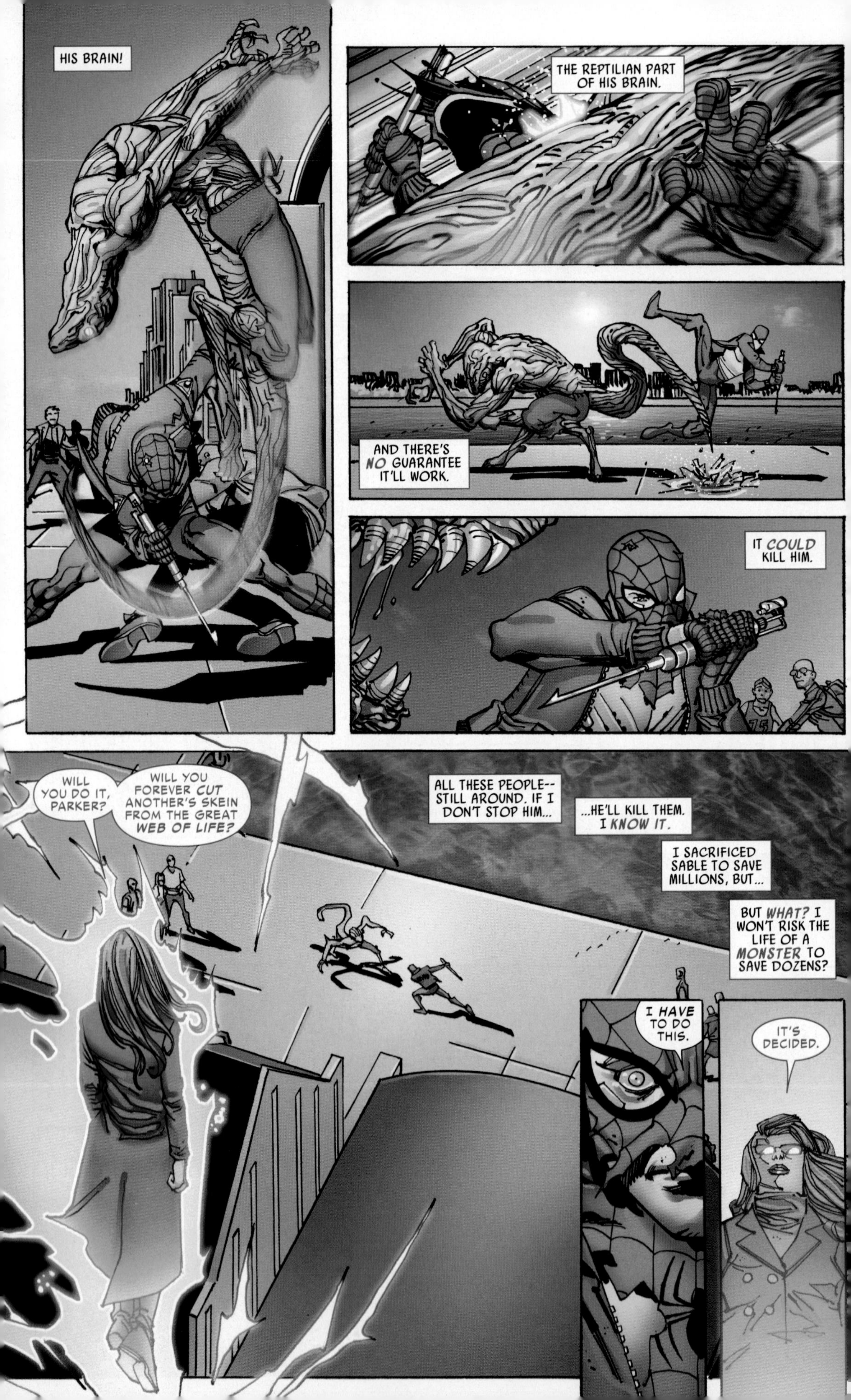
HIS BRAIN!
THE REPTILIAN PART OF HIS BRAIN.
AND THERE'S NO GUARANTEE IT'LL WORK.
IT COULD KILL HIM.
WILL YOU DO IT, PARKER?
WILL YOU FOREVER CUT ANOTHER'S SKEIN FROM THE GREAT WEB OF LIFE?
ALL THESE PEOPLE-- STILL AROUND. IF I DON'T STOP HIM...
...HE'LL KILL THEM. I KNOW IT.
I SACRIFICED SABLE TO SAVE MILLIONS, BUT...
BUT WHAT? I WON'T RISK THE LIFE OF A MONSTER TO SAVE DOZENS?
I HAVE TO DO THIS.
IT'S DECIDED.

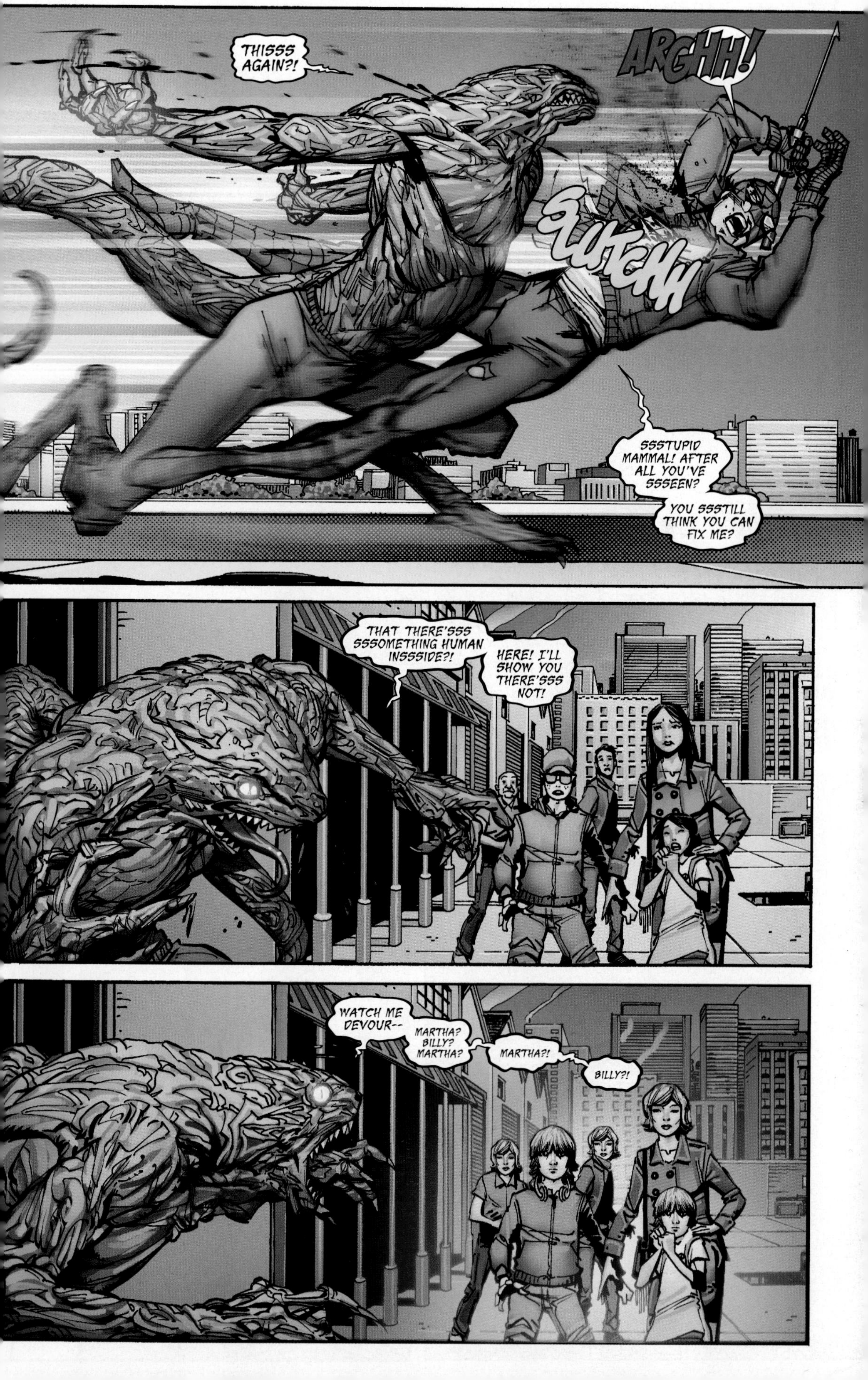
THISSS AGAIN?!
ARGHH!
SHLUKCHH
SSSTUPID MAMMAL! AFTER ALL YOU'VE SSSEEN?
YOU SSSTILL THINK YOU CAN FIX ME?
THAT THERE'SSS SSSOMETHING HUMAN INSSSIDE?!
HERE! I'LL SHOW YOU THERE'SSS NOT!
WATCH ME DEVOUR--
MARTHA? BILLY? MARTHA?
MARTHA?!
BILLY?!

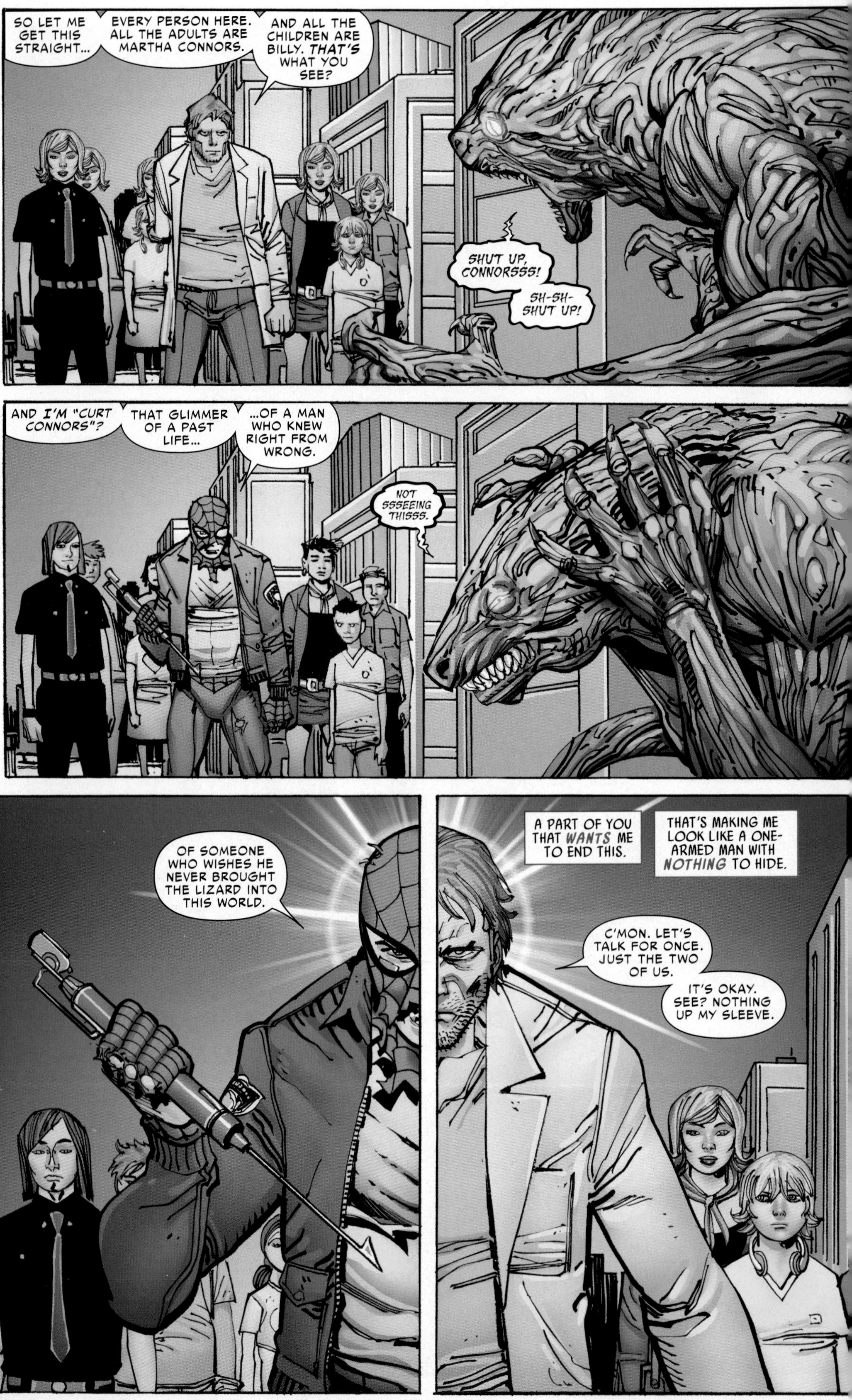
SO LET ME GET THIS STRAIGHT...
EVERY PERSON HERE. ALL THE ADULTS ARE MARTHA CONNORS.
AND ALL THE CHILDREN ARE BILLY. THAT'S WHAT YOU SEE?
SHUT UP, CONNORSSS!
SH-SH-SHUT UP!
AND I'M "CURT CONNORS"?
THAT GLIMMER OF A PAST LIFE...
...OF A MAN WHO KNEW RIGHT FROM WRONG.
NOT SSSEEING THISSS.
OF SOMEONE WHO WISHES HE NEVER BROUGHT THE LIZARD INTO THIS WORLD.
A PART OF YOU THAT WANTS ME TO END THIS.
THAT'S MAKING ME LOOK LIKE A ONE-ARMED MAN WITH NOTHING TO HIDE.
C'MON. LET'S TALK FOR ONCE. JUST THE TWO OF US.
IT'S OKAY. SEE? NOTHING UP MY SLEEVE.

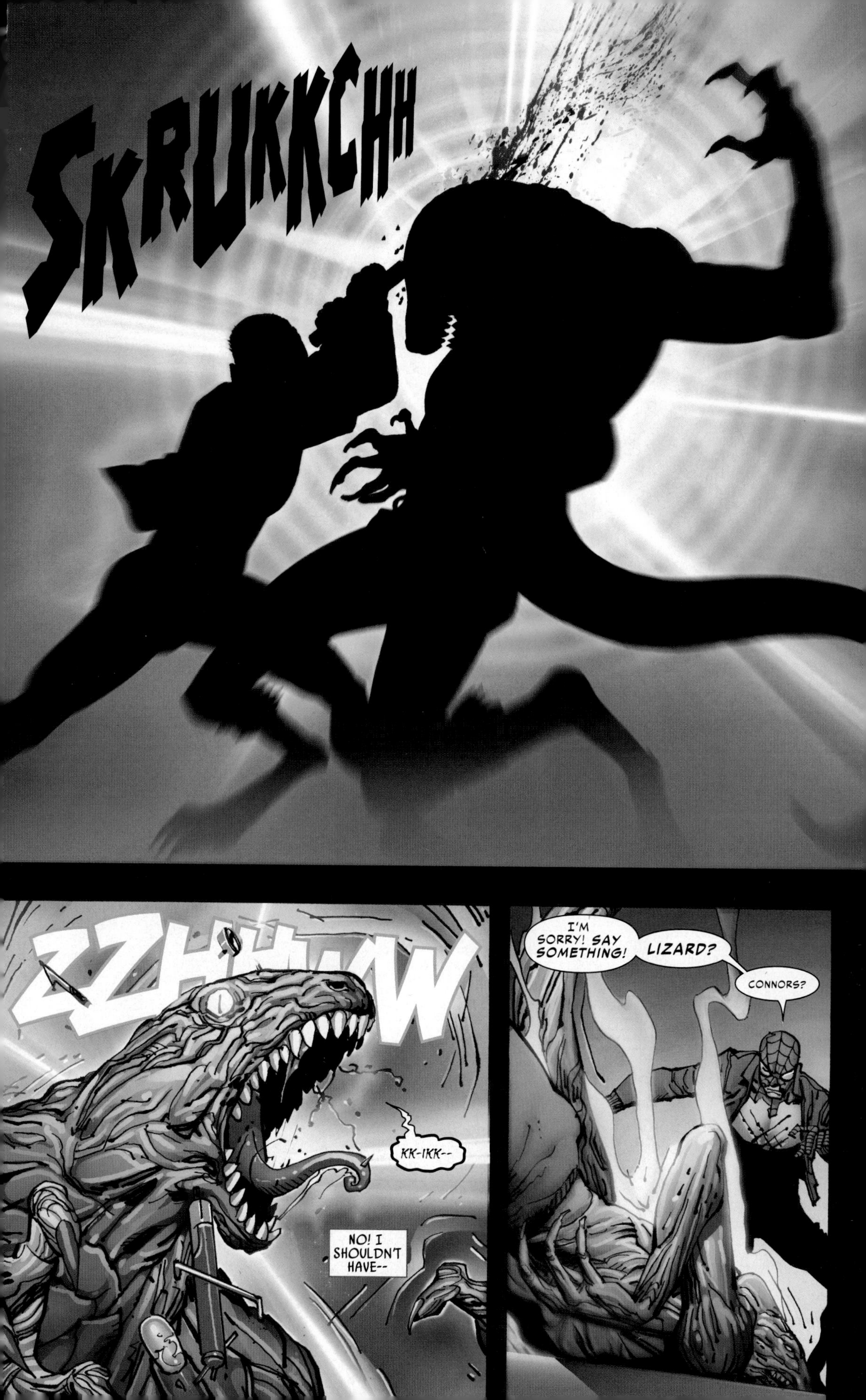
SKRUKKCHH
KK-IKK--
NO! I SHOULDN'T HAVE--
I'M SORRY! SAY SOMETHING!
LIZARD?
CONNORS?

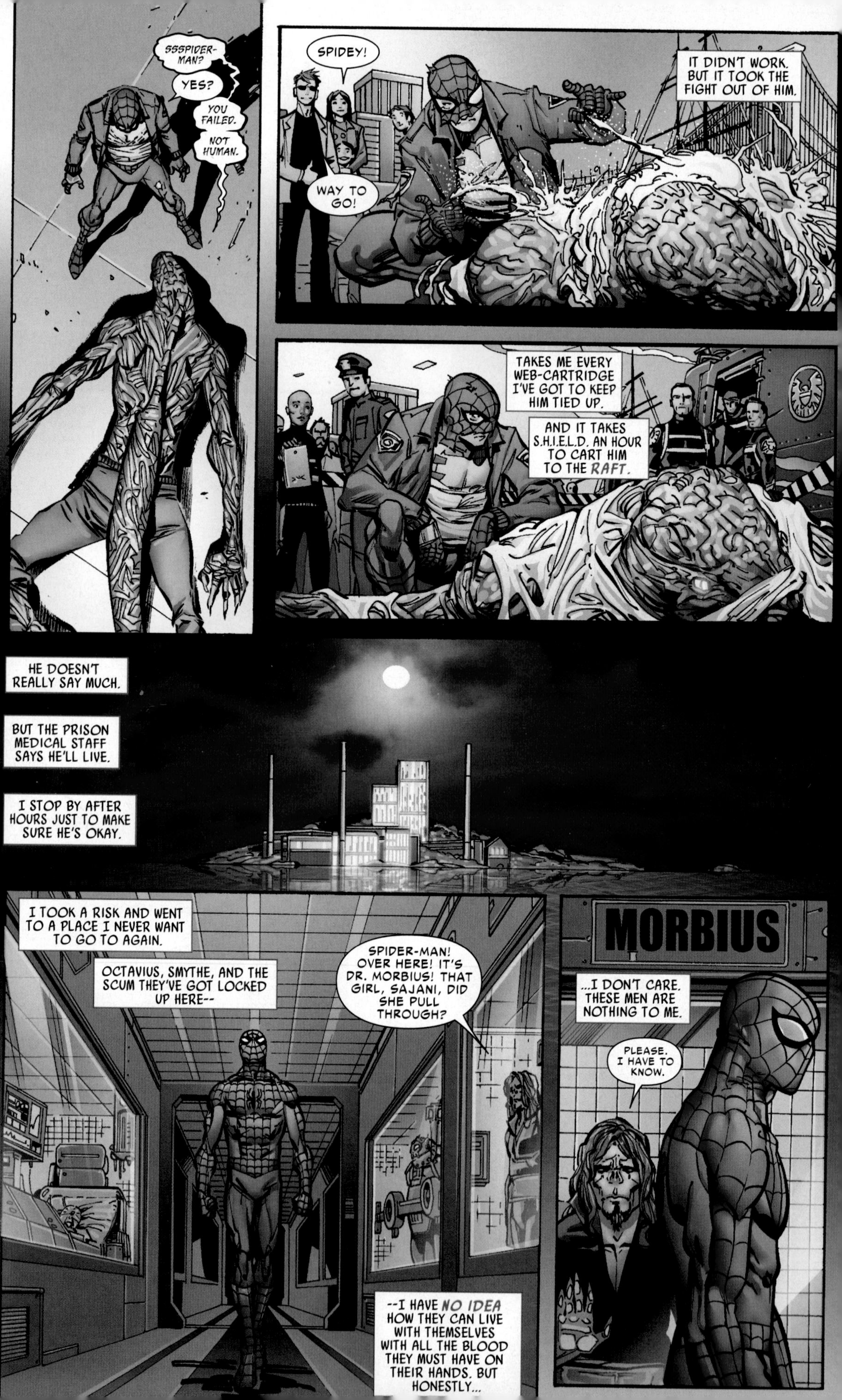
SSSPIDER-MAN?
YES?
YOU FAILED.
NOT HUMAN.
SPIDEY!
WAY TO GO!
IT DIDN'T WORK. BUT IT TOOK THE FIGHT OUT OF HIM.
TAKES ME EVERY WEB-CARTRIDGE I'VE GOT TO KEEP HIM TIED UP.
AND IT TAKES S.H.I.E.L.D. AN HOUR TO CART HIM TO THE RAFT.
HE DOESN'T REALLY SAY MUCH.
BUT THE PRISON MEDICAL STAFF SAYS HE'LL LIVE.
I STOP BY AFTER HOURS JUST TO MAKE SURE HE'S OKAY.
I TOOK A RISK AND WENT TO A PLACE I NEVER WANT TO GO TO AGAIN.
OCTAVIUS, SMYTHE, AND THE SCUM THEY'VE GOT LOCKED UP HERE--
SPIDER-MAN! OVER HERE! IT'S DR. MORBIUS! THAT GIRL, SAJANI, DID SHE PULL THROUGH?
--I HAVE NO IDEA HOW THEY CAN LIVE WITH THEMSELVES WITH ALL THE BLOOD THEY MUST HAVE ON THEIR HANDS. BUT HONESTLY...
MORBIUS
...I DON'T CARE. THESE MEN ARE NOTHING TO ME.
PLEASE. I HAVE TO KNOW.

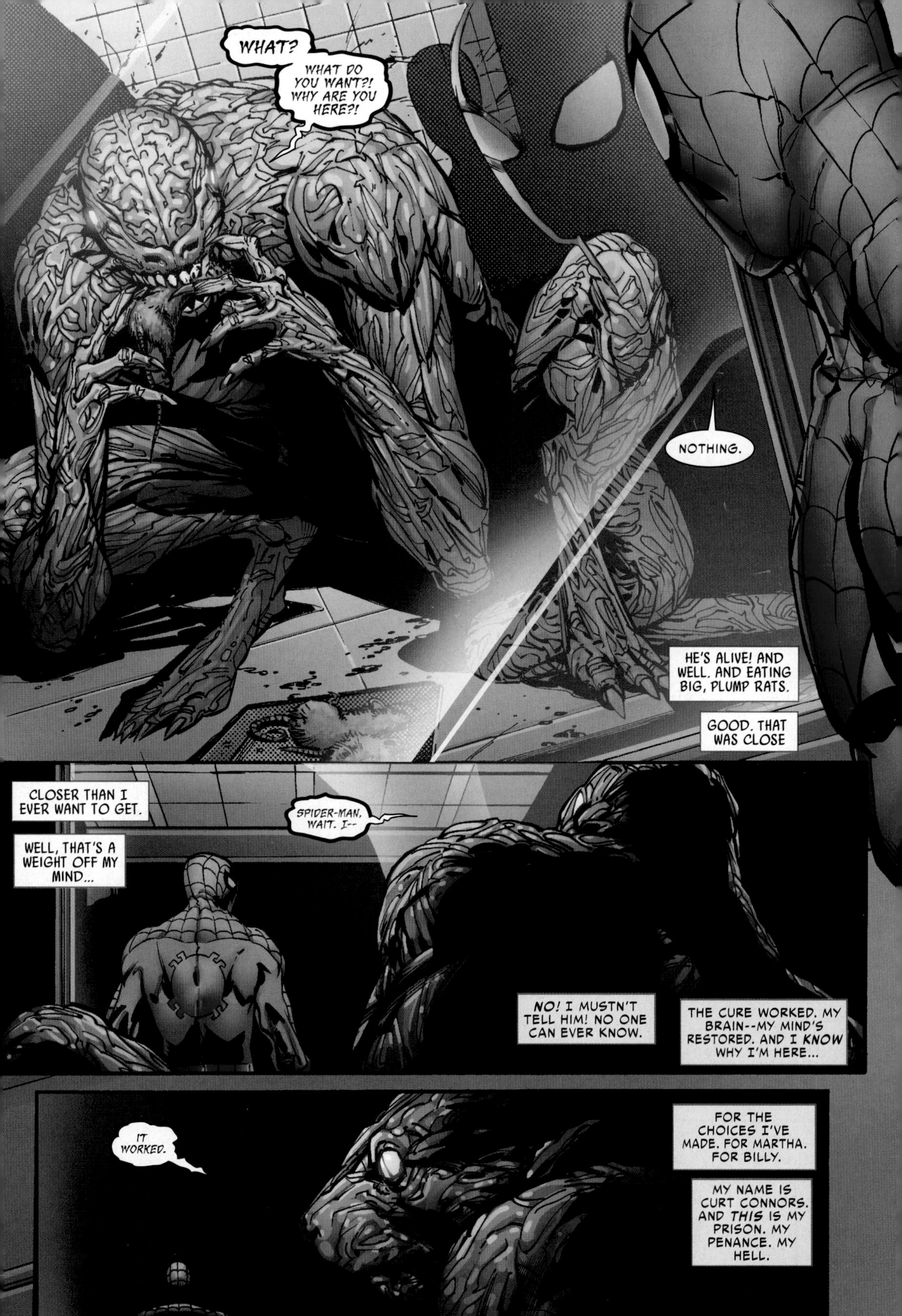
WHAT?
WHAT DO YOU WANT?! WHY ARE YOU HERE?!
NOTHING.
HE'S ALIVE! AND WELL. AND EATING BIG, PLUMP RATS.
GOOD. THAT WAS CLOSE
CLOSER THAN I EVER WANT TO GET.
WELL, THAT'S A WEIGHT OFF MY MIND...
SPIDER-MAN, WAIT. I--
THE CURE WORKED. MY BRAIN--MY MIND'S RESTORED. AND I KNOW WHY I'M HERE...
NO! I MUSTN'T TELL HIM! NO ONE CAN EVER KNOW.
IT WORKED.
FOR THE CHOICES I'VE MADE. FOR MARTHA. FOR BILLY.
MY NAME IS CURT CONNORS. AND THIS IS MY PRISON. MY PENANCE. MY HELL.

Horizon Labs.

HAVE WE DOUBLE-CHECKED?

YES. EVERYONE'S FINE.

WE'RE ALL BACK TO NORMAL? NO SIDE-EFFECTS?

PEOPLE ARE MAKING A LOT OF T-SHIRTS.

T-SHIRTS?

FOR THE ANNUAL *SOFTBALL GAME.* THIS YEAR IT'LL BE PEOPLE WHO TURNED INTO LIZARDS IN *THIS* FIASCO VERSUS EVERYONE WHO TURNED INTO SPIDERS IN OUR *LAST* FIASCO.

I HAVEN'T TURNED INTO ANYTHING.

GIVE IT TIME. IT'S ONLY MONDAY.

ASM #670.

SO, WE FINALLY... GOT TO THE TONGUE STAGE?

AS LIZARDS. YOU OKAY WITH THAT?

YEAH. I'VE BEEN IN...WEIRDER RELATIONSHIPS.

WELL, ONE THING'S BACK TO NORMAL.

YET *AGAIN* PARKER MISSED OUT ON ALL THE HEAVY LIFTING.

NOT JUST PARKER. MR. STONE'S ABSENT AS WELL.

HECTOR, IF YOU'D COME WITH ME, PLEASE.

WHAT'S THIS ABOUT?

I NEED YOU TO CHECK ME FOR...ANY REMAINING SCALES.

YOU KNOW, I COULD DO THAT AT HOME.

I KNOW.

I DIDN'T WANT TO DRAW ANY UNDUE ATTENTION...

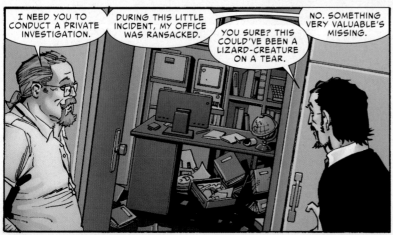

I NEED YOU TO CONDUCT A PRIVATE INVESTIGATION.

DURING THIS LITTLE INCIDENT, MY OFFICE WAS RANSACKED.

YOU SURE? THIS COULD'VE BEEN A LIZARD-CREATURE ON A TEAR.

NO. SOMETHING VERY VALUABLE'S MISSING.

AND I NEED TO KNOW WHO TOOK IT...

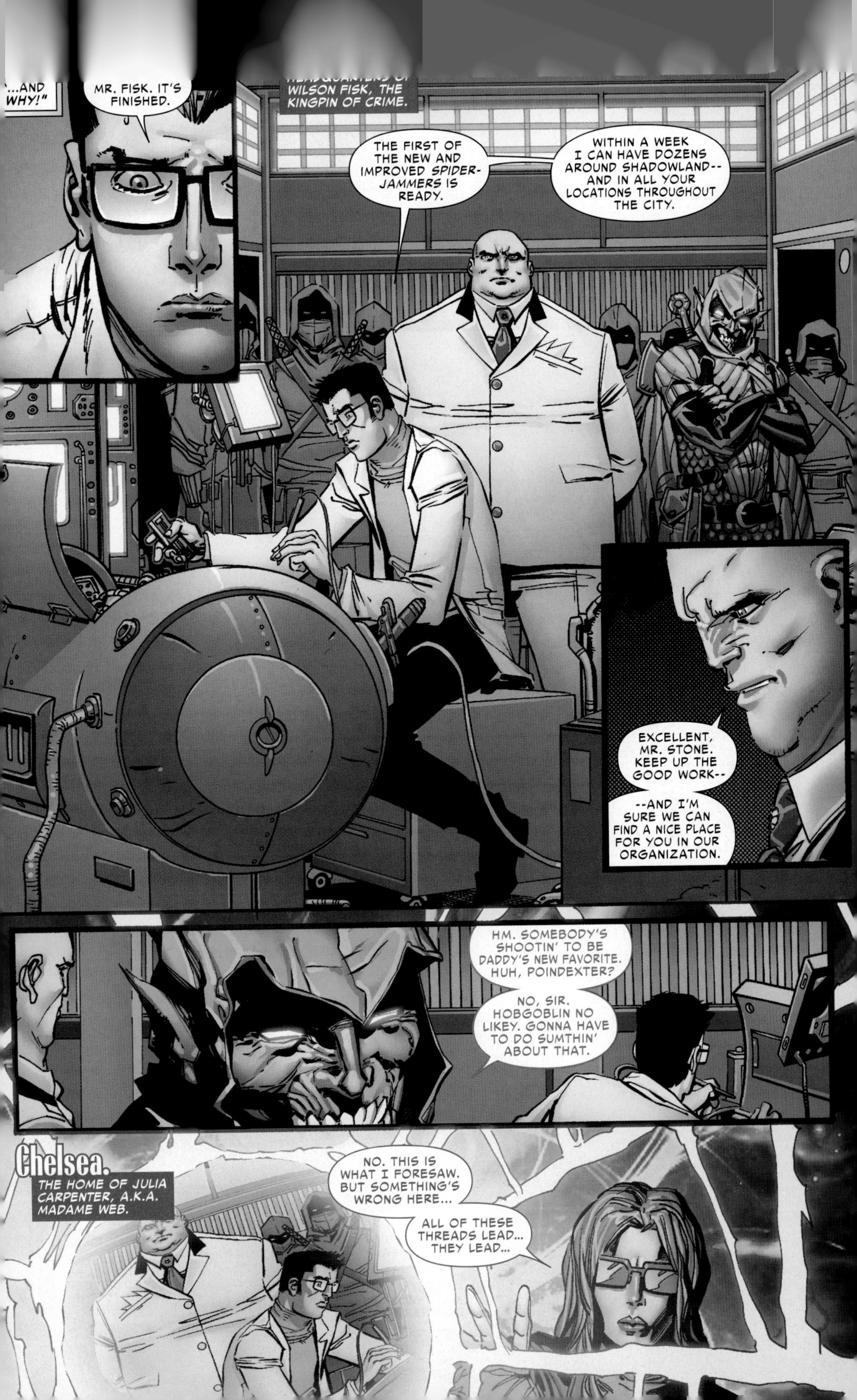
"...AND WHY!"
MR. FISK. IT'S FINISHED.
WILSON FISK, THE KINGPIN OF CRIME.
THE FIRST OF THE NEW AND IMPROVED *SPIDER-JAMMERS* IS READY.
WITHIN A WEEK I CAN HAVE DOZENS AROUND SHADOWLAND-- AND IN ALL YOUR LOCATIONS THROUGHOUT THE CITY.
EXCELLENT, MR. STONE. KEEP UP THE GOOD WORK--
--AND I'M SURE WE CAN FIND A NICE PLACE FOR YOU IN OUR ORGANIZATION.
HM. SOMEBODY'S SHOOTIN' TO BE DADDY'S NEW FAVORITE. HUH, POINDEXTER?
NO, SIR. HOBGOBLIN NO LIKEY. GONNA HAVE TO DO SUMTHIN' ABOUT THAT.
Chelsea.
THE HOME OF JULIA CARPENTER, A.K.A. MADAME WEB.
NO. THIS IS WHAT I FORESAW. BUT SOMETHING'S WRONG HERE...
ALL OF THESE THREADS LEAD... THEY LEAD...

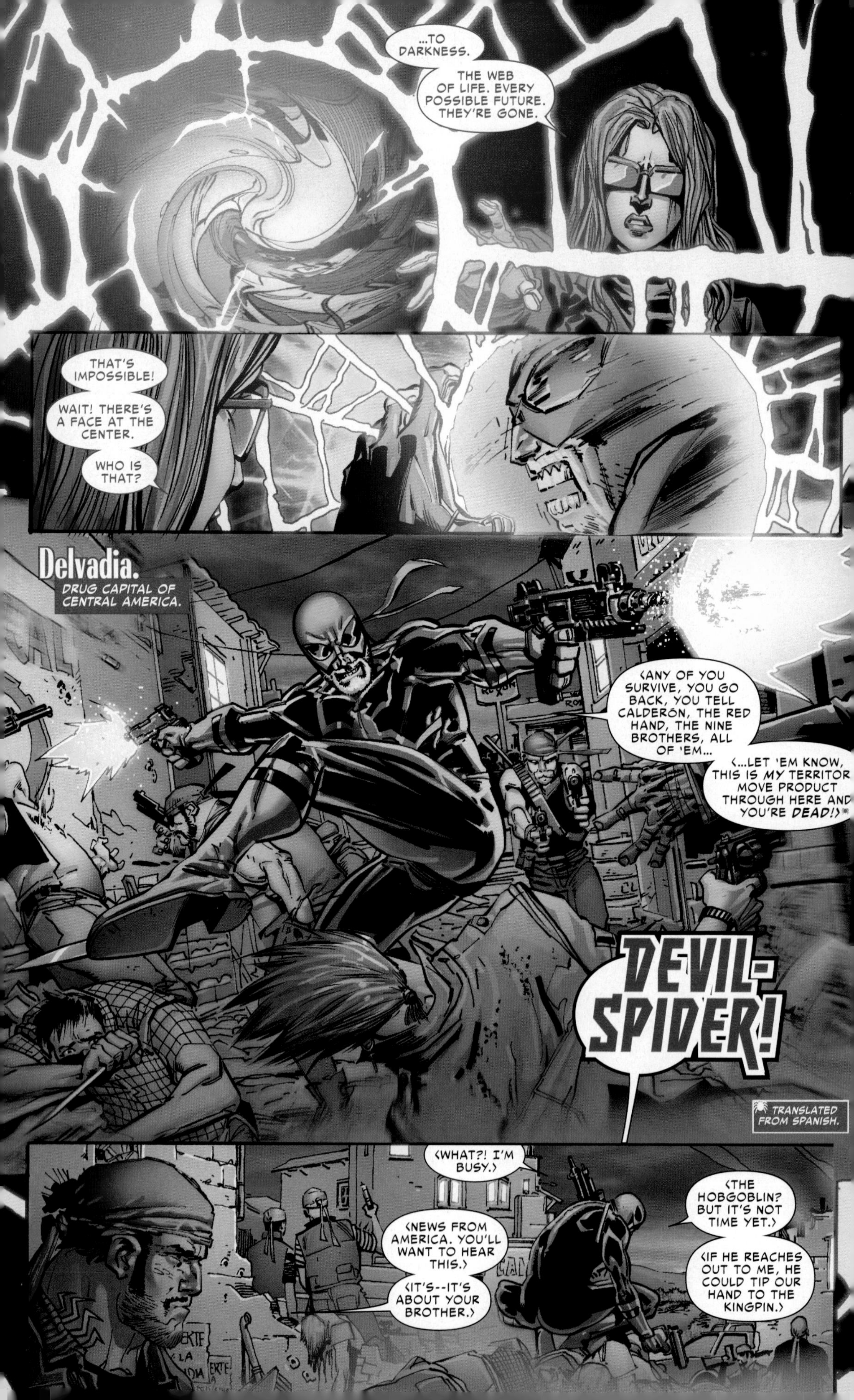
...TO DARKNESS.
THE WEB OF LIFE. EVERY POSSIBLE FUTURE. THEY'RE GONE.
THAT'S IMPOSSIBLE!
WAIT! THERE'S A FACE AT THE CENTER.
WHO IS THAT?
Delvadia.
DRUG CAPITAL OF CENTRAL AMERICA.
‹ANY OF YOU SURVIVE, YOU GO BACK, YOU TELL CALDERÓN, THE RED HAND, THE NINE BROTHERS, ALL OF 'EM...
‹...LET 'EM KNOW, THIS IS MY TERRITOR MOVE PRODUCT THROUGH HERE AND YOU'RE DEAD!›
DEVIL-SPIDER!
TRANSLATED FROM SPANISH.
‹WHAT?! I'M BUSY.›
‹NEWS FROM AMERICA. YOU'LL WANT TO HEAR THIS.›
‹IT'S--IT'S ABOUT YOUR BROTHER.›
‹THE HOBGOBLIN? BUT IT'S NOT TIME YET.›
‹IF HE REACHES OUT TO ME, HE COULD TIP OUR HAND TO THE KINGPIN.›

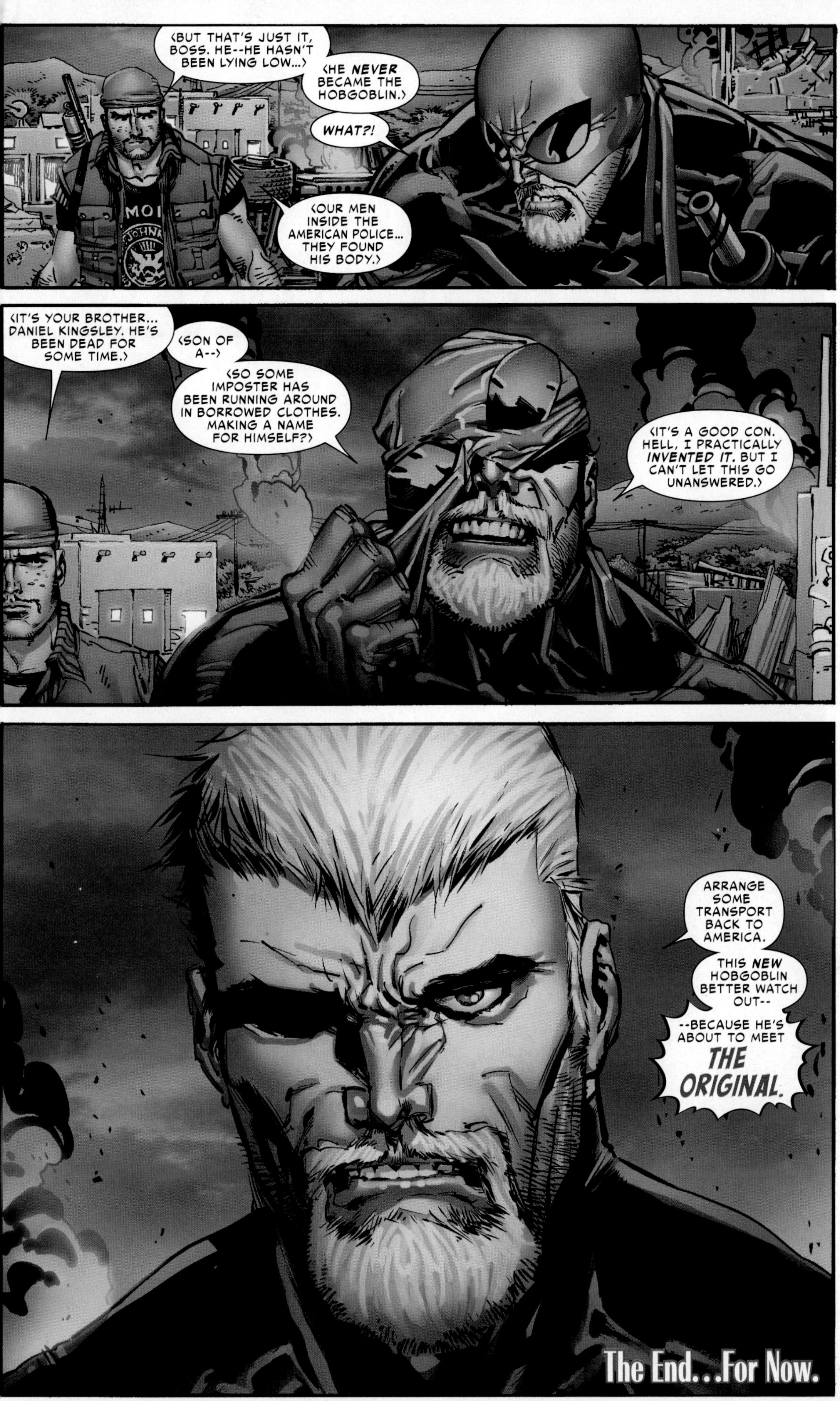
‹BUT THAT'S JUST IT, BOSS. HE--HE HASN'T BEEN LYING LOW...›
‹HE NEVER BECAME THE HOBGOBLIN.›
WHAT?!
‹OUR MEN INSIDE THE AMERICAN POLICE... THEY FOUND HIS BODY.›
‹IT'S YOUR BROTHER... DANIEL KINGSLEY. HE'S BEEN DEAD FOR SOME TIME.›
‹SON OF A--›
‹SO SOME IMPOSTER HAS BEEN RUNNING AROUND IN BORROWED CLOTHES. MAKING A NAME FOR HIMSELF?›
‹IT'S A GOOD CON. HELL, I PRACTICALLY INVENTED IT. BUT I CAN'T LET THIS GO UNANSWERED.›
ARRANGE SOME TRANSPORT BACK TO AMERICA.
THIS NEW HOBGOBLIN BETTER WATCH OUT--
--BECAUSE HE'S ABOUT TO MEET THE ORIGINAL.
The End. . .For Now.

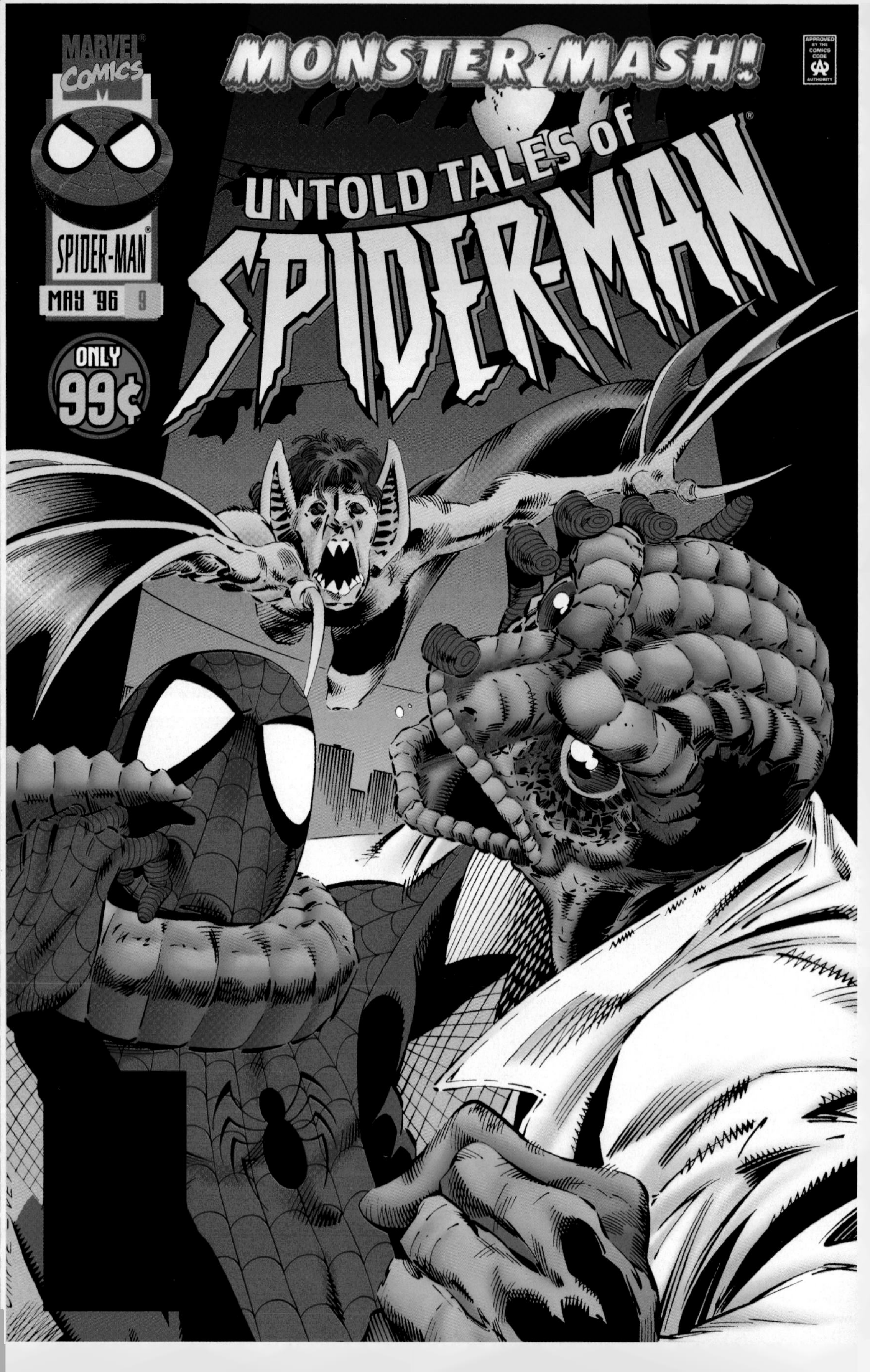
MARVEL COMICS
MONSTER MASH!
APPROVED BY THE COMICS CODE AUTHORITY
UNTOLD TALES OF
SPIDER-MAN
SPIDER-MAN
MAY '96 9
ONLY 99¢

Bitten by a radioactive spider, high school student **Peter Parker** gained the spider's powers, and soon became the costumed crimefighter the entire world would one day come to know as **Spider-Man!** In the early days of his career, when his amazing powers were still new to him, the teenaged Spider-Man struggled to learn about himself and his abilities, while trying to lead a **normal life!** It would **not** be easy...

STAN LEE PRESENTS... UNTOLD TALES OF SPIDER-MAN!

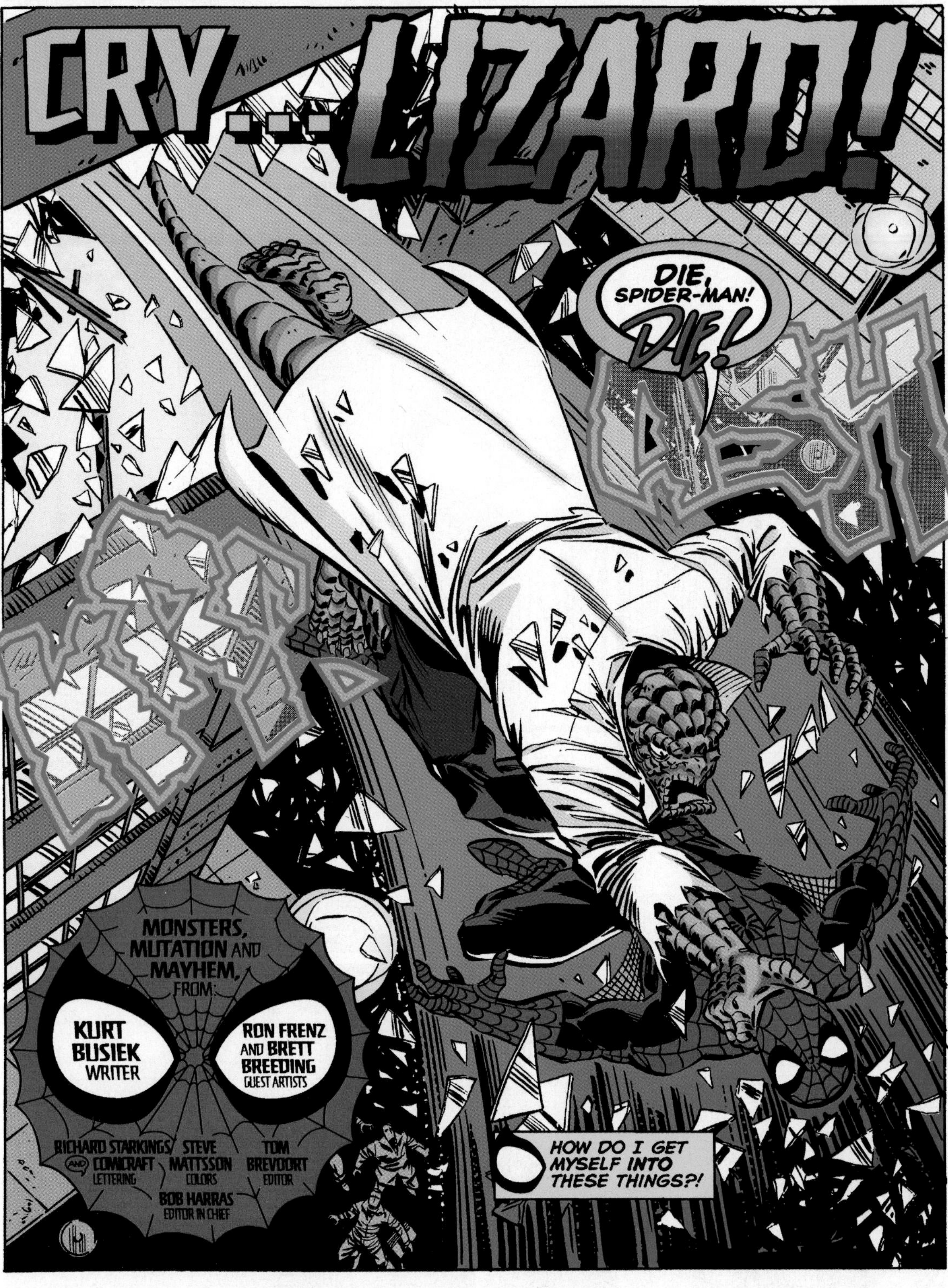
CRY... LIZARD!
DIE, SPIDER-MAN! DIE!
MONSTERS, MUTATION AND MAYHEM, FROM:
KURT BUSIEK WRITER
RON FRENZ AND BRETT BREEDING GUEST ARTISTS
RICHARD STARKINGS AND COMICRAFT LETTERING
STEVE MATTSSON COLORS
TOM BREVOORT EDITOR
BOB HARRAS EDITOR IN CHIEF
HOW DO I GET MYSELF INTO THESE THINGS?!

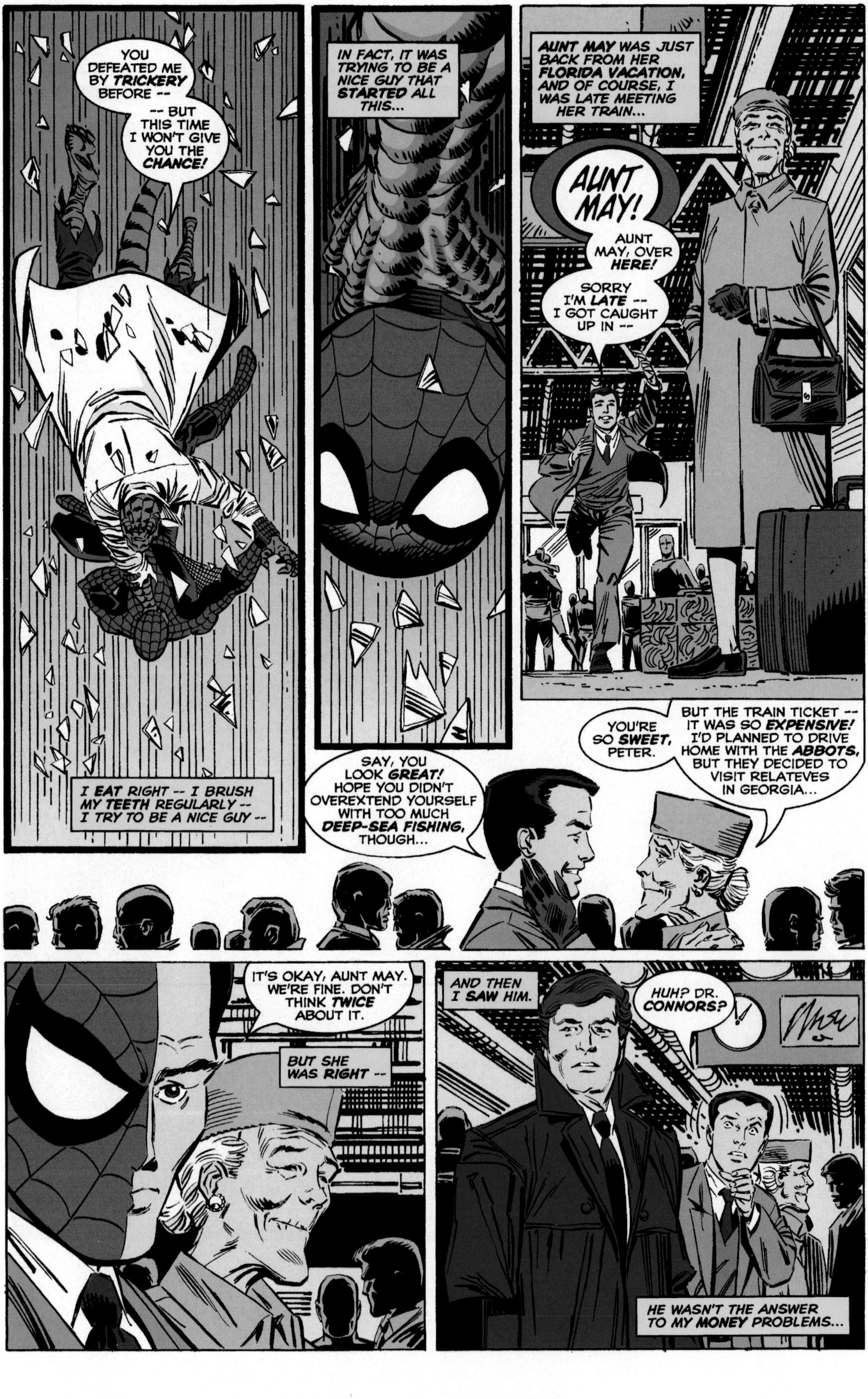

YOU DEFEATED ME BY TRICKERY BEFORE --
-- BUT THIS TIME I WON'T GIVE YOU THE CHANCE!
I EAT RIGHT -- I BRUSH MY TEETH REGULARLY -- I TRY TO BE A NICE GUY --
IN FACT, IT WAS TRYING TO BE A NICE GUY THAT STARTED ALL THIS...
AUNT MAY WAS JUST BACK FROM HER FLORIDA VACATION, AND OF COURSE, I WAS LATE MEETING HER TRAIN...
AUNT MAY!
AUNT MAY, OVER HERE!
SORRY I'M LATE -- I GOT CAUGHT UP IN --
SAY, YOU LOOK GREAT! HOPE YOU DIDN'T OVEREXTEND YOURSELF WITH TOO MUCH DEEP-SEA FISHING, THOUGH...
YOU'RE SO SWEET, PETER.
BUT THE TRAIN TICKET -- IT WAS SO EXPENSIVE! I'D PLANNED TO DRIVE HOME WITH THE ABBOTS, BUT THEY DECIDED TO VISIT RELATEVES IN GEORGIA...
IT'S OKAY, AUNT MAY. WE'RE FINE. DON'T THINK TWICE ABOUT IT.
BUT SHE WAS RIGHT --
AND THEN I SAW HIM.
HUH? DR. CONNORS?
HE WASN'T THE ANSWER TO MY MONEY PROBLEMS...

...BUT HE COULD MAYBE HELP ME OUT WITH A *DIFFERENT* SITUATION.

TURNED OUT HE WAS HERE TO GIVE A SERIES OF LECTURES ON HERPETOLOGY AT EMPIRE STATE UNIVERSITY, SO I SWUNG BY HIS TEMPORARY LAB...

PSST! DOC! HEY, *DOC!*

SPIDER-MAN?

I WAS WONDERING IF YOU COULD DO ME A *FAVOR*, DOC...

SPIDER-MAN, AFTER THE WAY YOU SAVED ME WHEN I TURNED MYSELF INTO...THAT *CREATURE*, YOU COULD ASK ME FOR THE *MOON*, AND I'D DO MY BEST.

IF NOT FOR YOU, I'D HAVE LOST...

...I'D HAVE LOST EVERYTHING THAT *MATTERS*...

YOU'RE A PAL, DOC. HERE'S WHAT I WANT TO DO...

NO! SCIENTISTS... WITH *NEEDLES!* THEY LOCK ME UP... NEVER LET ME OUT!

DOC CONNORS HAD DEVELOPED AN EXPERIMENTAL SERUM, BASED ON LIZARD REGENERATION, TO TRY TO REGROW HIS AMPUTATED ARM.

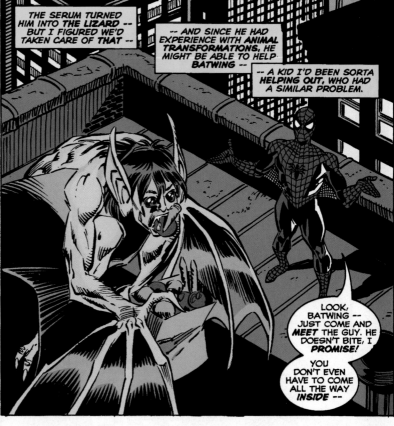

THE SERUM TURNED HIM INTO THE LIZARD -- BUT I FIGURED WE'D TAKEN CARE OF THAT --

-- AND SINCE HE HAD EXPERIENCE WITH ANIMAL TRANSFORMATIONS, HE MIGHT BE ABLE TO HELP BATWING --

-- A KID I'D BEEN SORTA HELPING OUT, WHO HAD A SIMILAR PROBLEM.

LOOK, BATWING -- JUST COME AND *MEET* THE GUY. HE DOESN'T BITE, I *PROMISE!*

YOU DON'T EVEN HAVE TO COME ALL THE WAY *INSIDE* --

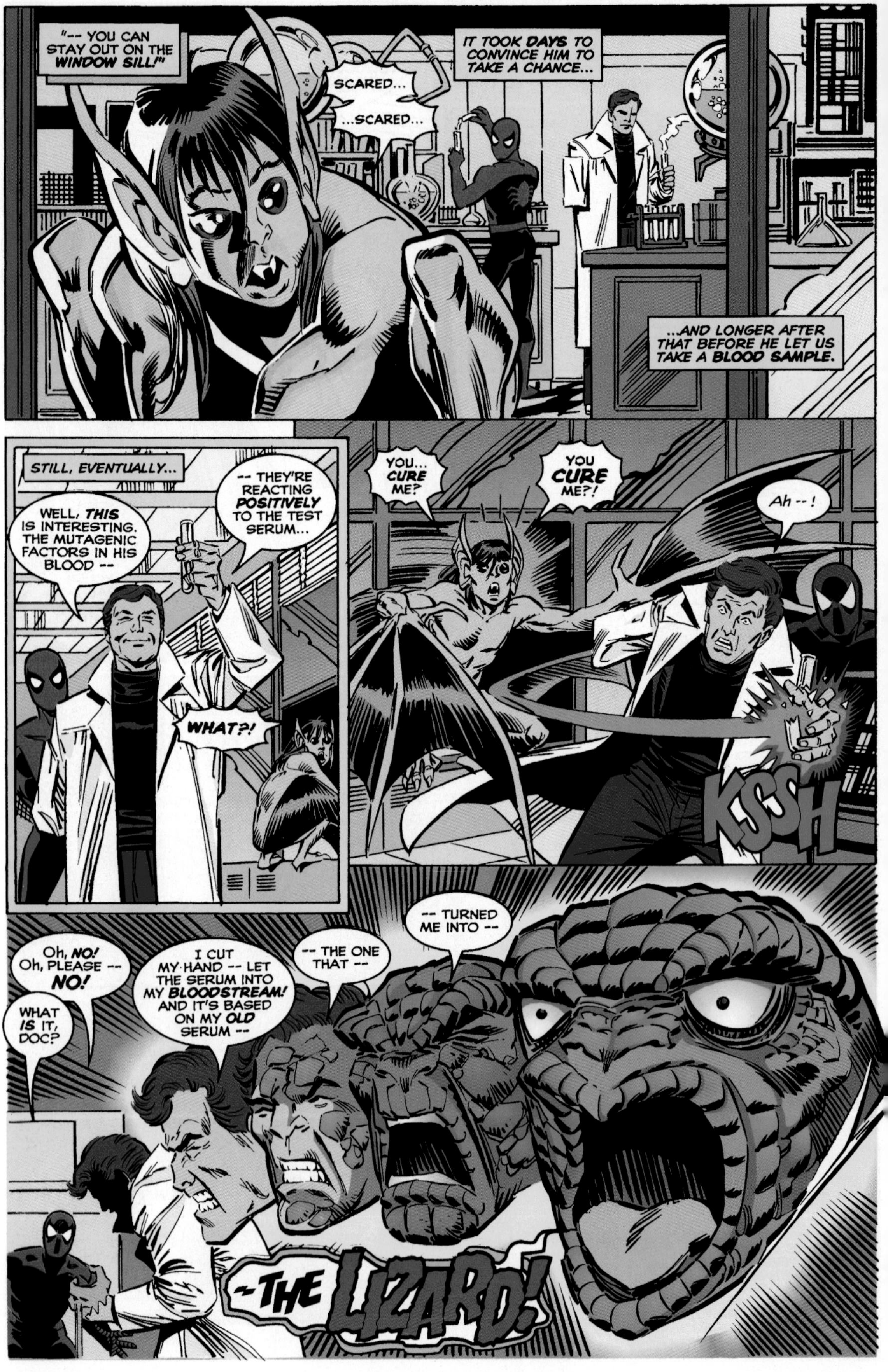
"-- YOU CAN STAY OUT ON THE WINDOW SILL!"
SCARED...
...SCARED...
IT TOOK DAYS TO CONVINCE HIM TO TAKE A CHANCE...
...AND LONGER AFTER THAT BEFORE HE LET US TAKE A BLOOD SAMPLE.
STILL, EVENTUALLY...
WELL, THIS IS INTERESTING. THE MUTAGENIC FACTORS IN HIS BLOOD --
-- THEY'RE REACTING POSITIVELY TO THE TEST SERUM...
WHAT?!
YOU... CURE ME?
YOU CURE ME?!
Ah --!
KSSH
Oh, NO! Oh, PLEASE -- NO!
WHAT IS IT, DOC?
I CUT MY HAND -- LET THE SERUM INTO MY BLOODSTREAM! AND IT'S BASED ON MY OLD SERUM --
-- THE ONE THAT --
-- TURNED ME INTO --
-- THE LIZARD!

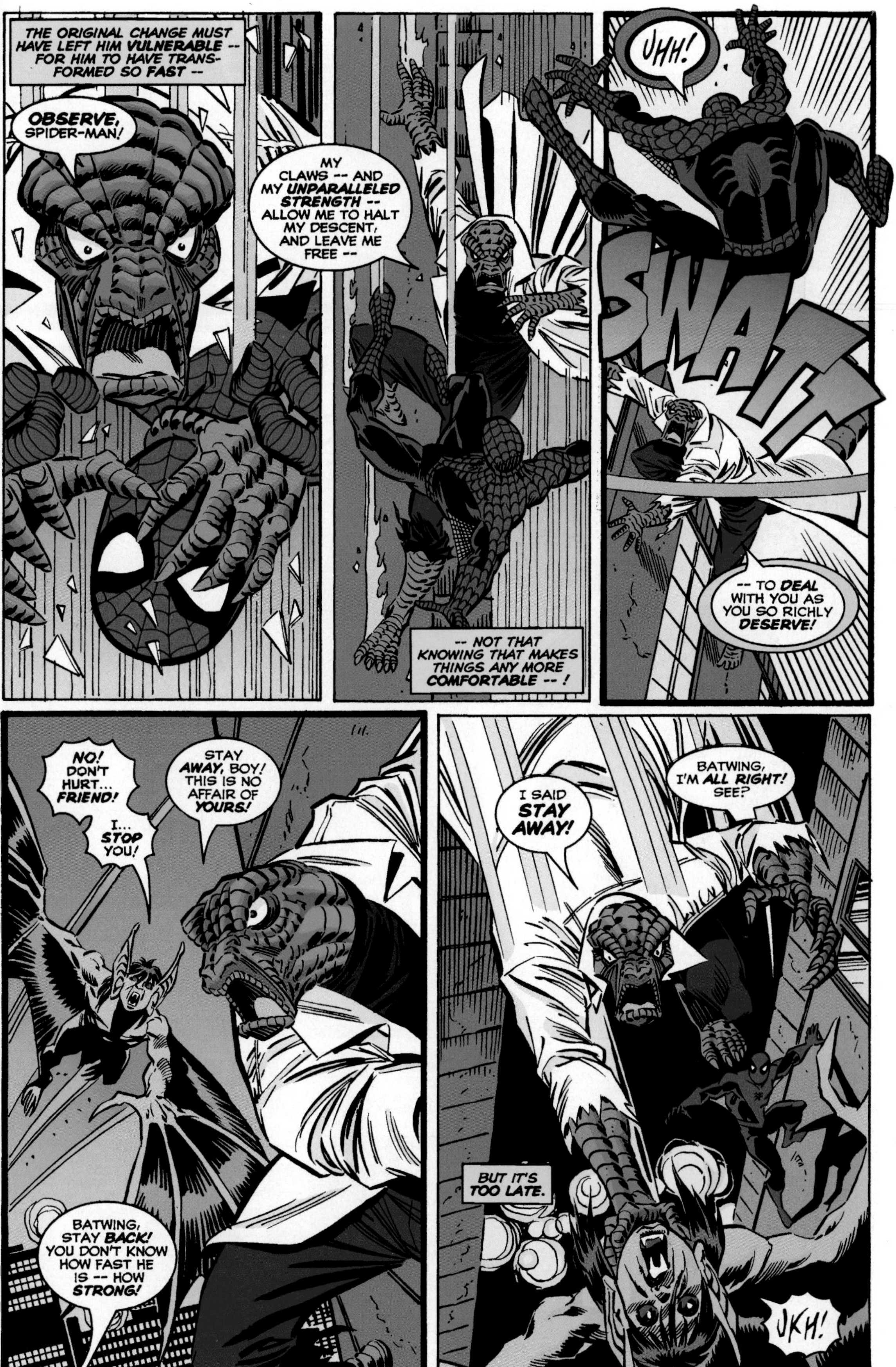

THE ORIGINAL CHANGE MUST HAVE LEFT HIM VULNERABLE -- FOR HIM TO HAVE TRANSFORMED SO FAST --
OBSERVE, SPIDER-MAN!
MY CLAWS -- AND MY UNPARALLELED STRENGTH -- ALLOW ME TO HALT MY DESCENT, AND LEAVE ME FREE --
-- NOT THAT KNOWING THAT MAKES THINGS ANY MORE COMFORTABLE -- !
UHH!
SWATT
-- TO DEAL WITH YOU AS YOU SO RICHLY DESERVE!
NO! DON'T HURT... FRIEND!
I... STOP YOU!
STAY AWAY, BOY! THIS IS NO AFFAIR OF YOURS!
BATWING, STAY BACK! YOU DON'T KNOW HOW FAST HE IS -- HOW STRONG!
I SAID STAY AWAY!
BATWING, I'M ALL RIGHT! SEE?
BUT IT'S TOO LATE.
UKH!

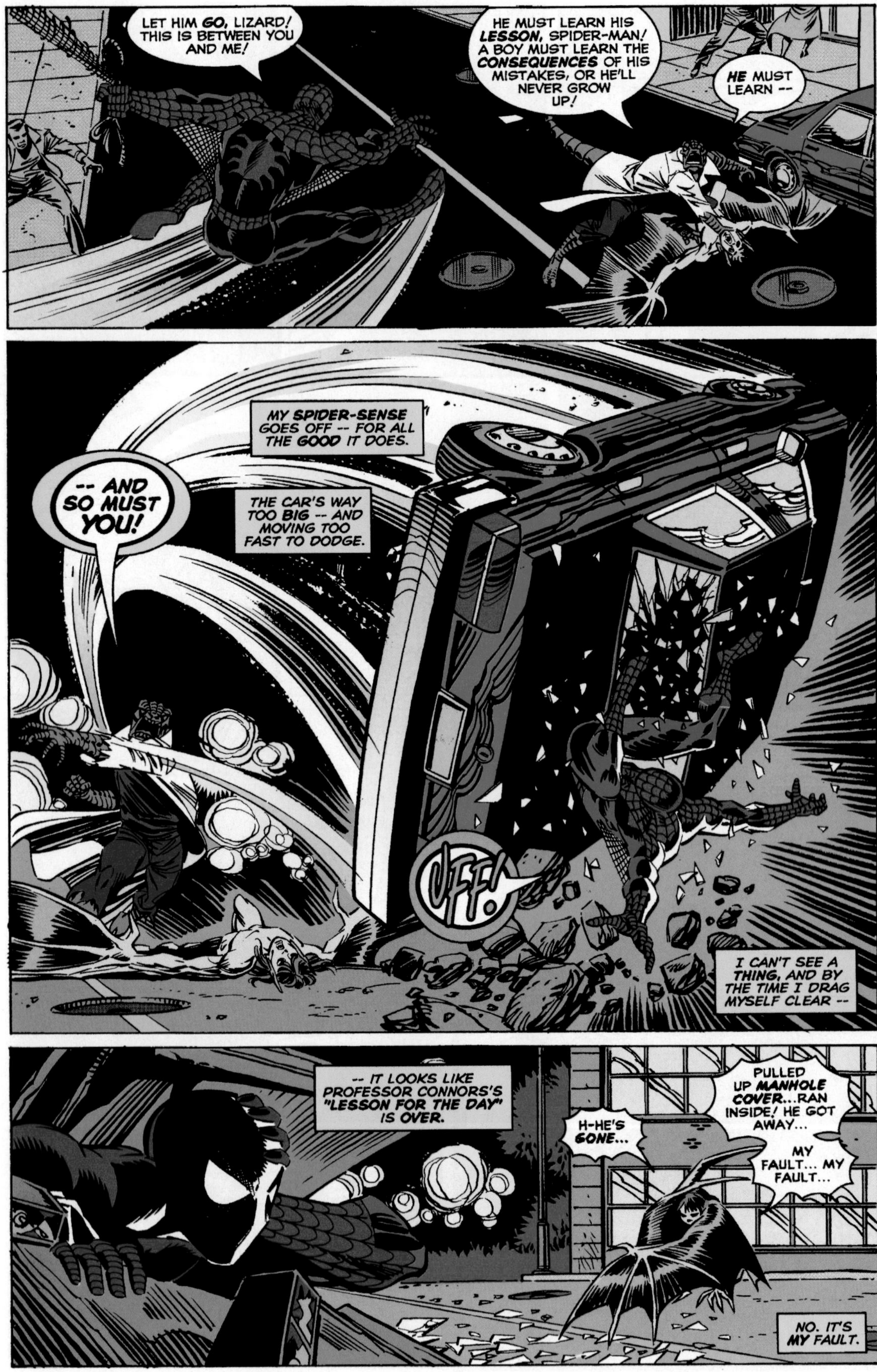

LET HIM GO, LIZARD! THIS IS BETWEEN YOU AND ME!
HE MUST LEARN HIS LESSON, SPIDER-MAN! A BOY MUST LEARN THE CONSEQUENCES OF HIS MISTAKES, OR HE'LL NEVER GROW UP!
HE MUST LEARN --
MY SPIDER-SENSE GOES OFF -- FOR ALL THE GOOD IT DOES.
-- AND SO MUST YOU!
THE CAR'S WAY TOO BIG -- AND MOVING TOO FAST TO DODGE.
UFF!
I CAN'T SEE A THING, AND BY THE TIME I DRAG MYSELF CLEAR --
-- IT LOOKS LIKE PROFESSOR CONNORS'S "LESSON FOR THE DAY" IS OVER.
H-HE'S GONE...
PULLED UP MANHOLE COVER...RAN INSIDE! HE GOT AWAY...
MY FAULT... MY FAULT...
NO. IT'S MY FAULT.

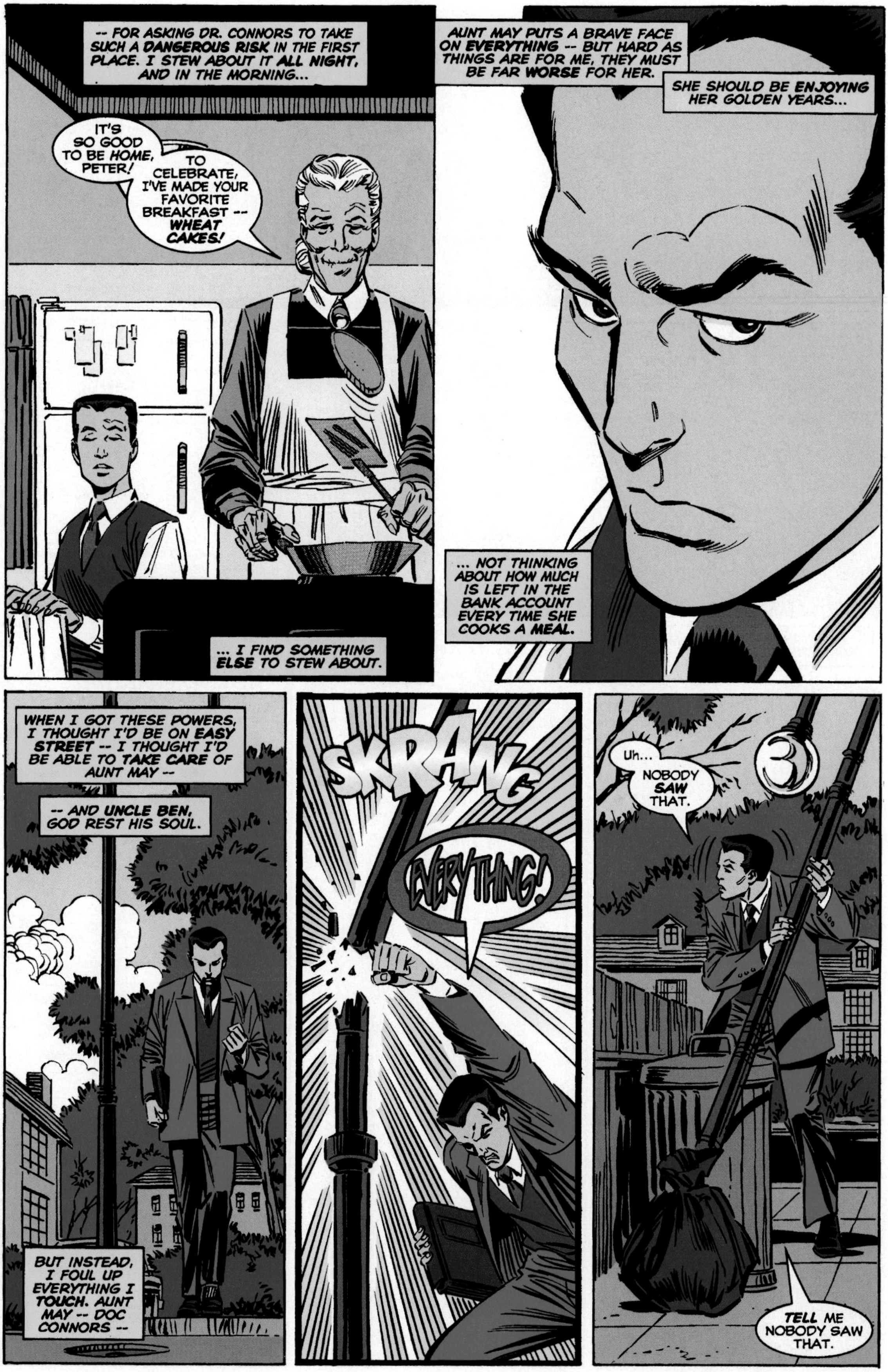
-- FOR ASKING DR. CONNORS TO TAKE SUCH A DANGEROUS RISK IN THE FIRST PLACE. I STEW ABOUT IT ALL NIGHT, AND IN THE MORNING...
IT'S SO GOOD TO BE HOME, PETER!
TO CELEBRATE, I'VE MADE YOUR FAVORITE BREAKFAST -- WHEAT CAKES!
... I FIND SOMETHING ELSE TO STEW ABOUT.
AUNT MAY PUTS A BRAVE FACE ON EVERYTHING -- BUT HARD AS THINGS ARE FOR ME, THEY MUST BE FAR WORSE FOR HER.
SHE SHOULD BE ENJOYING HER GOLDEN YEARS...
... NOT THINKING ABOUT HOW MUCH IS LEFT IN THE BANK ACCOUNT EVERY TIME SHE COOKS A MEAL.
WHEN I GOT THESE POWERS, I THOUGHT I'D BE ON EASY STREET -- I THOUGHT I'D BE ABLE TO TAKE CARE OF AUNT MAY --
-- AND UNCLE BEN, GOD REST HIS SOUL.
BUT INSTEAD, I FOUL UP EVERYTHING I TOUCH. AUNT MAY -- DOC CONNORS --
SKRANG
EVERYTHING!
Uh... NOBODY SAW THAT.
TELL ME NOBODY SAW THAT.

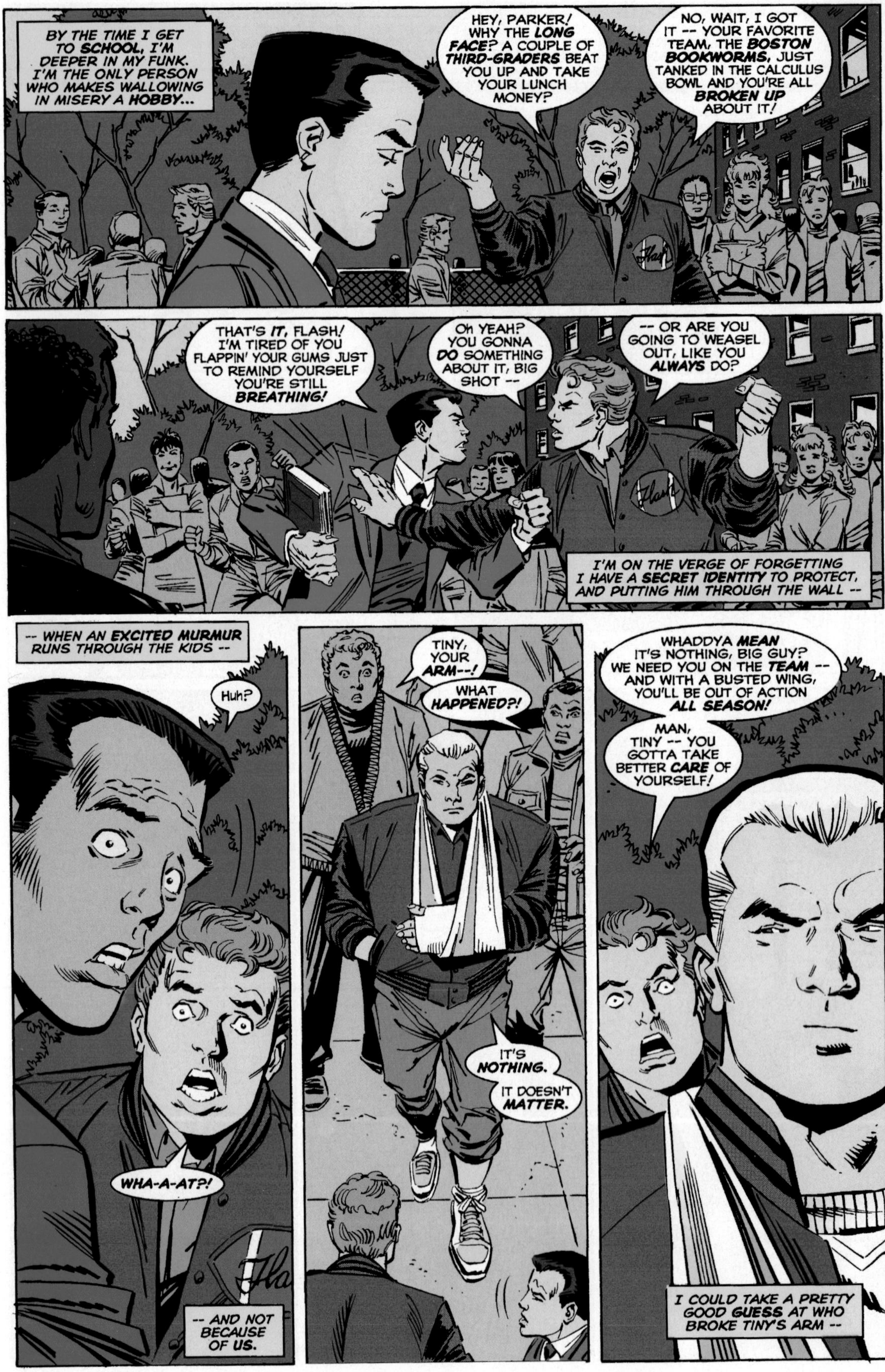
BY THE TIME I GET TO SCHOOL, I'M DEEPER IN MY FUNK. I'M THE ONLY PERSON WHO MAKES WALLOWING IN MISERY A HOBBY...
HEY, PARKER! WHY THE LONG FACE? A COUPLE OF THIRD-GRADERS BEAT YOU UP AND TAKE YOUR LUNCH MONEY?
NO, WAIT, I GOT IT -- YOUR FAVORITE TEAM, THE BOSTON BOOKWORMS, JUST TANKED IN THE CALCULUS BOWL AND YOU'RE ALL BROKEN UP ABOUT IT!
THAT'S IT, FLASH! I'M TIRED OF YOU FLAPPIN' YOUR GUMS JUST TO REMIND YOURSELF YOU'RE STILL BREATHING!
Oh YEAH? YOU GONNA DO SOMETHING ABOUT IT, BIG SHOT --
-- OR ARE YOU GOING TO WEASEL OUT, LIKE YOU ALWAYS DO?
I'M ON THE VERGE OF FORGETTING I HAVE A SECRET IDENTITY TO PROTECT, AND PUTTING HIM THROUGH THE WALL --
-- WHEN AN EXCITED MURMUR RUNS THROUGH THE KIDS --
Huh?
WHA-A-AT?!
-- AND NOT BECAUSE OF US.
TINY, YOUR ARM--!
WHAT HAPPENED?!
IT'S NOTHING.
IT DOESN'T MATTER.
WHADDYA MEAN IT'S NOTHING, BIG GUY? WE NEED YOU ON THE TEAM -- AND WITH A BUSTED WING, YOU'LL BE OUT OF ACTION ALL SEASON!
MAN, TINY -- YOU GOTTA TAKE BETTER CARE OF YOURSELF!
I COULD TAKE A PRETTY GOOD GUESS AT WHO BROKE TINY'S ARM --

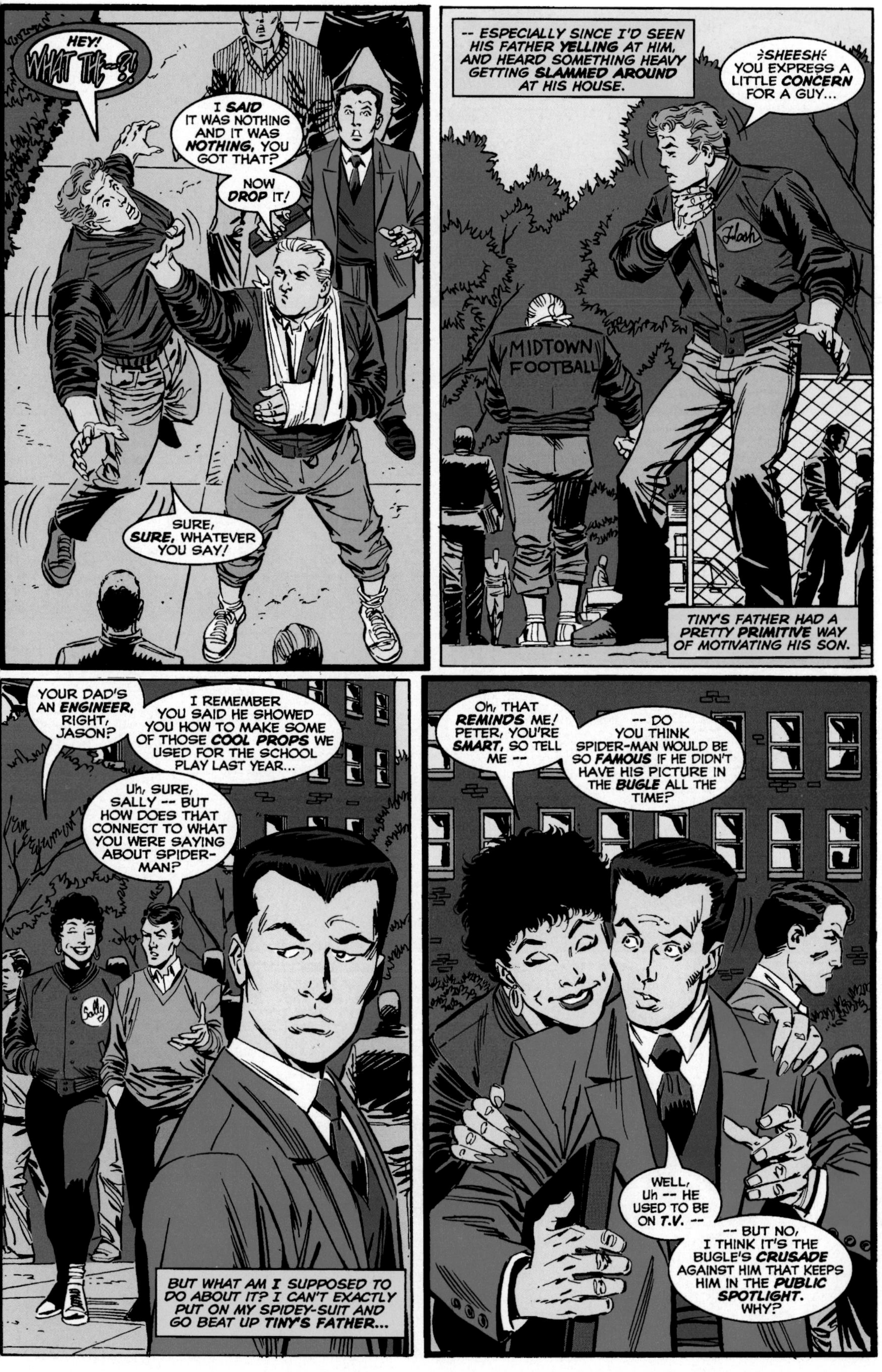
HEY! WHAT THE--?!
I SAID IT WAS NOTHING AND IT WAS NOTHING, YOU GOT THAT?
NOW DROP IT!
SURE, SURE, WHATEVER YOU SAY!
-- ESPECIALLY SINCE I'D SEEN HIS FATHER YELLING AT HIM, AND HEARD SOMETHING HEAVY GETTING SLAMMED AROUND AT HIS HOUSE.
SHEESH YOU EXPRESS A LITTLE CONCERN FOR A GUY...
MIDTOWN FOOTBALL
TINY'S FATHER HAD A PRETTY PRIMITIVE WAY OF MOTIVATING HIS SON.
YOUR DAD'S AN ENGINEER, RIGHT, JASON?
I REMEMBER YOU SAID HE SHOWED YOU HOW TO MAKE SOME OF THOSE COOL PROPS WE USED FOR THE SCHOOL PLAY LAST YEAR...
Uh, SURE, SALLY -- BUT HOW DOES THAT CONNECT TO WHAT YOU WERE SAYING ABOUT SPIDER-MAN?
Sally
BUT WHAT AM I SUPPOSED TO DO ABOUT IT? I CAN'T EXACTLY PUT ON MY SPIDEY-SUIT AND GO BEAT UP TINY'S FATHER...
Oh, THAT REMINDS ME! PETER, YOU'RE SMART, SO TELL ME --
-- DO YOU THINK SPIDER-MAN WOULD BE SO FAMOUS IF HE DIDN'T HAVE HIS PICTURE IN THE BUGLE ALL THE TIME?
WELL, Uh -- HE USED TO BE ON T.V. --
-- BUT NO, I THINK IT'S THE BUGLE'S CRUSADE AGAINST HIM THAT KEEPS HIM IN THE PUBLIC SPOTLIGHT. WHY?

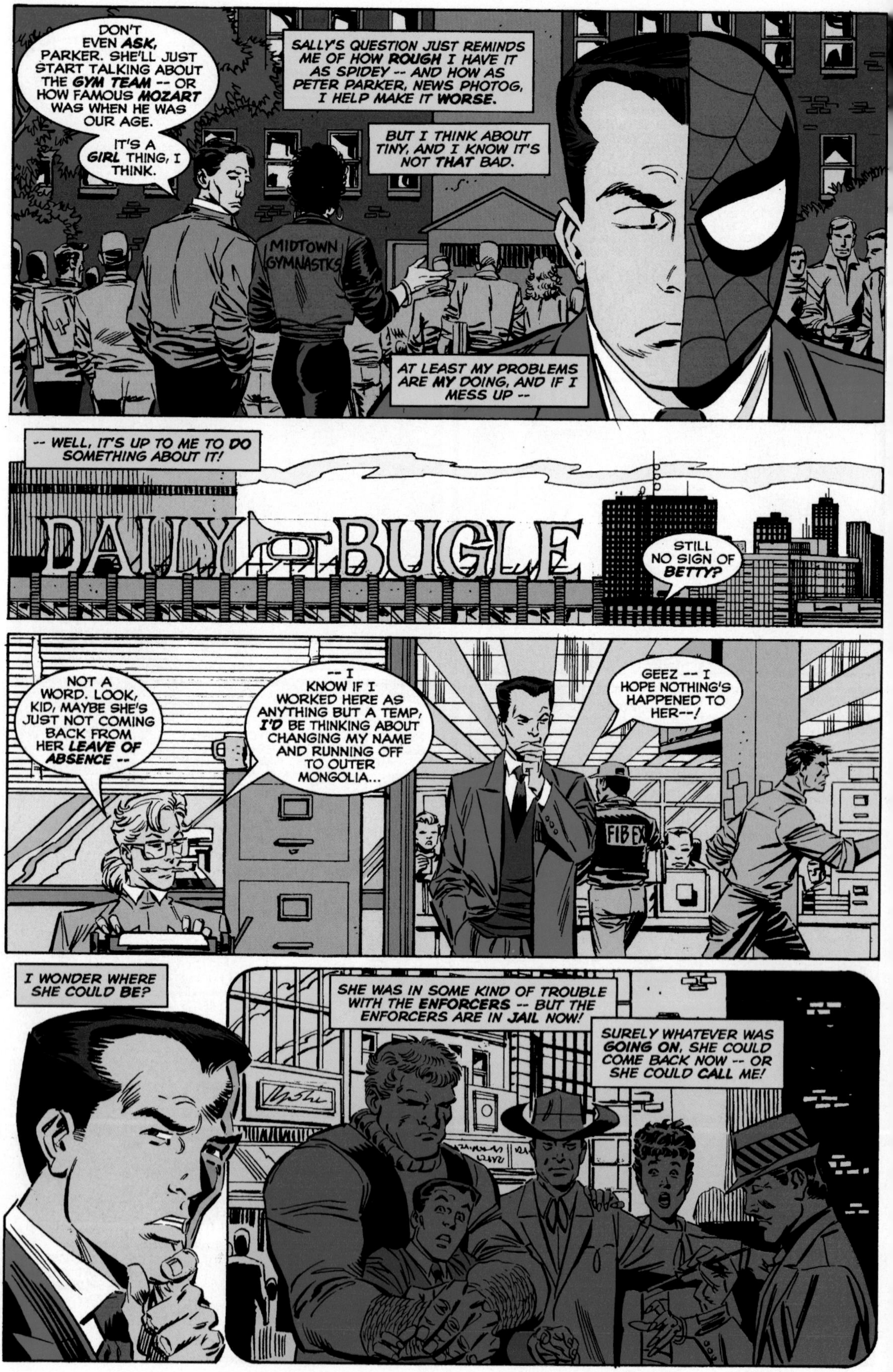
DON'T EVEN ASK, PARKER. SHE'LL JUST START TALKING ABOUT THE GYM TEAM -- OR HOW FAMOUS MOZART WAS WHEN HE WAS OUR AGE.
IT'S A GIRL THING, I THINK.
SALLY'S QUESTION JUST REMINDS ME OF HOW ROUGH I HAVE IT AS SPIDEY -- AND HOW AS PETER PARKER, NEWS PHOTOG, I HELP MAKE IT WORSE.
BUT I THINK ABOUT TINY, AND I KNOW IT'S NOT THAT BAD.
MIDTOWN GYMNASTKS
AT LEAST MY PROBLEMS ARE MY DOING, AND IF I MESS UP --
-- WELL, IT'S UP TO ME TO DO SOMETHING ABOUT IT!
DAILY BUGLE
STILL NO SIGN OF BETTY?
NOT A WORD. LOOK, KID, MAYBE SHE'S JUST NOT COMING BACK FROM HER LEAVE OF ABSENCE --
-- I KNOW IF I WORKED HERE AS ANYTHING BUT A TEMP, I'D BE THINKING ABOUT CHANGING MY NAME AND RUNNING OFF TO OUTER MONGOLIA...
GEEZ -- I HOPE NOTHING'S HAPPENED TO HER--!
FIBEX
I WONDER WHERE SHE COULD BE?
SHE WAS IN SOME KIND OF TROUBLE WITH THE ENFORCERS -- BUT THE ENFORCERS ARE IN JAIL NOW!
SURELY WHATEVER WAS GOING ON, SHE COULD COME BACK NOW -- OR SHE COULD CALL ME!

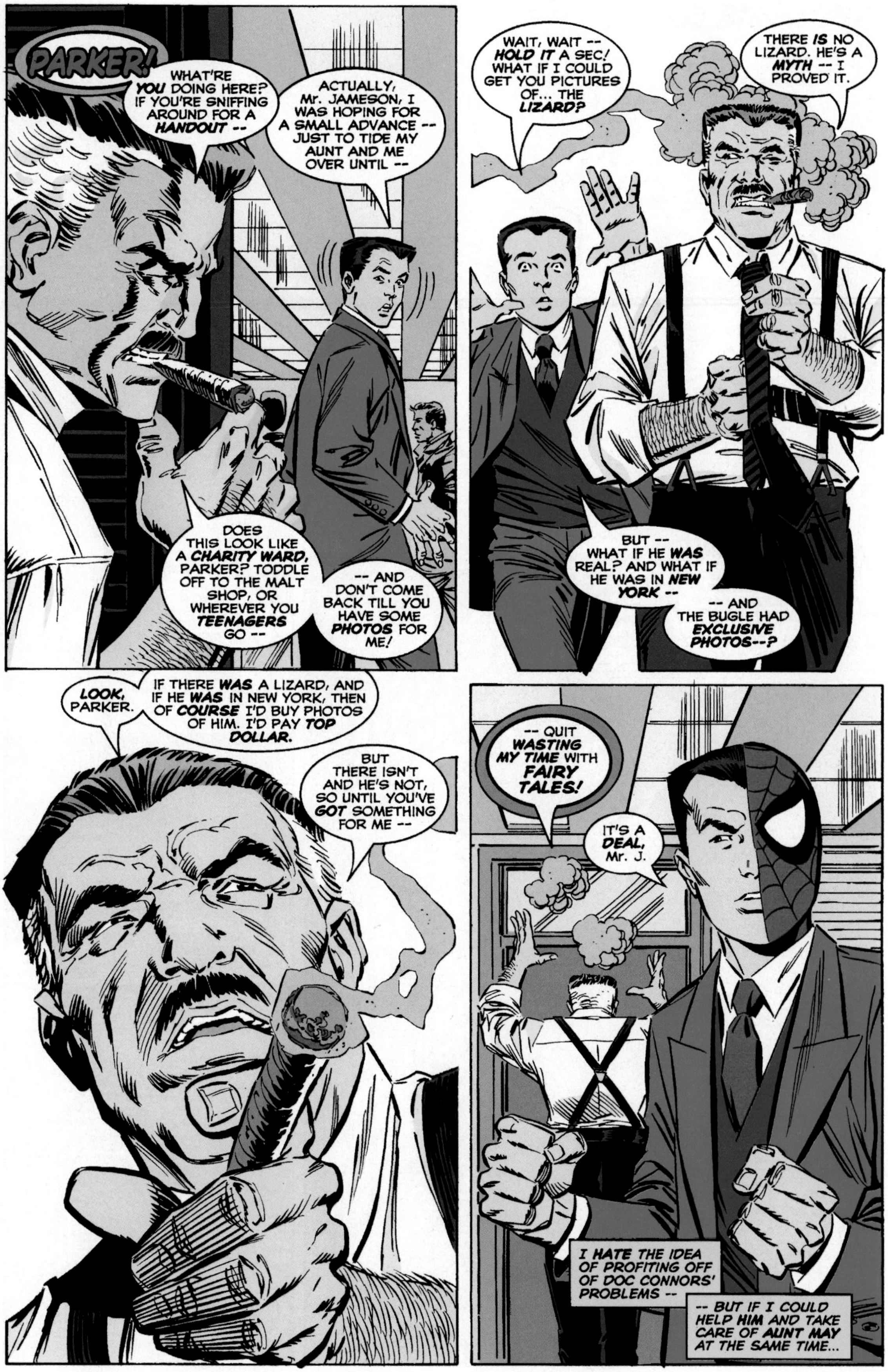
PARKER!
WHAT'RE YOU DOING HERE? IF YOU'RE SNIFFING AROUND FOR A HANDOUT --
ACTUALLY, Mr. JAMESON, I WAS HOPING FOR A SMALL ADVANCE -- JUST TO TIDE MY AUNT AND ME OVER UNTIL --
DOES THIS LOOK LIKE A CHARITY WARD, PARKER? TODDLE OFF TO THE MALT SHOP, OR WHEREVER YOU TEENAGERS GO --
-- AND DON'T COME BACK TILL YOU HAVE SOME PHOTOS FOR ME!
WAIT, WAIT -- HOLD IT A SEC! WHAT IF I COULD GET YOU PICTURES OF... THE LIZARD?
THERE IS NO LIZARD. HE'S A MYTH -- I PROVED IT.
BUT -- WHAT IF HE WAS REAL? AND WHAT IF HE WAS IN NEW YORK --
-- AND THE BUGLE HAD EXCLUSIVE PHOTOS--?
LOOK, PARKER.
IF THERE WAS A LIZARD, AND IF HE WAS IN NEW YORK, THEN OF COURSE I'D BUY PHOTOS OF HIM. I'D PAY TOP DOLLAR.
BUT THERE ISN'T AND HE'S NOT, SO UNTIL YOU'VE GOT SOMETHING FOR ME --
-- QUIT WASTING MY TIME WITH FAIRY TALES!
IT'S A DEAL, Mr. J.
I HATE THE IDEA OF PROFITING OFF OF DOC CONNORS' PROBLEMS --
-- BUT IF I COULD HELP HIM AND TAKE CARE OF AUNT MAY AT THE SAME TIME...

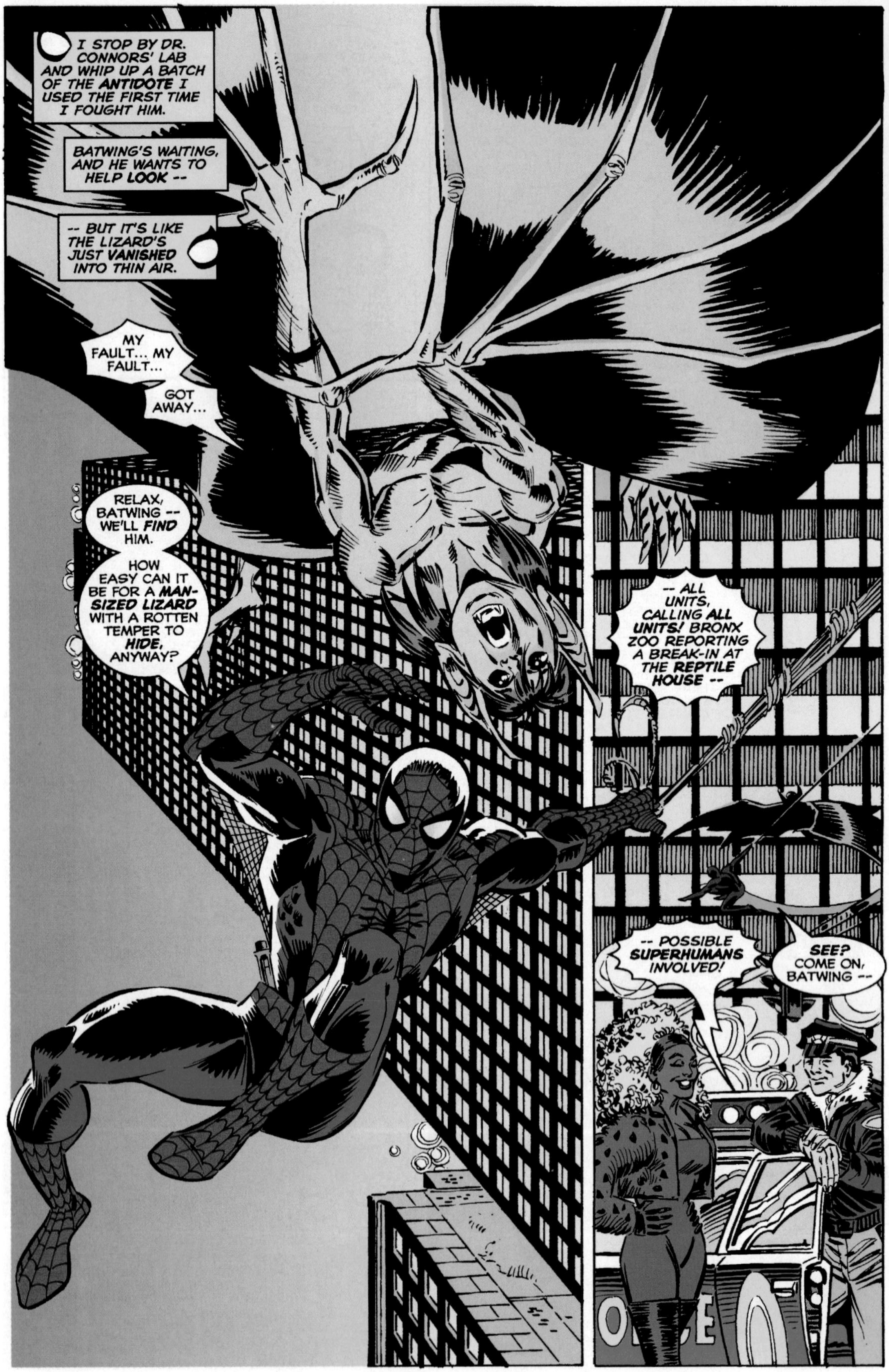
I STOP BY DR. CONNORS' LAB AND WHIP UP A BATCH OF THE ANTIDOTE I USED THE FIRST TIME I FOUGHT HIM.
BATWING'S WAITING, AND HE WANTS TO HELP LOOK --
-- BUT IT'S LIKE THE LIZARD'S JUST VANISHED INTO THIN AIR.
MY FAULT... MY FAULT...
GOT AWAY...
RELAX, BATWING -- WE'LL FIND HIM.
HOW EASY CAN IT BE FOR A MAN-SIZED LIZARD WITH A ROTTEN TEMPER TO HIDE, ANYWAY?
-- ALL UNITS, CALLING ALL UNITS! BRONX ZOO REPORTING A BREAK-IN AT THE REPTILE HOUSE --
-- POSSIBLE SUPERHUMANS INVOLVED!
SEE? COME ON, BATWING --

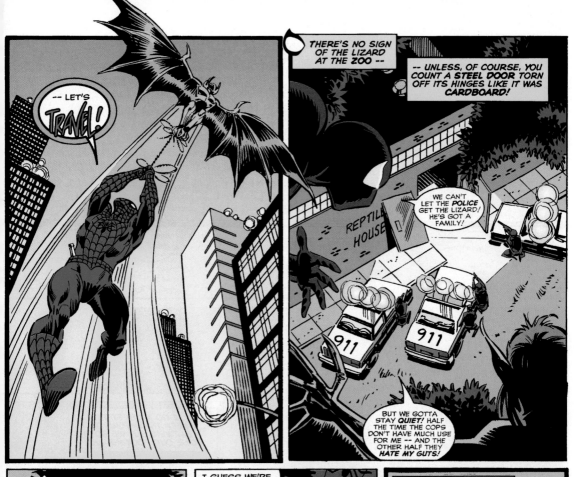

-- LET'S **TRAVEL!**

THERE'S NO SIGN OF THE LIZARD AT THE **ZOO** --

-- UNLESS, OF COURSE, YOU COUNT A **STEEL DOOR** TORN OFF ITS HINGES LIKE IT WAS **CARDBOARD!**

WE CAN'T LET THE **POLICE** GET THE LIZARD! HE'S GOT A **FAMILY!**

REPTILE HOUSE

911

911

BUT WE GOTTA STAY **QUIET!** HALF THE TIME THE COPS DON'T HAVE MUCH USE FOR ME -- AND THE OTHER HALF THEY **HATE MY GUTS!**

YOU IN THE **REPTILE HOUSE!**

WE HAVE YOU **SURROUNDED** -- COME OUT WITH YOUR **HANDS UP!**

WHADDYA THINK, BILL? THE NIGHT WATCHMAN ON THE **SAUCE** --

-- OR HE REALLY **DID** SEE A GIANT ALLIGATOR WEARIN' CLOTHES?

I GUESS WE'RE GONNA HAVE TO SNEAK PAST THEM...

NO!

OVER THERE... NEAR SEWER!

"I **SEE** IT, BATWING! REPTILES -- FREED BY THE LIZARD, NO DOUBT! AND WHEREVER **THEY'RE** HEADED --

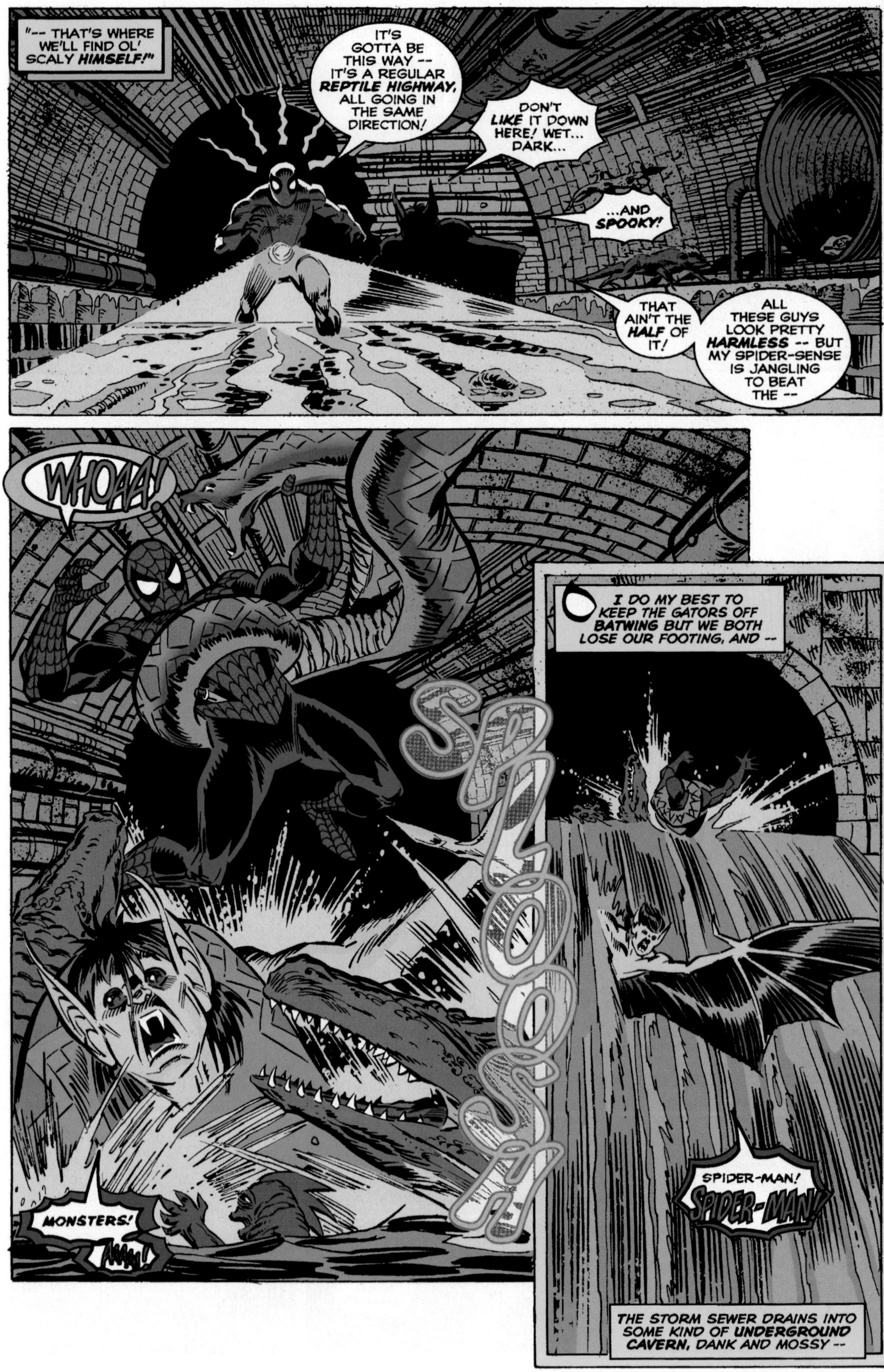
"-- THAT'S WHERE WE'LL FIND OL' SCALY HIMSELF!"
IT'S GOTTA BE THIS WAY -- IT'S A REGULAR REPTILE HIGHWAY, ALL GOING IN THE SAME DIRECTION!
DON'T LIKE IT DOWN HERE! WET... DARK...
...AND SPOOKY!
THAT AIN'T THE HALF OF IT!
ALL THESE GUYS LOOK PRETTY HARMLESS -- BUT MY SPIDER-SENSE IS JANGLING TO BEAT THE --
WHOAA!
SPLOOOSH
MONSTERS!
AAAH!
I DO MY BEST TO KEEP THE GATORS OFF BATWING BUT WE BOTH LOSE OUR FOOTING, AND --
SPIDER-MAN!
SPIDER-MAN!
THE STORM SEWER DRAINS INTO SOME KIND OF UNDERGROUND CAVERN, DANK AND MOSSY --

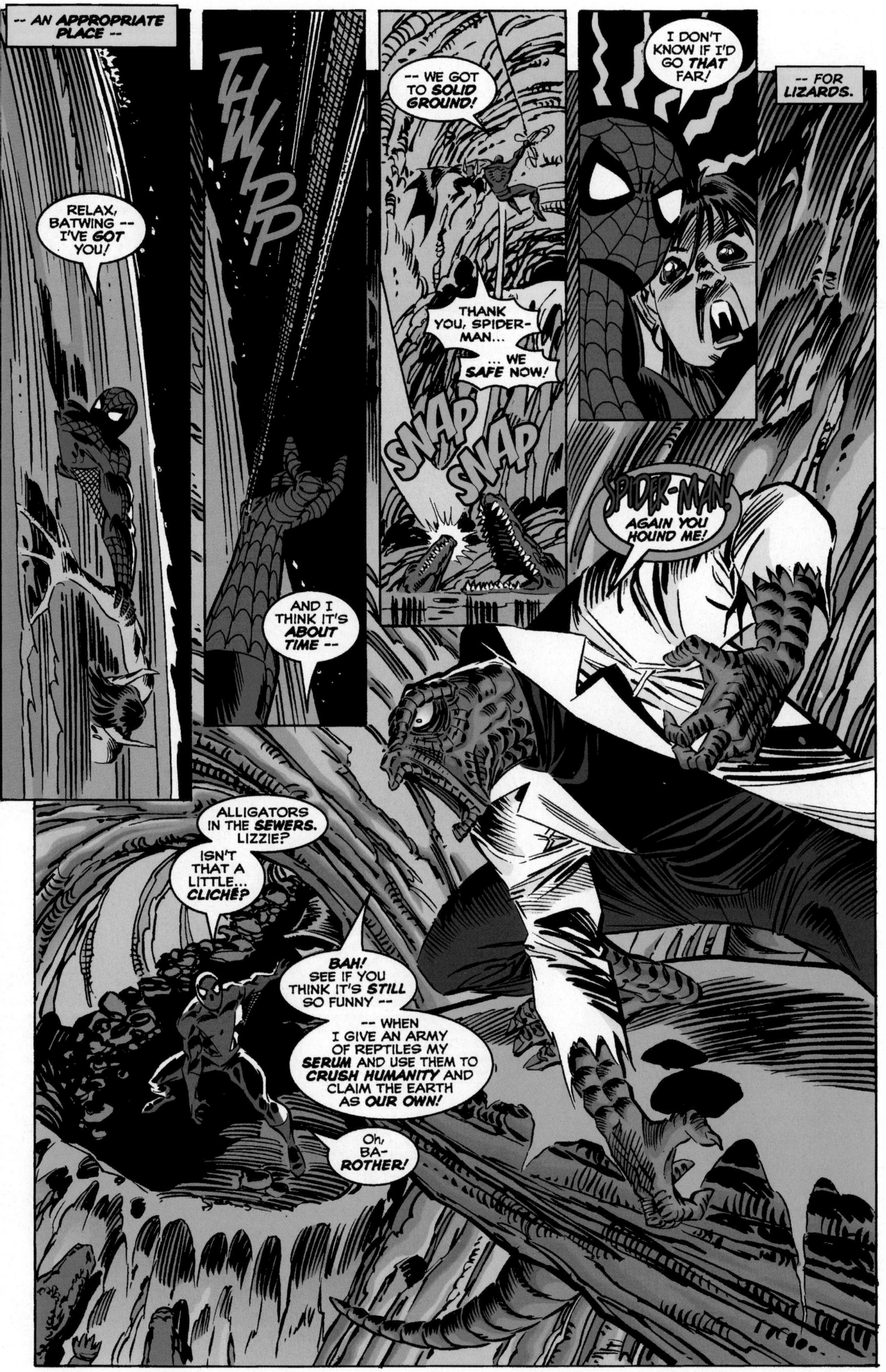
-- AN APPROPRIATE PLACE --
RELAX, BATWING -- I'VE GOT YOU!
THWIPP
AND I THINK IT'S ABOUT TIME --
-- WE GOT TO SOLID GROUND!
THANK YOU, SPIDER-MAN...
... WE SAFE NOW!
SNAP SNAP
I DON'T KNOW IF I'D GO THAT FAR!
-- FOR LIZARDS.
SPIDER-MAN! AGAIN YOU HOUND ME!
ALLIGATORS IN THE SEWERS. LIZZIE?
ISN'T THAT A LITTLE... CLICHÉ?
BAH! SEE IF YOU THINK IT'S STILL SO FUNNY --
-- WHEN I GIVE AN ARMY OF REPTILES MY SERUM AND USE THEM TO CRUSH HUMANITY AND CLAIM THE EARTH AS OUR OWN!
Oh, BA-ROTHER!

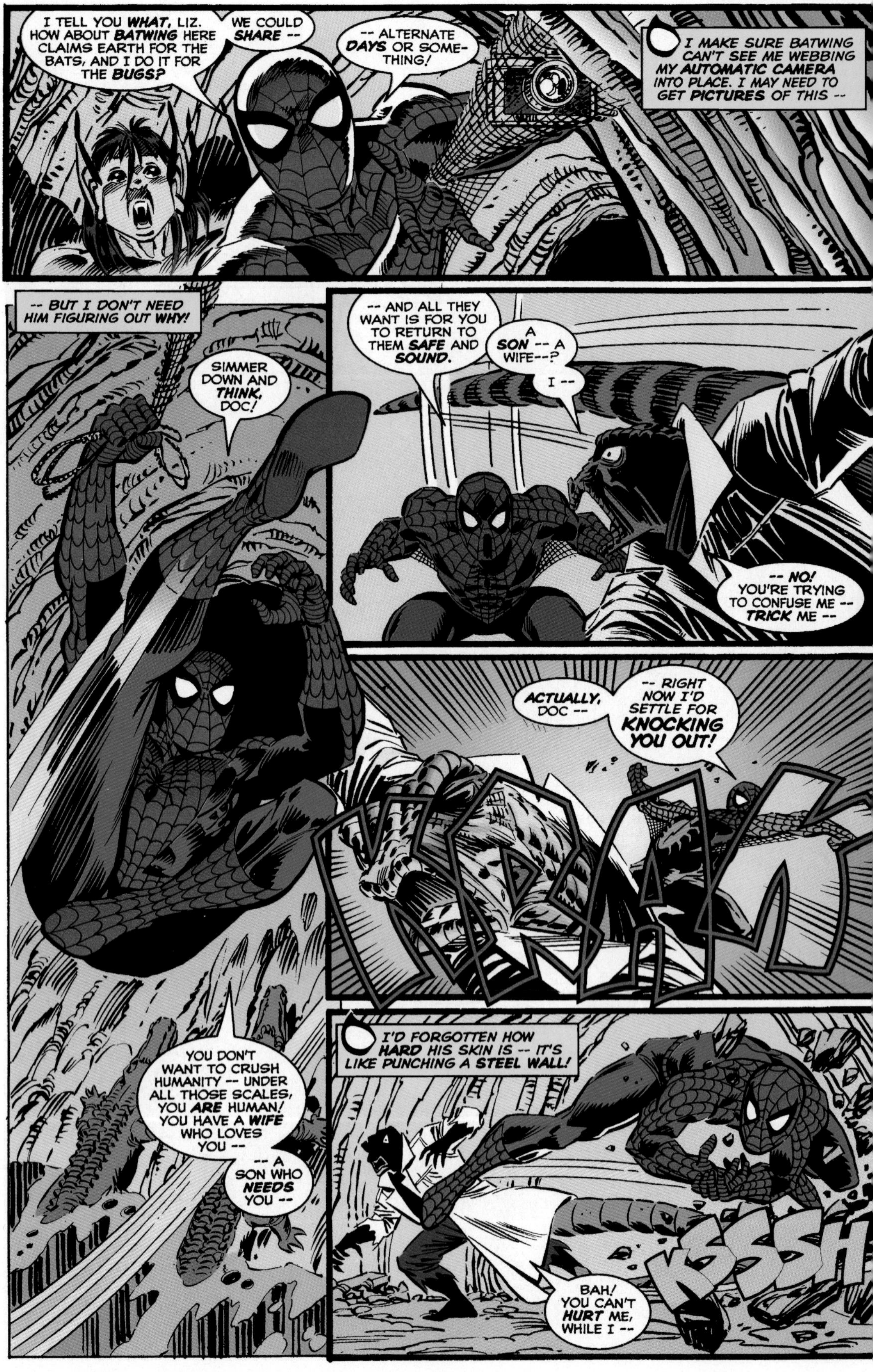
I TELL YOU WHAT, LIZ. HOW ABOUT BATWING HERE CLAIMS EARTH FOR THE BATS, AND I DO IT FOR THE BUGS?
WE COULD SHARE --
-- ALTERNATE DAYS OR SOMETHING!
I MAKE SURE BATWING CAN'T SEE ME WEBBING MY AUTOMATIC CAMERA INTO PLACE. I MAY NEED TO GET PICTURES OF THIS --
-- BUT I DON'T NEED HIM FIGURING OUT WHY!
SIMMER DOWN AND THINK, DOC!
YOU DON'T WANT TO CRUSH HUMANITY -- UNDER ALL THOSE SCALES, YOU ARE HUMAN! YOU HAVE A WIFE WHO LOVES YOU --
-- A SON WHO NEEDS YOU --
-- AND ALL THEY WANT IS FOR YOU TO RETURN TO THEM SAFE AND SOUND.
A SON -- A WIFE--?
I --
-- NO! YOU'RE TRYING TO CONFUSE ME -- TRICK ME --
ACTUALLY, DOC --
-- RIGHT NOW I'D SETTLE FOR KNOCKING YOU OUT!
KRAK
I'D FORGOTTEN HOW HARD HIS SKIN IS -- IT'S LIKE PUNCHING A STEEL WALL!
KSSSH
BAH! YOU CAN'T HURT ME, WHILE I --

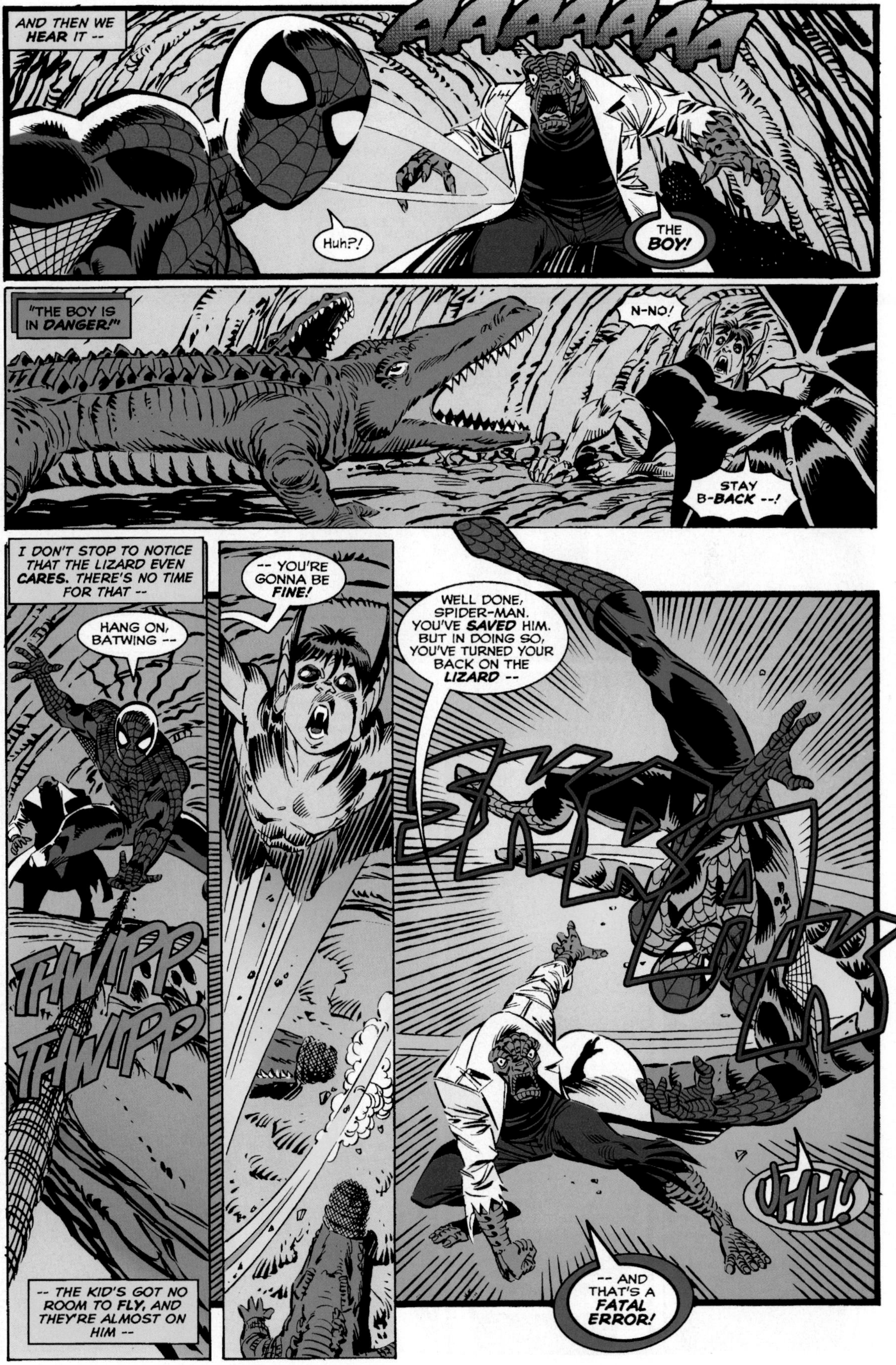
AND THEN WE HEAR IT --
AAAAAAA
Huh?!
THE BOY!
"THE BOY IS IN DANGER!"
N-NO!
STAY B-BACK --!
I DON'T STOP TO NOTICE THAT THE LIZARD EVEN CARES. THERE'S NO TIME FOR THAT --
HANG ON, BATWING --
THWIPP
THWIPP
-- THE KID'S GOT NO ROOM TO FLY, AND THEY'RE ALMOST ON HIM --
-- YOU'RE GONNA BE FINE!
WELL DONE, SPIDER-MAN. YOU'VE SAVED HIM. BUT IN DOING SO, YOU'VE TURNED YOUR BACK ON THE LIZARD --
UHH!
-- AND THAT'S A FATAL ERROR!

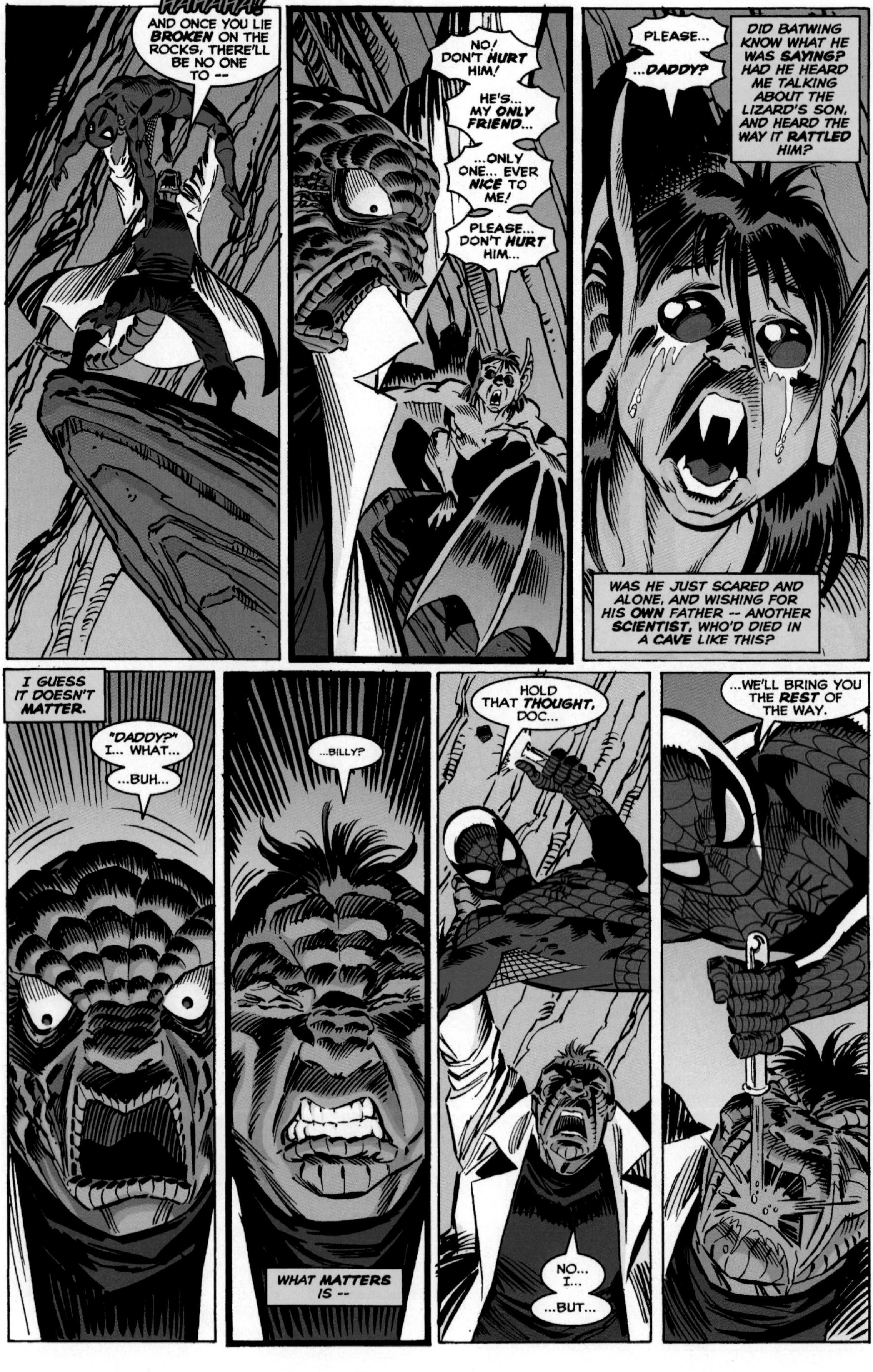
HAHAHA!
AND ONCE YOU LIE BROKEN ON THE ROCKS, THERE'LL BE NO ONE TO --
NO! DON'T HURT HIM!
HE'S... MY ONLY FRIEND...
...ONLY ONE... EVER NICE TO ME!
PLEASE... DON'T HURT HIM...
PLEASE...
...DADDY?
DID BATWING KNOW WHAT HE WAS SAYING? HAD HE HEARD ME TALKING ABOUT THE LIZARD'S SON, AND HEARD THE WAY IT RATTLED HIM?
WAS HE JUST SCARED AND ALONE, AND WISHING FOR HIS OWN FATHER -- ANOTHER SCIENTIST, WHO'D DIED IN A CAVE LIKE THIS?
I GUESS IT DOESN'T MATTER.
"DADDY?" I... WHAT...
...BUH...
...BILLY?
WHAT MATTERS IS --
HOLD THAT THOUGHT, DOC...
NO... I...
...BUT...
...WE'LL BRING YOU THE REST OF THE WAY.

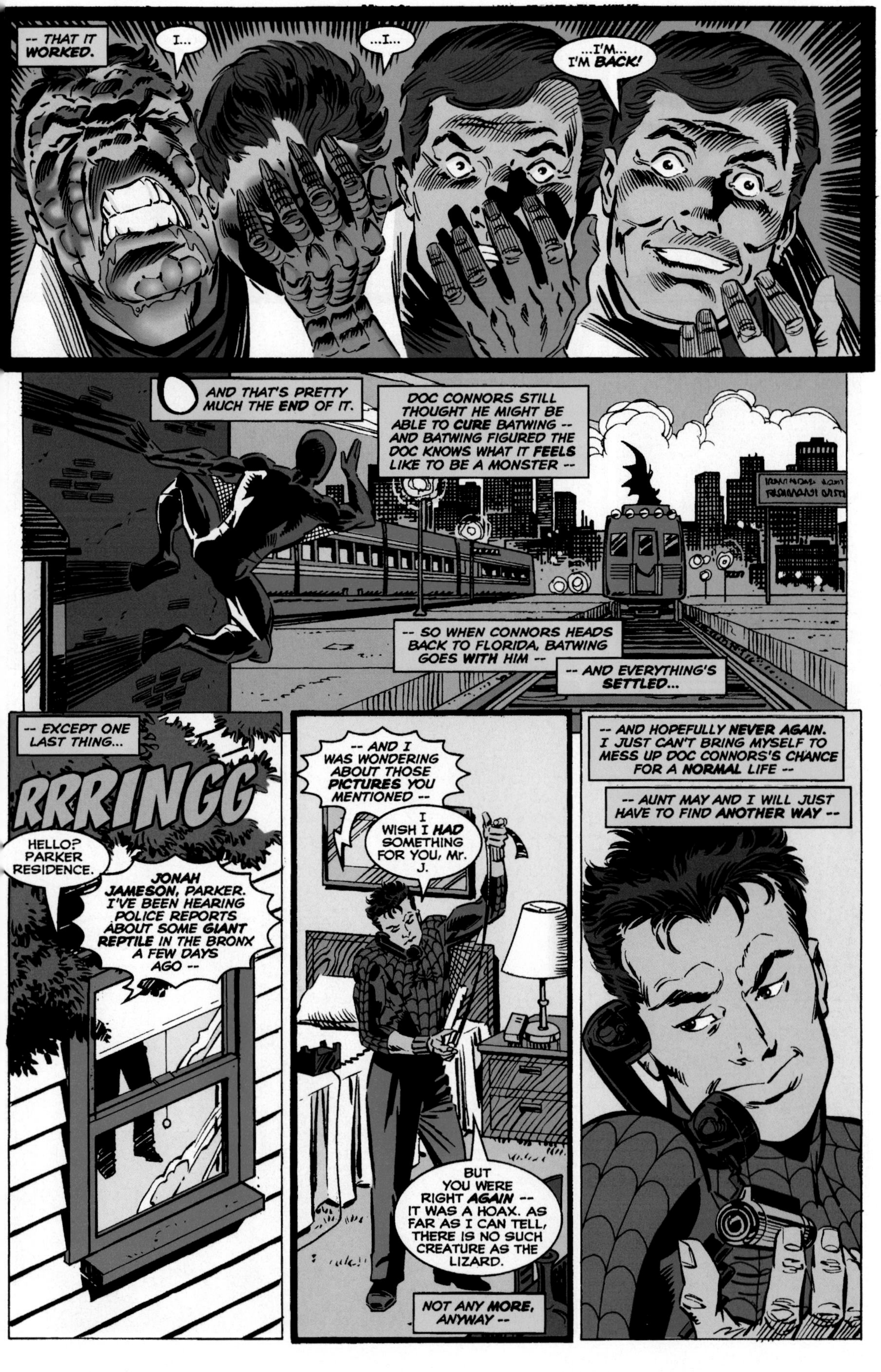
-- THAT IT WORKED.
I...
...I...
...I'M... I'M BACK!
AND THAT'S PRETTY MUCH THE END OF IT.
DOC CONNORS STILL THOUGHT HE MIGHT BE ABLE TO CURE BATWING -- AND BATWING FIGURED THE DOC KNOWS WHAT IT FEELS LIKE TO BE A MONSTER --
-- SO WHEN CONNORS HEADS BACK TO FLORIDA, BATWING GOES WITH HIM --
-- AND EVERYTHING'S SETTLED...
-- EXCEPT ONE LAST THING...
RRRINGG
HELLO? PARKER RESIDENCE.
JONAH JAMESON, PARKER. I'VE BEEN HEARING POLICE REPORTS ABOUT SOME GIANT REPTILE IN THE BRONX A FEW DAYS AGO --
-- AND I WAS WONDERING ABOUT THOSE PICTURES YOU MENTIONED --
I WISH I HAD SOMETHING FOR YOU, Mr. J.
BUT YOU WERE RIGHT AGAIN -- IT WAS A HOAX. AS FAR AS I CAN TELL, THERE IS NO SUCH CREATURE AS THE LIZARD.
NOT ANY MORE, ANYWAY --
-- AND HOPEFULLY NEVER AGAIN. I JUST CAN'T BRING MYSELF TO MESS UP DOC CONNORS'S CHANCE FOR A NORMAL LIFE --
-- AUNT MAY AND I WILL JUST HAVE TO FIND ANOTHER WAY --

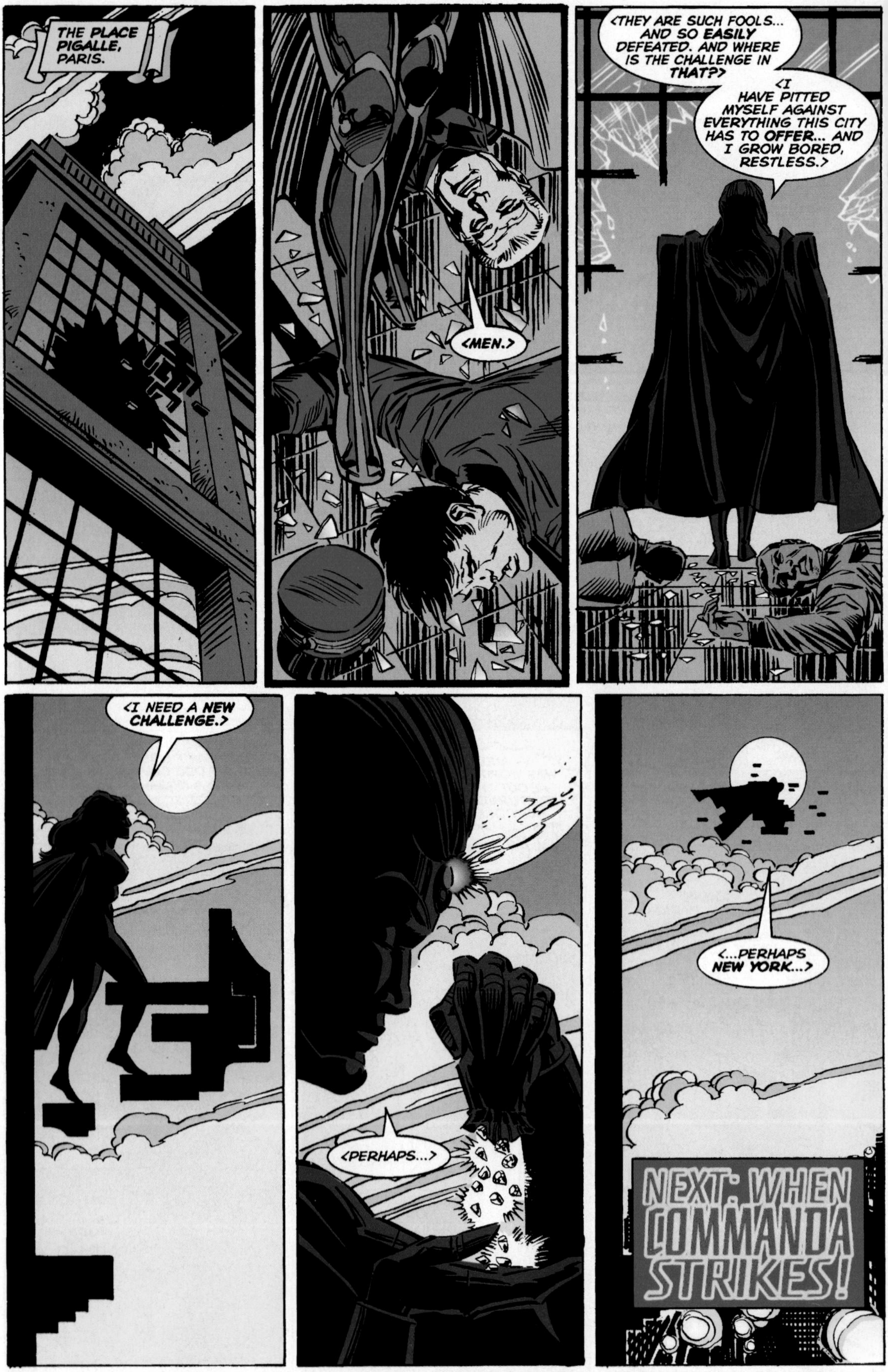
THE PLACE PIGALLE, PARIS.
<MEN.>
<THEY ARE SUCH FOOLS... AND SO EASILY DEFEATED. AND WHERE IS THE CHALLENGE IN THAT?>
<I HAVE PITTED MYSELF AGAINST EVERYTHING THIS CITY HAS TO OFFER... AND I GROW BORED, RESTLESS.>
<I NEED A NEW CHALLENGE.>
<PERHAPS...>
<...PERHAPS NEW YORK...>
NEXT: WHEN COMMANDA STRIKES!

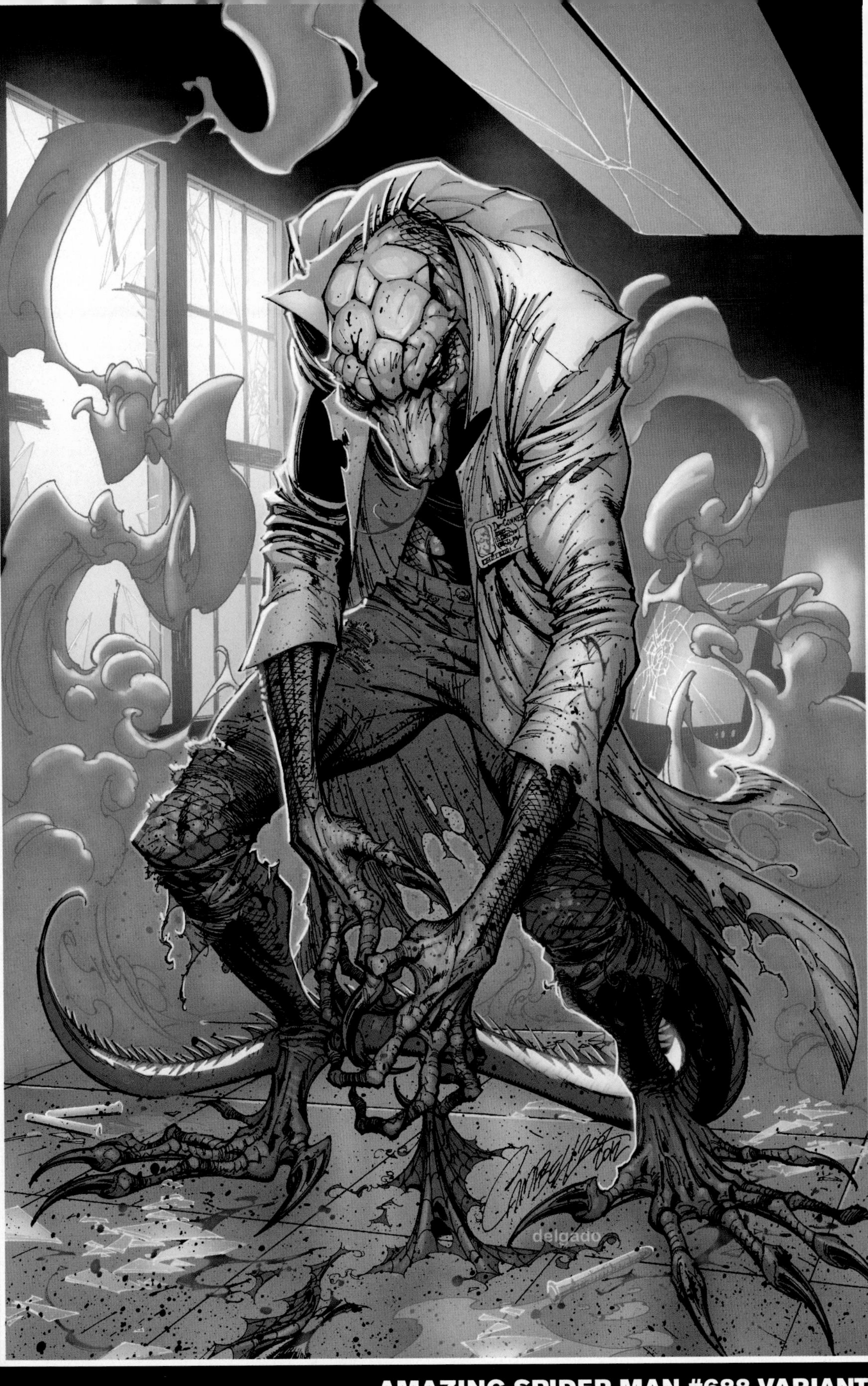
delgado

AMAZING SPIDER-MAN #688 VARIANT

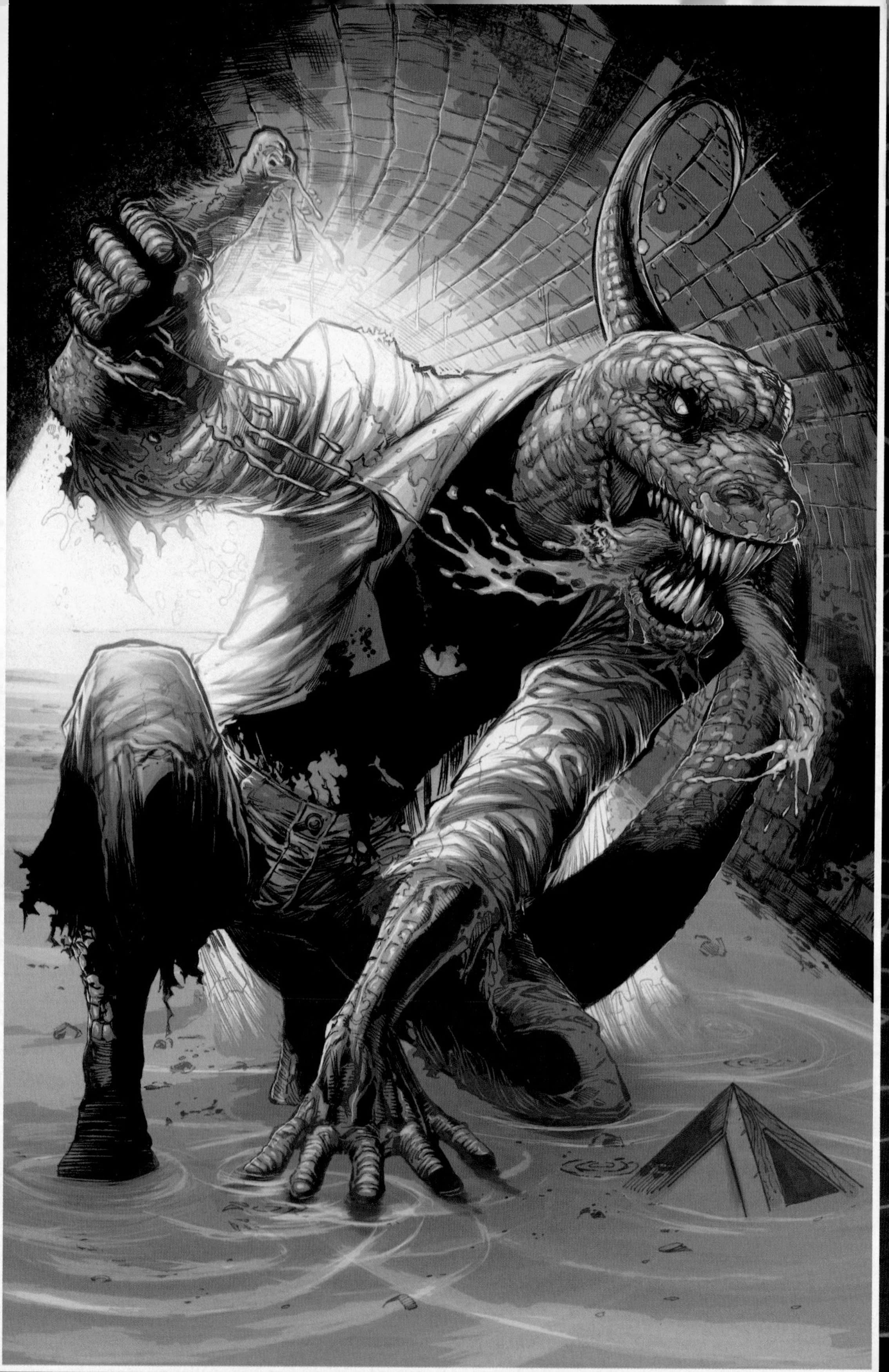

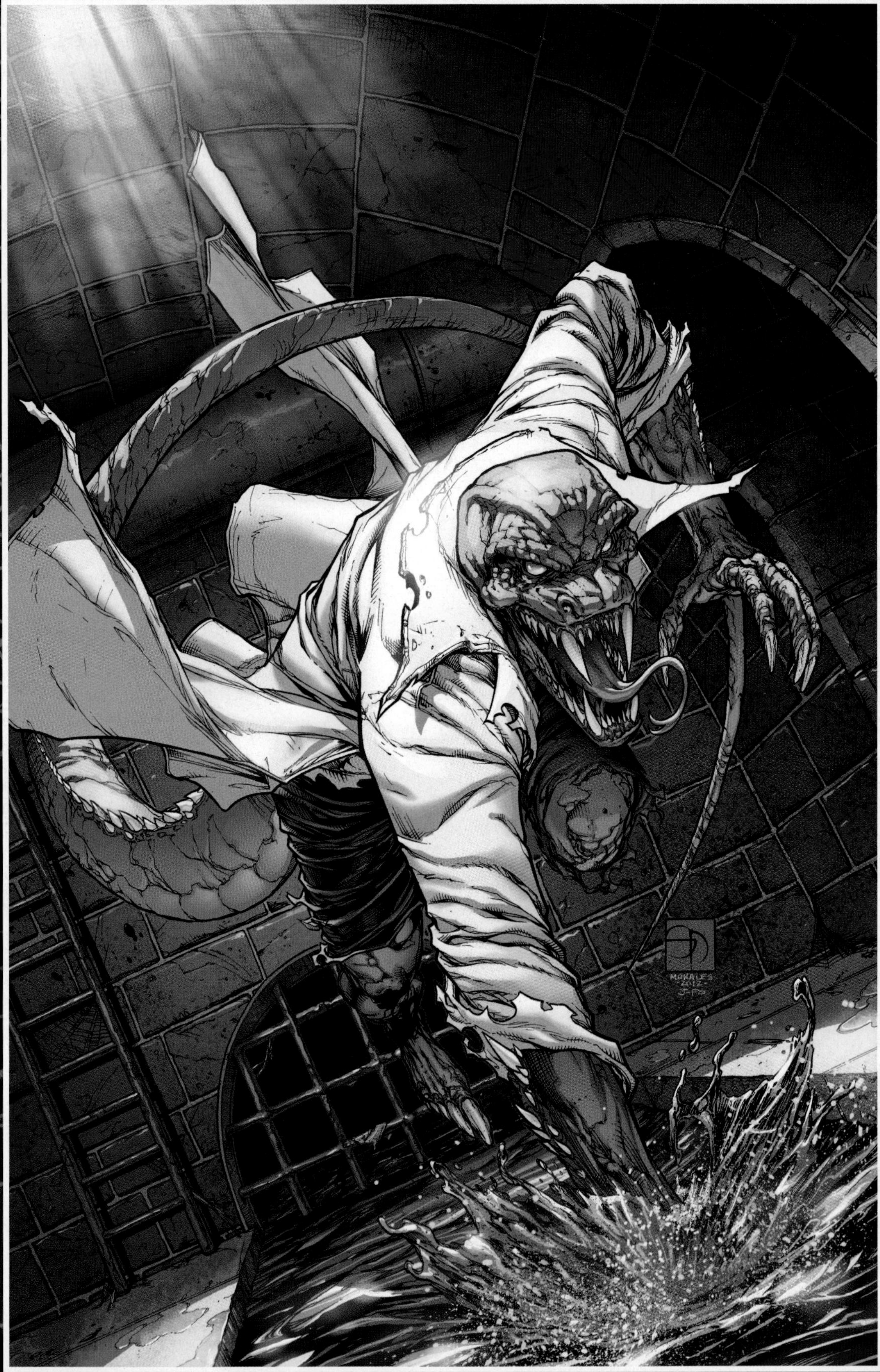

AMAZING SPIDER-MAN #690 VARIANT
COVER BY SHANE DAVIS, MARK MORALES & JUSTIN PONSOR

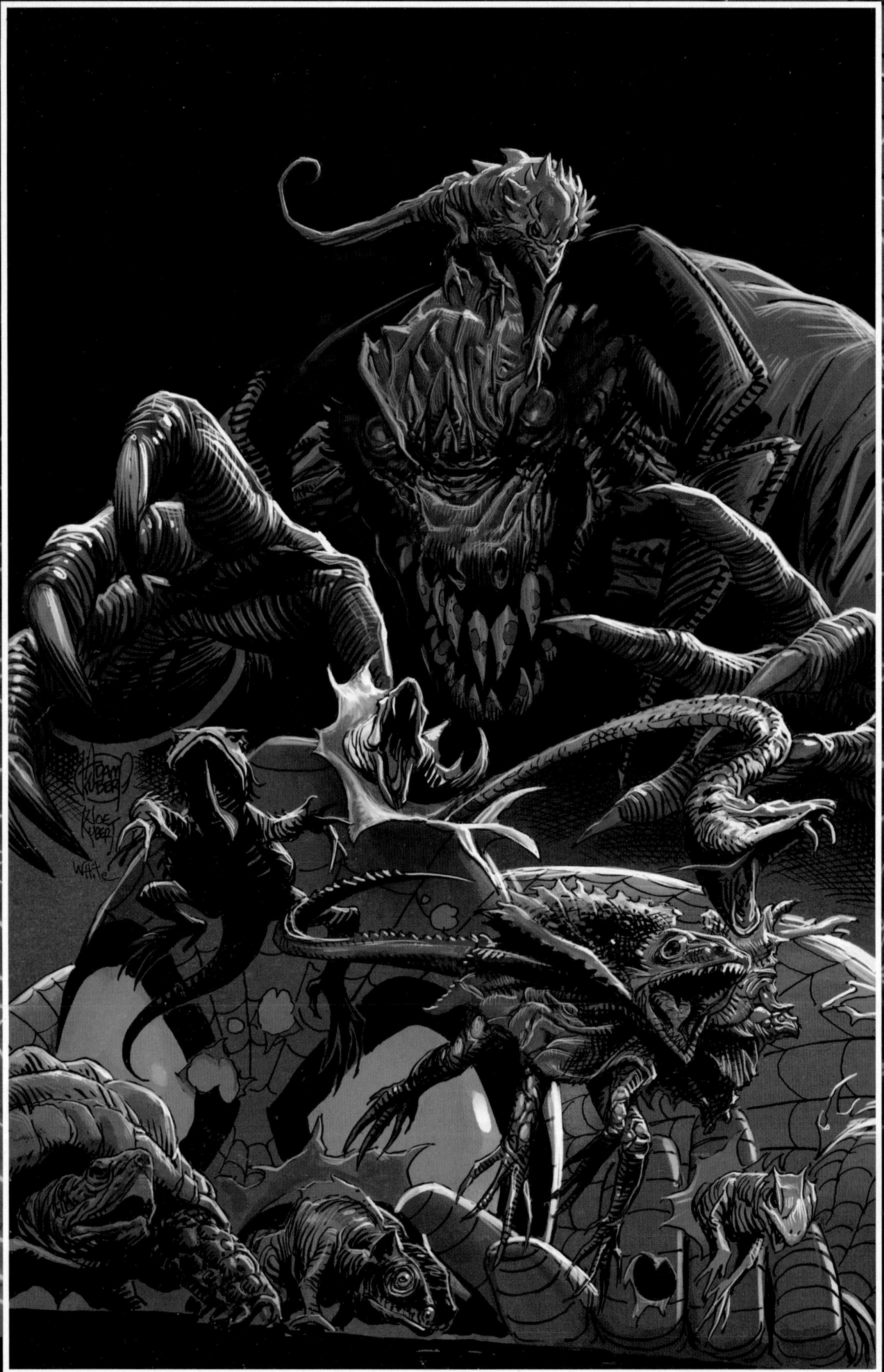

AMAZING SPIDER-MAN #691 VARIANT
COVER BY JOE KUBERT, ADAM KUBERT & DEAN WHITE